NEXT-LEVEL KNIFEMAKING

Jason Fry, Editor

Salem Straub Tracy Mickley Geoff Keyes Larrin Thomas
Brad Stallsmith Dave Ferry Tom Lewis Bob Ohlemann
Mark Bartlett Ed Braun Lin Rhea Erin Healy
Dustin Rhodes Joshua Swanagon Jim Cooper Ed Caffrey
John Gulso Shanna Jantz Kemp Nathan Carothers

Next-Level Knifemaking

ISBN 978-1-7321930-4-8

www.reddinkpress.com

CONTENTS

SECTION ONE

Introduction to Knifemaking

CHAPTER 1

Introduction

Jason Fry

THIS ISN'T A typical knifemaking book. There are dozens of examples of fine books that will take you from bar stock through the grinding and forging processes, through finish work, and so forth, until you will know (at least on paper) what there is to know about how to build a knife. This book is nothing like that.

A knifemaker will fairly quickly and easily reach a certain point at which they can make a knife that will cut and that has a decent enough heat treat and level of fit and finish. They'll sell a few to their friends and family and get the idea that maybe a knife show is their ticket to the big bucks. That first encounter with other knifemakers, or with educated customers, is often an eye-opening disappointment. The knives you make aren't as good as you thought they were. This is your book.

Progress beyond "good," progress to the next level of knifemaking, is about really only two things: your technique and your mind-set. At this point, technique is best learned from others, not from a book. You know the rudiments, and you need to see how the techniques of the experienced begin to chip away at the flaws in your work. You need to learn to see these flaws and then learn how to fix them. Learning to see is often harder than learning to fix. Your technique will also evolve as your equipment improves. There are chapters in this book about some of the choices you'll make as you upgrade your equipment. Each upgrade will often result in an improvement in your overall work quality.

I began my journey with files and sandpaper, then a Craftsman two-by-forty-two belt sander. One hundred and fifty knives later, I finally built a two-by-seventy-two, and I thought I had arrived. Two years after that, I upgraded to variable speed and realized there were an infinite number of levels of improvement. Your "good enough" had better keep on creeping upward. If you're searching for what that philosophy of continuous improvement can do for you, this is your book.

Beyond simple equipment and technique (which, of course, isn't really simple at all), continuous progress is a function not only of your hands but also of your mind. In this book, there are chapters about philosophy, about art, about marketing, and about photography. Your knowledge of technique will take you far. Your integration of ideas from other walks of life will take you further. Your ability to learn is your greatest tool, more useful than a grinder, a milling machine, or a heat-treat oven.

This book is like no other in this field for one other important reason that bears mention in the foreword. Many have set out to know enough about knifemaking that they can write a book on the subject. Many more of us, however, know a subject or two very deeply. At the foundation of this project is the idea that we should all share what we know best. While I (Jason) am the editor, so my voice and thoughts color the whole piece, I've collected a group of material by experts in the field about the things they know best. It is unprecedented to have this level of expertise from cover to cover in a knifemaking book.

One more thing, then you can get to reading. While I've worked hard to make sure that the perspectives in this book are true and accurate and that the authors know the material that they presented, *you* are the hero of this book. Using my style tips, or Mickley's abrasive selections, or Cooper's photo tips won't help *us*. They will help *you*. We're not the heroes who have killed the dragons, stormed the castles, and saved the maidens. We're the guides to help you succeed in *your* quest to become a next-level knifemaker. We'll give the guidance. The heroics are up to you.

CHAPTER 2

Knifemaking 101

Jason Fry

THERE'S A GOOD chance this isn't your first knifemaking book. But if it is, I'd like to start at the beginning. I say in a later chapter that the master knows the questions that the beginner doesn't yet know to ask. The first chapter of this book will be a basic overview of the knifemaking process. This material, or something like it, can be found in how-to-make-a-knife books all over the world. For almost all of these topics, there's a chapter or two of advanced material later in this book. Even so, the beginning is a place to start.

The knife is an old tool. Perhaps it was the second tool, right after the hammer. First, our ancestors hit with the rock. Then the rock split, and they learned to use the sharp edge of the rock to make tasks easier. The rest is history. We eventually moved beyond simple rocks to finely crafted knapped tools, and then later to copper, bronze, and iron. Steel came later, and we now enjoy an age when there are literally hundreds of types of steel that can make knives that greatly outperform the cutting tools from any other time in history.

Design Rule Number One: Form Follows Function

At its simplest essence, a knife is a cutting edge and a means by which to hold that edge. Throughout the history of mankind, the form of a tool has often been based on the tool's intended function. Hammers are heavier on the head end than the handle end. Wheels are round so that they'll roll. A smith need only look to his collection of tongs to understand that the different jaw types are useful for holding different sizes and styles of work pieces. For a working tool, the form of the tool should be suited to the job for which it is designed.

You should design your knives to do a job. The first question a knifemaker should consider is, "What is this knife designed to do?" Knives can be made for peeling potatoes, carrying in the pocket, stabbing bad guys, skinning varmints, chopping jungle underbrush, and many other tasks. Not surprisingly, a pen blade on a stockman folder isn't the same shape and size as a kukri or a machete. When designing a knife with function in mind, one should consider what characteristics of the knife make it well suited to the intended job. A single knife has many design elements that fall under "form" that ultimately influence its functionality.

A knife blade may be ground or forged from stock that is thick or thin. In general, thick knives are more durable, have greater chopping power, feel heavier in the hand, and are often capable of non-knife work like digging or prying. Thin knife blades are generally less durable, not likely to excel at clearing brush, but are much more efficient at cutting and slicing. We all recognize that you *could* slice a tomato with a katana or skin a bear with a paring knife, but we also intuitively recognize that the knife should be suited to each particular task with regard to its thickness and cutting characteristics.

Before we move on, I want the reader to note that I included "ground or forged" in the first sentence of the last paragraph without any further qualifying information. In times past, and perhaps even today, the argument over the relative merits of forging versus stock removal is a rabbit trail to nowhere. Given today's modern steel manufacturing techniques, and given the availability of quality heat-treating equipment and information, I can confidently say that there's no functional difference in the end product between forged and stock-removal knives. Sure, some steels do better with one process or the other, and some makers take advantage of the different characteristics of the two processes, but in the end, the cutting performance of two equal knives will be identical, regardless of whether the steel was forged or ground. Any differences in performance between equivalent, properly hardened forged and stock-removal knives will be the result of grind geometry and steel selection.

Cutting performance is greatly influenced by the way in which the maker grinds the knife. Flat grinds cut differently than hollow grinds. A flat ground knife is a simple wedge and may be thick or thin. A hollow ground knife has a slightly concave bevel, which makes it thinner behind the cutting edge. Convex grinds have slightly rounded bevels, while Scandi grinds are often a short, flat grind with no secondary bevel. Each grind will have different cutting characteristics. A good knifemaker will consider whether the grind of the knife is suited to the chosen task.

The size and shape of the knife should also be suited to the task. A long, thin blade may be ideal for filleting fish, but useless for shucking oysters. A sword isn't a suitable substitute for a skinner, nor a bowie for a barber's razor. The shape of the blade, whether drop point, trailing point, or clip, and the shape and length of the handle have an impact on the knife's performance. You can't split a whitetail's sternum with your skinner if the blade is too thin or the handle too short. You can't whittle sticks on the porch all day without blisters if the handle is too blocky or there are sharp angles. Some knives are safer to use when designed with a guard or deep finger groove. Other knives function better without a guard.

As you consider each attribute of the knife you have in mind, consider first whether that particular attribute compliments the knife's intended function. The form of your final design should have characteristics that lend themselves to the knife's assigned task. Form follows function.

The Very Basics

Here is a basic outline of the knifemaking process.

1. Obtain suitable steel.
2. Shape the steel to near the final shape, either by forging or removing material.
3. Harden the steel by heating it and then cooling it rapidly.
4. Draw back the hardness by tempering to improve performance.
5. Polish or otherwise finish your blade.
6. Install a handle.

Suitable Steel

Steel is fundamentally a uniform mix of iron and carbon atoms, with occasional other elements mixed in. Each alloy element beyond simple iron changes the properties of the final product. In a broad generality, hardenable knifemaking steel typically contains between 0.6 and 1.5 percent carbon. There's a chapter later in this book that goes into great detail about how and why carbon and iron work together to make knife steel.

Another critical question for the beginner is, "What steel is suitable?" That question is perhaps best answered by naming a few steels that are *not* suitable, and a few other steels that seem easy but really are not. Steel from the local big-box hardware store isn't suitable, as it does not contain enough carbon to harden properly. Railroad spikes are not suitable steel to make a high-performance knife. Even those spikes marked "HC" for "high carbon" only have around 0.3 percent carbon and will not make a knife that will hold an edge. Free things are fun, and much has been written in other places about places to find knife steel among free junk. Commonly mentioned are old files. How do you know if a file is old, and how old is old enough? Next will be mentioned lawnmower blades. While I am quite sure there have been suitable knives made out of lawnmower blades, and I know of at least one master smith who made lawnmower blades out of hardened O1 knife steel, most modern lawnmower blades are made overseas to minimum specifications by the lowest bidder. Do you want to start with the cheapest material the manufacturer could get by with? I don't. Next, folks will recommend leaf springs. I myself have personally made quality knives out of leaf spring material. I've also put time and effort into leaf spring knives only to have the steel fail miserably due to either unseen flaws or insufficient carbon content. Leaf spring knives take a level of experience to do well. If you're just starting out, don't start with leaf springs.

Steel is among the cheapest part of your final product. Consider that a four-foot bar of 1084 may cost twenty-four dollars, or six dollars a foot. A three-foot bar of 154CM stainless may cost sixty dollars, or twenty dollars a foot. Fine Damascus steel may cost twenty dollars an *inch*. Even so, when made into an eight-inch blade, the steel cost is four dollars in 1084, $13.33 in 154CM, and $160 in Damascus. Considering that out of my shop a standard eight-inch knife in 1084 might bring $300–400 in carbon or stainless, my steel cost represents somewhere between 1 percent and 3 percent of the final price in standard steels. Even in high-priced Damascus, my steel cost is at maximum around 25 percent. Given that math, and that you will never find quality Damascus for free in a junk pile, what do you save by using "free" steel? Three percent of your final cost. With found steel, you risk putting time and effort into a piece that may not perform properly, all so that you can save 3 percent. With "free" steel, you sink expensive hours of labor, as well as utility and abrasive costs, into steel for which there's no heat-treat recipe, no assurance of quality, and no guarantee of performance. I highly recommend you don't take that risk. Don't try to save 3 percent by assuming the risks of "free" steel. Buy your knife steel from a reputable supplier.

I will also say that there are reasons to use found steel, but that these reasons aren't related to cost. If you want to make a knife out of your grandfather's file, out of your customer's farm implement, or out of a classic car's leaf spring, go for it. The cool factor sometimes makes free steel worth the risks involved.

Shaping Your Blade

There are two basic approaches to taking your steel from bar stock to a knife shape. One way is to forge the steel. This involves heating the steel up in a fire, most often coal or propane, and hammering it into shape. This requires a heat source, some way to hold your work, a hammer, and something to hit against. There are later chapters about building forge burners and about choosing a suitable anvil.

The other way to shape a knife is to buy bars of steel and grind them to shape using abrasives. Simply put, you grind off everything that *isn't* a knife. Basic stock-removal tools may include files, bench grinders, angle grinders, or belt grinders. There's a chapter about belt grinders and other professional-grade equipment later in the book as well.

There several areas to consider with regard to shape. First, consider the profile of the knife. Make it suited to the chosen function. You'd not expect a competition chopper-style tip on a hunting knife, nor a thin bird-and-trout-style tip on a castrating knife, for example. Next, consider the grind of your knife. Make your edge thickness suited to the task. A chopper needs a thicker edge than a kitchen knife. The more common error is to make your edge too thick, not too thin.

A final factor that goes to shape is the symmetry of the grind. On a fine knife, the transition from handle flats to the blade bevels, which is called the plunge cut, will be even and symmetrical. The edge will be centered, and the curves of the plunge will be the same on both sides. I've been making knives for twelve years so far, and I have to pay attention to every single plunge. There are things you'll learn with experience, but you'll always have to work to make sure the plunges are even.

Hardening

Steel is hard compared to wood or silly putty, but the knife steel you buy is soft relative to its final state. In order to make your knife steel into a performing knife, you must harden it. The basic hardening process requires heating steel to its critical temperature. The critical temperature of steel is determined by its carbon content and its alloy content and may also include a soak time in order for the knife to harden properly. Once the steel has reached critical temperature and soaked the right amount of time, it is quickly cooled. This is called *quenching* the steel. Some steels quench properly simply by cooling in air. These are called *air-hardening* steels. They also can be hardened by placing them between aluminum plates in a process called *plate quenching.*

Other steels quench properly in oil. The type of oil must be suited to the composition of the steel. Some things that don't work well for quenching are used motor oil and water. Motor oil is made as a lubricant for moving metal parts. The reason we change the oil in our cars is because its properties degrade over time, and because it becomes contaminated. Do you want to quench your knife in worn out, contaminated oil? I don't.

As far as recommendations for quench oils, I suggest you start first with something that you know what it is. Canola or vegetable oil present some long-term challenges, but are a suitable quench medium for some steels. Mineral oil also is a suitable alternative and is often sold as livestock laxative. If you choose your steel to match the properties of these oils, you can make a fine knife that is properly hardened. Later on, I suggest you choose your oil to fit the properties of your steel. As you advance, buy engineered quench oil from a reputable supplier. Doesn't it make sense to use an oil whose only job is quenching, whose characteristics are carefully built for that purpose? Or you can use french fry oil, or horse laxatives. Your choice.

You may also read about water hardening steels such as W1. You're right, the *w* stands for water. What you may not know is that water hardening of thin pieces of steel such as a knife is a dangerous proposition. Water cools the steel both very quickly and very unevenly. This combination of fast and uneven temperature transfer can destroy your knife, resulting in cracks or complete destruction of the steel. Water quenching is a great way to make your one-piece knife into a two-piece knife.

There's a chapter later in this book about how the hardening process works at the atomic level, and about the various technicalities of the heat-treating process.

Some people confuse the terms *heat-treating*, *hardening*, and *tempering*. In my mind, heat-treating is the entire process of taking a knife from raw stock to finished blade. Heat-treating includes both hardening and tempering, as well as optional steps such as normalizing, annealing, thermal cycling, or cryogenic cooling. Hardening is the process I described above, bringing the steel to critical and then cooling it quickly. Tempering is the process by which your hardened steel knife is made less brittle, so that your edge will perform well. While hardening may require special equipment and temperatures between 1,500 and 2,000 degrees Fahrenheit, tempering can often be completed in your kitchen oven's temperature range.

Another consideration is the final hardness of the knife. In general, a quality knife will have a Rockwell C hardness of fifty-eight to sixty-one. There will be exceptions, and you should choose the final hardness of your knife based on how you want it to perform. Knives on the softer end of the range will sharpen more easily. Knives on the harder end of the range will hold an edge longer, but will be more likely to chip. There's further information about the tradeoffs involved in heat-treating in a later chapter.

Finish Before You're Done

A blade straight out of the heat-treating process will require some finish work. This most commonly involves using abrasives of increasingly finer grit to remove metal until you reach the level of smoothness that you require. There's a chapter later in the book that talks about abrasives and the machine polishing process. A typical user-grade knife is finished to at least 400 grit, while many fine knives are hand finished to 1,500 grit, or are machine polished to a mirror finish. The higher the grit number, the finer the finish.

There are several keys to a clean, uniform finish. First and foremost, start with a good grind. Whether flat or hollow, your primary grind should have no little bobbles, dips, wiggles, or anything else other than a clean grind at your chosen grit. If there are thirty-six grit scratches showing under your 120-grit finish, you're not ready to move to 220 yet.

Second, you have to set your grit progression up with your end in mind. It is often recommended to finish one grit at forty-five degrees to the blade, then switch ninety degrees on the next grit (which points you forty-five in the opposite direction), and then switch to parallel to the blade for the final grit. I have found this to be best practice, as it lets you more easily see the previous grit's scratches that still need to be removed.

I recommend that you use the best quality sandpaper you can find. If you start with big-box hardware store paper, you'll be amazed at the cutting characteristics of quality paper. Your blade should be firmly clamped to a hard surface, and you should use a hard sanding stick. I've used sanding sticks made of steel, Micarta, plastic, and sticks covered in leather. Each has their place.

Finally, use some kind of sanding lubricant. WD-40, synthetic motor oil, Simple Green, or other cutting fluid will make your sandpaper cut longer and cleaner, as it lifts away the fine metal shavings that the sandpaper creates and also makes a slurry of the sandpaper abrasive.

Your final finish should be uniform, with no underlying heavier grit grind marks. Your final finish should also be in one direction. The way to get a single direction finish is *not* to scrub back and forth, but rather to make long pulls in only one direction down the blade. The area around the plunge line is always the hardest to get polished evenly. Don't get so caught up in finishing your blade flats that you forget to finish the spine of your knife to an equally fine finish.

Can You Handle It?

When it comes to handle design, consider again how form follows function. Is the size of your handle suitable to the task at hand, and suitable to the blade you've constructed? Any sharp corners left on your handle will impact the end user's experience in negative ways. There should be no sharp corners on a custom knife's handle. There are other design considerations in later chapters, but for this introduction, I'll only make one more point. Most new makers make their handles too fat and too square. Your handle should be at least oval or egg shaped in profile, not a square with rounded corners. This happens because the new maker is subconsciously scared to remove too much material. Don't be afraid. Remember this: Thin is in, and light is right.

The handle material you choose should also be suited to the knife's intended purpose. The basic categories are wood, synthetic, and animal products such as bone, horn, or ivory. Each has its place in the knife world. Regardless of what you choose, don't you *ever* put your knife in the dishwasher.

Handles are typically fastened with glue and mechanical fasteners. Modern two part epoxy is the glue of choice. Generally, the slower the cure time, the higher the strength. Don't waste your time with five- minute epoxy, as it won't serve you well. Epoxy joints have very good strength perpendicular to the joint, but tend to be weaker when sheared across the joint. Therefore, the vast majority of knives will include pins in the handle material to increase the shear strength of the handle to blade junction. Others prefer the belt-and-suspenders approach and use a true mechanical fastener such as a Corby or Loveless bolt in addition to the glue joint. Another factor that influences the strength of your glue joint is the preparation of the surfaces prior to glue up. Surfaces should be a bit rough, or even dimpled, while maintaining no gap around the edges. Surfaces must also be 100 percent clean, free of oils and gunk. Many makers use acetone or denatured alcohol for final cleaning prior to gluing.

It's Simple, but It Isn't

In the end, the process sounds simple. The truth is that there are steps within the steps, and details within the details. As you progress, you'll make mistakes and learn how to fix them. You'll think of questions you never thought of, and then you'll find the answers. You'll develop preferences on what kinds of materials, shapes, and designs that you like best. Every maker has something to learn, no matter what they've accomplished, and every maker has something to teach, no matter how long they've been on the journey. This introductory overview is simply introductory. Dive in to the advanced material in the chapters to come. The information may be dense, advanced, or beyond your immediate skill level, but it represents the best knowledge available to the industry, brought to you by experts. Read on, my friend!

CHAPTER 3

Behavior Change for Knifemakers

Jason Fry

MOTIVATION IS A funny thing, and it varies considerably from person to person. Some of us have an internal drive, and we just keep looking for the next mountain to climb. Others of us require some external or situational motivation in order to excel. Whatever your motivation, behavior change seldom just happens. One of the primary truisms of the human experience is that, "If you do what you've done, you'll get what you've got." Put another way, "If nothing changes, then nothing changes." There's not a requirement that improvement must begin from a critical position, where you must decide your work was bad or previously unworthy, but if you want to improve your work, you must do something differently than you were doing before. It is a fact of life that growth requires change. Change by definition means that something will be different than it was before, and most of us are fairly content with the way things are in the moment. Change by nature generates moments of incompetence, where we must learn and adapt to a new situation, where we must develop skills we've not had before. We tend to dislike feeling incompetent, and so we resist the changes that generate those small moments.

Later in this book, there are chapters on next-level knifemaking tools and techniques to improve your work. There are advanced chapters about abrasives, steel, and knife organizations. There are stories of the journeys some of us took in our knifemaking, and there are tips and tricks for increasing your sales. There's one thing I can promise you with absolute certainty: if you read this book and don't change anything about your processes or approach, then nothing will change about the knives you produce. Improvement in the craft begins with changing discrete behaviors, simply doing small things differently than you did before. In this chapter, we'll explore some behavior change tools to help you as you work to the next level.

I am a knifemaker on my nights and weekends, and I've worked hard over the last twelve years to get to this point in the journey. I'm a voting member of the national Knifemakers' Guild, and the president of the Texas Knifemakers' Guild. I was a finalist on *Forged in Fire.* Some of you reading this book may know these things about me already. What many of you don't know is that I am a behavior analyst in my day job. The science of behavior change is how I've spent the last twelve years of my professional life, even as I've advanced in knifemaking outside of business hours. It is from the other side of my life, as a behavior analyst, that I bring you this introductory chapter.

Goal Setting for Knifemakers

One of the most common recommendations given in the behavior change and self-help arena is a suggestion to make goals. For some folks, the goal-setting approach works well to generate behavior change. A good goal is specific, measurable, achievable, relevant, and time limited. A bad goal is poorly defined or unrealistic, or may be beyond the realm of possibility. Look at the list below and decide for yourself if these goals are good or bad.

- I will pass the Journeyman Smith performance test by March.
- I will make a bowie knife that is worth more than $500 this year.
- I want to make my knives better and sell more.
- I will increase my Instagram followers by 10 percent this month.
- I will attend three major knife shows this year.

The two weakest of these goals are the bowie knife and the vague "make my knives better." For the bowie, you're talking about sales price, not quality.

For the "make my knives better," you haven't defined better. You have no indication of how you plan to do so, nor any specific timeline. The Journeyman Smith goal could be good or bad, depending on how realistic it is. If this is your first knifemaking book, and you just got it for Christmas, JS by March is nearly impossible. A bulleted list isn't a place to be specific enough to make a great goal. Each of these requires being broken down into specific behavioral components, specific tasks, or sub-deadlines.

For example, if your goal is to pass the JS performance test within three months, some of the steps might look like:

- Read the chapter in this book by Ed Caffrey about how to build a knife to pass the JS performance test.
- Order a couple of bars of 5160.
- Forge four identical knives in one session.
- Normalize and anneal all four the same way.
- Do two different heat-treat methods on two of the knives, one full quench and one edge quench.
- Put both knives through the performance test: rope, chop, and bend.
- Do the third knife the same way you did the one that performed best, making any necessary changes based on the results of the testing.
- Test the third knife. It should pass, but likely be destroyed.
- Make the fourth knife just like the third.
- Take the fourth knife to a master smith's shop for the official test.

It is good to have top-level goals that you can easily remember, like "Pass the JS test." It is better to break these simple goals down into specific tasks that, when completed in order, will lead to the desired result.

Set Up Structures to Help You Perform

Most of us don't mind following rules once in a while. We may not work on Sundays, or we may not order more than two drinks at the bar. We also tend to gravitate toward set routines. We put our socks on before our pants, or we put our car keys in the same spot immediately when we walk in the door. What if you built a few rules to guide your knifemaking routines? You'll have to do this for yourself, but here are a few of my rules and routines. They are specifically designed habits that I use to push myself in the craft.

I build something outside the box for every show. I want one piece on the table that is crazy, somehow pops, or is a representation of the top end of my skill set. Honestly, a significant portion of the time, I end up bringing that knife home. On the other hand, these are the knives with which I've won awards, and knives that have been published. They draw customers to your table and showcase your talents.

I do something special for the milestones. I started this back with knife one hundred, which was the first one I'd built with guide pins and a file-worked spacer. Every hundredth, and sometimes the fifties as well, get special treatment or a new technique. Each time you try something new, you learn something new.

I always build an extra knife or two in between orders. I will never have knives for a show or for my customers who want one if I focus on orders all the time. I plan these extra knives into my work flow, and I quote order times to allow for the slack.

I only take orders that I want to build, and I never take money in advance. Being selective keeps me from building ugly, unsellable knives should the customer back out. Not taking money in advance keeps me from running into financial problems when life gets in the way of my knifemaking. By following these two rules, I build knives that I'm proud of that will sell quickly, and I keep my finances in order as much as possible.

Take Advantage of Social Pressure

Another way to push yourself is to take advantage of social pressure to compete with those around you. Consider Peyton and Eli Manning. Venus and Serena Williams. Those Kardashians, if anyone still tries to keep up with them. All the way back to Cain and Abel, the bonds and competition between siblings have made life...interesting. Whether it's the older trying not to be outshone by the younger, or the younger trying to escape the older's shadow, sibling relationships are often characterized by a spirit of friendly competition. In 2015, my brother Travis and I took advantage of sibling rivalry as a way to push each other to more complex knife work, and the results were spectacular!

The story began with an eleven-by-one-and-a-quarter-inch piece of 154CM in my shop. Travis and I were brainstorming over the phone about what to do with the piece, since it was too large for one knife, but too small for two. As various ideas were tossed around, we ultimately settled on Travis's suggestion: split the bar down the middle lengthwise and make two thin daggers. The terms of the deal were simple: start with two identical blades, with each brother making a knife after their own style. The only rule was *no compromises.* The knife had to represent the maker's best work, with quality materials and no shortcuts.

The two halves of the original bar were roughed out to the same profile and heat-treated. At the family Christmas gathering, each brother took a piece to make their blade. I set my sights on the Lone Star Knife Expo in June of 2015, with an eye toward ICCE in September, where I would be judged for voting membership into the Knifemakers' Guild. Travis traveled a lot with his job, so his timing was more open-ended.

I decided on a frame handle design with mother-of-pearl and a carved shell motif. I finished my knife on schedule, and it won the best of show award at the Lone Star show. The knife was presented to the Guild judging panel, and I passed my voting membership examination. Travis went an entirely different direction, building an ivory-handled, ABS master-smith-style quillon dagger with carved fluting, twisted silver-wire inlay, and a faceted, hexagonal motif.

Jason's Dagger

154 CM, fourteen-inch overall length, with a nine-inch blade. Frame handle and fittings are 416 stainless. The frame handle is rope file worked, with coined spacers and mother-of-pearl scales. The rear bolster, guard studs, and quillon ends are carved with a shell motif.

Travis's Dagger

154 CM, fourteen-inch overall length, with a nine-inch blade. Preban fluted elephant-ivory handle with twisted argentum silver-wire inlay. Fittings are 416 stainless with a hexagonal, faceted motif.

Travis and I hoped that the pair of knives could stay together, but our primary customer base at the time was high-end hunting knives, not art daggers. Efforts were made to sell the knives individually, but ultimately, both knives were purchased as a set by a single collector who both of us had both done business with previously. The collector is one of four brothers, and he understood the dynamics at play and was intrigued by the story.

So who won the challenge? I've always considered Travis the better artist, but our styles are so different it's hard to compare. My dagger won best of show, but his never got the chance to compete before it was sold. Travis said we both won. "We both made great knives, and neither of us compromised. The challenge gave us something to do together and pushed us to better work, so it doesn't matter if we ever declare a winner."

What among your personal social situations can you take advantage of? A local knifemaking group? A national guild? A public commitment to your Facebook or Instagram followers? If you can create a healthy social pressure, it can push you to do better work.

Climb the Ladder

Most knifemakers know that there are organizations that can help you advance your work. One of the ways that they do this is by providing certifications. Some folks think that if they make JS or voting member in the Guild that they *should* somehow deserve more money for their work. I think that's not how it works at all. The process of submitting your work to scrutiny by these organizations, of meeting the established advancement criteria, that's what pushes your work to the point where it can command a higher price. It's the quality improvement that drives the pricing, and the certification process pushes you to improve your quality.

In addition to the natural progression that comes from working toward a certification, the social pressure of living up to an organization's standards tends to keep your quality high and moving forward. Some people may reach up to a certification, and then come back down, so that their MS test knives are the best knives they will ever make. I think this is the exception, not the rule. Most people who choose to grow enough to gain a rank continue to keep growing. At the very least, once you've gained a Guild membership or ABS stamp, you don't want that mark on a substandard knife, so you continue to make knives at a high standard. Later in this book, there's a chapter that further explores the benefits of joining local and national knifemaking organizations.

Go for It!

In the end, it's up to you. Behavior tricks alone won't make you a better knifemaker. Reading this book is a start, but it won't make you any better unless you learn something in the process of digesting the information. If nothing changes about your mind-set, about the techniques by which you complete your work, or about your sources of information and education, nothing will change about your final product. Next-level work doesn't come naturally, but is the result of continued baby steps of improvement. You can do it!

SECTION TWO

Basic Knifemaking Equipment

CHAPTER 4

Basic Knifemaking Machines

Salem Straub

THE PRIMARY TOOLS used to make knives are fairly universal across different shops and the makers that inhabit them. Many are the tools one would find in a common home machine shop or garage in which cars are maintained. Others are tools that would be found in a cabinet shop or luthier's workshop. Still others are those specific tools best suited to the blacksmith or leatherworker. The competent knifemaker will use a variety of both manufactured and homemade tools as he works to transform bars of steel and blocks of wood into well-functioning examples of cutting tools.

This chapter will discuss the main powered tools found in the shops of the bladesmith, as well as the stock-removal maker, with an eye to relative suitability of various types and capacities of available equipment to the maker's needs. We'll discuss some basic advantages to each machine, with a nod to requisite tooling, and then pass on to briefly cover some more specialized tools as well as a few tools of the hand-powered sort.

In some ways, to move to next-level knifemaking requires next-level tools. What can a better tool do for you? A better tool can improve quality, speed of production or surface finishes, or even widen your range of possible materials and styles of work. The right tool can increase the repeatability and evenness of surface finishes and the accuracy of mechanisms. Every maker will not need every tool. Some choose to work in one way, others in another. One may prefer to efficiently make relatively simple, yet clean, knives in batches of ten or more, while another may like making more detailed pieces one at a time at a slower pace. Figure out what kind of maker you are, as this will drive what tools you need to be successful.

The Basic Knife Shop

Undoubtedly, the most essential machine to the majority of knifemakers is the belt grinder. The most common size uses a belt that is two inches wide and seventy-two inches long, usually noted as a two-by-seventy-two. Not long ago, there were only a handful of solid options on the market for the maker to choose from. Now, there are perhaps fifteen or twenty companies and individuals who make a knifemaking two-by-seventy-two grinder. Regardless of the manufacturer, all knife grinders have a few features in common.

First, the belt tracking needs to be adjustable and stay solidly where it's set with any attachment being used. Second, a range of tooling needs to be available upon purchase, either as part of the initial package or as upgrades later. Tooling should change out easily. Third, variable speed in a grinder is so useful, and so relatively cheap now, that I wouldn't recommend a professional maker use anything else.

The modern knife grinder can have a variety of tooling options. A flat platen or large contact wheel are usually standard, depending on whether the maker prefers to flat or hollow grind. Platen wheels may be aluminum, or they may be rubber contact wheels of different diameters. Special arms are made that hold small wheels, ranging from as small as a quarter-inch, up to three-inch diameters. A half- or three-quarter-inch wheel is very versatile. Various work rests, some static and some adjustable, come in handy. Some grinders are built horizontally, or are built to run both vertically and horizontally. There are grinders built for slack belt grinding. There are special air-cooled rotary platens. There are even surface-grinding attachments available for your two-by-seventy-two.

A nice thing to have in a well-tooled production shop is a row of grinders, each dedicated at least temporarily to a specific part in the overall process of the work being done. Belt and tooling changes take time, especially if a series of belts need to be changed along with every tooling change on a single grinder doing all the work.

Disc grinders fit well into knife work, as they are a quick way to ensure that your parts are truly flat. Many times, a part needs a quick reflatten or skim/deburr with a 220-grit sheet after drilling holes or a lock cut. A disc is useful when a precise flat grind is wanted, to true up the work off the belt grinder platen. Finally, discs with adjustable work rests are invaluable for work that needs angles matched, such as dovetail bolsters or handle frames, and even match-grinding pattern weld tiles after cutting for a Filicietti flip.

These grinding tools depend on cloth- or paper-backed abrasives in order to remove material. The science of abrasives continues to evolve. Don't be afraid to try new belts over time, look for better deals, or find new suppliers. It's a competitive industry, with new materials becoming available often, and who doesn't want to cut grinding time and expense down? Throw those belts away when they're not cutting anymore, and don't be afraid to use roughing belts to get as close to size as you are able. It saves time and grinds cooler too.

Another basic requirement for the knife shop is a way to drill holes. Of course, the drill press is used for the great majority of this in many knife shops, but not all drill presses are created equal. A drill press is a basic machine tool, and like machine tools in general, weight is often an indicator of quality. A hefty press with a fair range of speeds works well for a main drill and should have a big table, optimally with crank height adjustment. This all helps when doing things like cutting screw slots or liner lock bars with an abrasive wheel in the chuck. Look for a long spindle travel of at least four inches, so handle blocks won't need the bit reset or risers used. Adjustable quill stops in both directions are very handy. A row of presses can be used to advantage, particularly for folder work—one set slow, one set fast, one with a tapping head, one with a countersink, and so on. For those who can't afford a Tapmatic immediately, a modified drill press can make a very good manual tapping fixture, with the motor removed and a handwheel added to the top spindle pulley.

A professional knife shop needs a way to cut metal and wood, and a band saw fits the bill. The band saw cuts not only wood, metal, and basically everything else, but is a safe and versatile machine in skilled hands. Because of blade speed, a metal saw is capable of cutting wood, while a wood saw won't cut most metals we might need. With that in mind, my first recommendation to the novice would be a Portaband with bench mount. In a pro shop, hopefully we have the budget and space to have more than one saw, which is really what's called for.

For the bladesmith, a horizontal saw is useful for processing stock for pattern welding, as well as for resectioning or tile cutting during billet-working processes. A vertical floor model is a wonderful thing to have, with my preference being for a throat of twenty inches or more and variable speed to enable cutting all materials on one saw. This capacity allows resawing of larger blocks of hardwood, as well as a nice, big, flat table to work on when sawing multiple parts from large sheets of material.

Older domestic machines, such as DoAll or Grob brand vertical metal saws, will usually achieve speed reduction and various speeds through the use of multiple pulleys, variable sheaves, and the like, while newer import machines, such as JET and Grizzly, will feature variable speed through a variable-frequency drive. Either way is good; and, indeed, a large three-phase wood saw can be converted fairly easily to cut metal with the addition of a variable-frequency drive and perhaps a jackshaft. Regardless of your saw, break all of your blades in by sawing at slow speeds and feeds on large, solid, mild steel stock, with coolant, to condition those sharp, delicate new points on the teeth. Much like your new grinding belts, you'll strip the life off of them if not careful. Also, I do like having the Portaband still as an option to cut harder metals or abrasive materials like carbon fiber. You can trash an eight-dollar Portaband blade on one handle and not worry about it, but a-hundred-and-fifty-inch, bimetal blades are expensive for that big saw.

Another saw deserves quick mention—the abrasive chop saw. While this is often more of a fabricator's tool, they are quite handy for the pattern welding shop. Billets and bars can be sawed without much regard to hardness, or even at dull, red heat. Like band saws, all are not equal. The brushed-motor type, fourteen-inch saws typically used by contractors will work, but much better is to find an industrial cutoff saw with a larger induction motor and belt drive. These are more durable, cut with more torque, and are quieter to boot. Try thin Flexovit or Sait wheels, and you'll never look back. Glazing halfway through a thick, solid billet will be a memory.

Heat treatment is of utmost importance, as is of course the associated equipment. We do have a couple of chapters on the subject in this book, so I'll just quickly say a couple things about the equipment. Regarding quality of heat treatment, having a digital oven to thermal cycle, normalize, and quench from is an enormous asset. One oven is nearly essential, two are very handy, and even three will be called for at times. After all, temper needs to follow quench much sooner than your one oven would cool down to the correct tempering range, and some stainless steels can benefit from a two-oven process when heating for the quench.

Each oven will vary slightly from others, so one needs to evaluate results rather than just trust the heat-treating recipe. Testing by practical methods helps, and a Rockwell tester comes in handy as well. Make sure to keep your tester calibrated within spec, understand the surface finish necessary for the procedure, and keep the machine well-maintained and in trim. Testers are touchy, and care is necessary for accuracy.

The Machine Shop.

The next step up from a drill press is a milling machine, ideally a vertical knee-mill, such as a Bridgeport. These have the lever spindle like a drill press, as well as the spindle crank or knee for Z-axis. A mill is generally capable of drilling a more precise, perpendicular hole than a drill press, and this is important for folder pivots in particular. Of course, the ability to actually mill is useful for a variety of task. One thinks of guard slotting immediately, but there are many other uses as well—flattening and sizing handle stock, counterboring holes in handle work, roughing fittings to shape, mortising handle scales, and fabricating jigs and fixtures, just to name a few.

Much has been debated about whether to buy new or used, a benchtop or floor model, a domestic or an import. If you can at all fit it into your shop, a full-sized, used, domestic machine, such as a Bridgeport or Index, is far and away the best choice in terms of value, quality, and rigidity. Otherwise, do try to at least find a machine with square or otherwise dovetailed column/Z-ways. Staying indexed while adjusting the available Z-axis travel is important, particularly when swapping between a drill chuck and different lengths of end mills, reamers, or other cutters.

To start with, you'll need at least a decent milling vise (AngLock type—the jaw won't lift badly when clamping), a set of collets, a drill chuck, set of parallels, an edge finder, a dial test indicator and holder, a clamp set, and some one-two-three blocks. As far as actual cutters, they can be acquired over time to suit certain jobs. I'd start with at least a range from one-eighth to half an inch of four-flute single or double end mills in HSS, and another set in carbide, ideally. A fly cutter and face mill are good to have as well for truing larger surfaces and thickness-sizing stock.

If you can obtain a mill with a digital readout, or DRO, or otherwise retrofit a DRO to whatever machine you may have, you'll find it very handy for locating features on workpieces or jigs. The graduated dials on a machine with no DRO will serve fine as well, especially if a calculator and notebook are kept in the machining area and if methods for dealing with any backlash that may exist in the table are understood and followed.

Those knifemakers who have a surface grinder in their shops will likely never care to have to do without one again. I know I use mine all the time and would miss it terribly. I won't go too far into the "stones versus belts" debate. Stones are preferred for dimensional tolerances and fine finishes, while belts cut on a whole new level of stock removal and render the surface grinder into a very effective tool in pattern welding and fabrication in general. Match-grinding bars and tiles, roughing billets to size clean and flat for restack, and mill and forge scale removal all are easily managed by an abrasive belt surface grinder. Do try to hold out for a machine with an automatic table—and a magnetic chuck is essential. Shims can be used to grind tapered parts flat, or vice versa. Blocks can be used to trap parts on the chuck, and super glue or double-sided tape enable thickness-grinding of nonferrous metals and even handle materials.

Opportunities to use a metal lathe in the knife shop abound. A short list would include making or modifying custom pins, bolts, and other fasteners for handles, making or modifying stop pins, pivots, standoffs, screws, and other folder hardware, turning Damascus quillons, pommels, and other fittings, creating custom bolts or nuts for frame handles and other takedown knives, creating or modifying contact wheels, idlers, and fabricating parts for your belt grinders and other machines.

Combination lathe/mill machines and other small and light bench-sized machines are to be avoided. A useful sized lathe for a knife shop is twelve by thirty-six. I'd stay away from anything much smaller, if possible. You won't often be turning pieces thirty-six inches long, but that bed space will be taken up by the tailstock, chuck, and a drill bit, all of which are used quite frequently. A taper attachment is nice, but not that essential to knife work. A three-jaw chuck is very useful, while a four-jaw chuck is slower to dial in, yet more versatile. Both should be considered essential, but one can make do with either alone quite often. You'll need a chuck to fit your tailstock, a live center (with bearings) for the tailstock, and some variety of tool post or holder for your cutters (a lever-lock, quick-change tool post is very convenient). Some lathe tooling can be shared with the mill, such as the dial test indicator and centering drills, and a DRO is likewise quite handy here, although each machine will need to have its own. Knowledge of how to grind various cutters and what types to buy is very helpful, and can be obtained through self-study online and in print. Single-point threading is an involved skill, and while it can occasionally be of use in the knife shop, it falls outside the scope of this article. Most lathes of a size useful for knives will have this capability, and I'd consider it an unfortunate limitation to buy a lathe without working threading functions.

For a home production or light industrial shop, now is a fortunate time to be in the market for used machine tools. Huge sections of stateside manufacturing shops have been being liquidated for the past two or three decades, and this process continues. Consequently, good-quality manual machine tools abound in the used market. I cannot stress enough that compared to buying relatively small, expensive, weak, imported machines, the best value—and, by far, the most capable and enjoyable machines—will be older, used, and made in the USA. Machinery dealers, online auctions, classifieds online and in print, and last, but certainly not least, good old networking through machine shops and other metalworkers, should yield a range of options to the motivated shopper. Your prospects are even better if any population center or former industrial area of any size is fairly close to hand. Keep in mind, when buying used machine tools, always do your homework and know what to look for as far as common problems or wear points. Try to keep your head screwed on straight and be objective in your assessments of condition, as well as honest with yourself about your resources regarding rebuilding skills and repair budget. I've certainly dragged home a few machines that were a bit more than I bargained for, but in the end, I've gotten each running and have been paid back amply by both the work that they've done and the lessons that I learned along the way. It is my assertion that for a machine to be used safely and efficiently, the operator should be well-educated in its mechanical functions; and overhauling a machine prior to putting it back into service affords the operator a very good familiarity with, and respect for, all the moving parts.

The Hot Shop

There has been some debate over whether a hydraulic forging press or a power hammer would be a better choice for pattern welding, should a shop be able to have only one. First, if you are serious about pattern welding, ultimately, you'll need both. You'll catch the bug, and you won't stop until the machines as well as the space to house them are obtained. That said, my vote would nevertheless go to the press as a first power-forging aid. It is slower and more controllable, more versatile, and can move thicker stock with less investment in a large machine and the related infrastructure.

Ram speed and tonnage are the two primary indicators of the capacity of a forging press. Ram speed should be at least one inch per second extending speed, while two inches per second is really more acceptable. Below a push force of sixteen tons or so, a press won't be powerful enough for most billet work. It is typical in the common presses built by and sold to bladesmiths for the pump to be a two-stage type, to maximize speed and power when a smaller motor (down to five horsepower) is needed. Where more electric power and a greater budget are available, a single-stage press of ten horsepower or more will move the steel with even more efficiency.

Either a C- or an H-frame press will work well, provided that the frame is built as heavy and stiff as it needs to be, given the design. A C-frame can be nice, as it offers unrestricted access on three sides, and an H can be nice as it inherently will tend to rack less under high load. Ultimately, if a large power hammer is acquired, the press will get relegated to being mostly a patterning tool, so it's good if the frame and die holders will lend themselves to use with a wide range of tooling.

The press will normally include its own hydraulic power unit. Later, with quick-change hoses, other tools such as hydraulic twisting or rolling machines can be powered from the same unit. The press itself can also be accessorized with additional hydraulic circuits for automatic retract or reciprocation, adjustable depth stopping, and the like.

A power hammer is perhaps the most spectacular machine that a smith will own. They are a powerful and impressive tool when integrated into pattern welding work, and will perform some tasks better than a press. Drawing out of thinner stock is the classic example of a hammer's strengths, but that's far from the only reason to add one if you already own a press.

A smaller hammer, such as those of seventy-five-pound ram weight or less, will work best when equipped with mild-crowned drawing dies. This shape will still be versatile and capable of forging tapers and bevels, but with the reduced area of contact and directional effect, will best exploit the available power of the machine. A larger hammer, of one-hundred-pound ram weight or more, can be used with such dies, but it will be a more versatile and valuable tool if equipped with flat dies. These enable the use of top or bottom handheld or saddle-mounted tooling, and can be excellent for quickly forge welding billets of large surface area.

Unlike a press, heat isn't sucked aggressively from the work's surface by the hammer's dies, and a hammer of larger-ram weight can often be seen to keep the stock hot longer through energy transfer. This can be a major asset. For example, my three-hundred-pound Beaudry will keep a large billet at a near-welding heat until almost entirely drawn out for restacking. The speed of a large hammer with flat dies can be a very nice thing when closing up complex forge welds without the use of flux.

The primary drawbacks of a power hammer are that a large foundation is normally required, power requirements can be considerable, larger hammers may not work with neighbors, and you may grow addicted to hammers and ruin your life always trying to drag another one home.

The hot shop will need some type of arc welding machine. At the basic level, this can be no more than a 225-amp AC tombstone-type stick welder. This type of machine represents a lot of bang for the buck, and much great pattern welding has been done supported by one of these alone. I'll briefly describe the other main choices though, and why a maker might prefer to have more than just the most basic of welding machines on hand.

MIG, also known as *wire-feed welding* gets my vote for the most used, most convenient type of welding in a bladesmithing shop. It is very fast and works great for complete closing of seams in dry-welding and San Mai work. I have found that it is less touchy than TIG with regard to cracking upon air cooling after welding hardenable steels in thin sections, since it adds a lot of mild filler wire to lower the carbon content of the weld pool. The use of flux-cored wire is little better than stick welding. I recommend setting up with shielding gas right from the start. Be sure to get at least a 140-amp welder with a decent duty cycle. If you can afford it, a 200-amp, 240-volt machine is what I'd consider a capable size for general bladesmith work.

TIG welding is the most difficult common type of welding to learn, but can be very useful and versatile when called for. As a general-use process around the shop, it's slower and more laborious than MIG. However, if you want to be able to fusion weld not only mild steel, but also to complete delicate welds in stainless, bronze, or copper for fittings and the like, TIG is where it's at. It's good for Damascus work where the use of filler metal isn't wanted, and when you're not using that argon bottle for TIG welding, you can route it over to your heat-treating kiln for an inert atmosphere.

The bottom line is, when shopping for welding equipment, do your homework. Don't just buy the red brand or the blue brand or the cheapest one you can find. Look for performance and value and talk to professionals in the field, and, if possible, try some machines or take a welding class before buying anything.

This chapter works on the assumption that the primary knifemaking tools can be bought. Another category deserves mention, though, and that is the tools that can be made by the knifemaker himself. This requires the use of your most important tools, your brain and hands. Many times, I have found myself doing a task in a way that works, but is clearly not the best or most efficient way. At these moments, I have learned to listen to that voice that tells me to stop, think about it, and create a tool or jig that will enable me to do a cleaner or faster job in the future.

When you have cultivated the practice of making tools as needed, the creativity and innovation that this process breeds will certainly manifest itself in your knives as well. Jigs and hammer or press tooling for patterning in Damascus will give your steel a distinctive look. Stamps you invent for tooling leather will yield patterns no one else has. Scrapers made for fullering blades will enable you to do work that is beyond the capability of average smiths. All of these add to your capability in ways that will make your work unique.

To me, my shop and machines have become extensions of my brain and body, much like an added set of limbs. At this point, I don't know how I'd manage without that space and potential. It is my hope that you who read this will go on to build and outfit the shops of your dreams, and to make the knives in your heads become reality. May you succeed in creating lasting quality and beauty in this world.

CHAPTER 5

Understanding Abrasives

Tracy Mickley

ABRASIVES LIKE BELTS, discs, and sheets are one of the most significant expenses in knifemaking. What you don't know about them can cost you a lot of wasted money and time. If you get nothing else out of this chapter, please take the time to understand this:

What you read on the internet or hear from a buddy about a belt may or may not work for you.

There are many excellent and well-respected knifemakers who share their experience on the internet. Even though one guy says, true to his experience, that you should use XYZ belt because it's the best ever, that belt might not work out as the best belt ever for you. Here is why.

Abrasives are engineered to break down under use at specific speeds and pressures. As the abrasive granules are consumed and break down, they create sharp, new edges in the granule. These sharp edges are what gets the job done. This fracturing is designed into the abrasive and is measured by a term called *friability*. The more friable an abrasive granule is, the easier it breaks down, exposing sharp new edges. This breakdown continues until the abrasive is exhausted. If you use an abrasive that requires high speed and pressure to break down, such as a using ceramic-based abrasive at a low speed or pressure, the granule sharp edges will simply wear smooth, and the abrasive will go dull and stop cutting. The belt will work as if it were exhausted, but there will still be plenty of abrasive left. It just won't work well. It will still grind slowly, but it will generate more heat and require more pressure or speed to work. Conversely, if you use a highly friable abrasive like aluminum oxide (typically called AO) on hardened steel, it will break down very quickly—so quickly, in fact, that you will exhaust the abrasive in little to no time, forcing you to change to another belt.

That Brings Us to Rule #1

Match the abrasive to your needs and how you grind or sand, and not based on what someone says is the best belt. Gather recommendations and test to be sure. But in the end, what is best for you won't simply come from an internet recommendation. The material you're grinding, the speed you run the belt, the amount of pressure you apply, and your grinding method (flat platen, slack belt, contact wheel) all affect how the abrasive granule breaks down in use. Use different abrasives for different applications. There's no universal best abrasive. It doesn't exist. You will have to experiment and find what works best for the way you grind.

General Rules of Thumb about Abrasive Types

Aluminum oxide (AO) works well for plastics, woods, leather, and phenolics. It's highly friable and breaks down quickly. AO abrasives are generally the cheapest. Sheets, belts, and discs are all available in AO. In fact most nine-by-eleven sheets are AO. There are several quality levels in AO abrasives. Super-cheap AO belts don't screen the abrasive granule size as rigorously as more expensive belts, and so you may see odd scratch marks in your uniform grind finish. That is one reason they are cheap. You will absolutely want to use AO in certain applications, so don't dismiss it automatically because they are the cheapest of the abrasives.

SC, or silicon carbide, is often used in the automotive body repair industry and sees some use in the cutlery trade. It is slightly less friable than AO. Generally, you won't find many knifemakers using SC belts, and they can be difficult to find. SC is generally sold in discs or hand sheets. It is usually inexpensive and can be found everywhere. The problem is it wears very quickly in the knifemaking process. I don't know of any knifemaker using it on regular basis other than hand sanding, and even then, there are more cost-effective AO abrasives for hand sanding.

Zirconium oxide, commonly called simply *zircs*, is an abrasive that is less friable than SC. It is a decent midrange abrasive that might be in the sweet spot for you and how you grind. It does well on metal, G10 and other man-made handle materials. It is usually priced a bit higher than AO-based abrasives. It also is almost always screened better than cheap AO abrasives, so the scratch pattern is more uniform.

Ceramic abrasives are the hardest and least friable abrasives. Ceramics love tough materials, and perform best with high-speed and high-pressure applications. They work well for stainless steels, hardened carbon steels, and tough materials like titanium. These abrasives are almost always the most expensive initially, but may outlast two or three other less-expensive abrasives. Ceramic abrasives are found in belts and discs, but rarely in sheets. You most likely will not find any ceramic abrasives smaller than 120-grit as that is the current practical limit to manufacturing technology.

I will say it again because it is worth repeating. *The correct abrasive to use is the one best suited to the material, the speed, and the pressure you use in grinding or sanding.* Matching the abrasive to your process will save you a lot of expense, maximize your belt life, and overall improve the quality of your knife. The guy who recommends a certain type of abrasive as "the best" may be using it in an entirely different way than you.

Just like the TV infomercial guy says, "But wait! There's more," so is there more to abrasives than just type. Keep in mind most abrasive companies put out different quality levels, like *good, better, best.* Let's have a look at some of the variables that impact price and performance.

Open-Coat versus Closed-Coat Abrasives

You may find some abrasives listed as either open- or closed-coat. The belt manufacturing process, overly simplified, is that open-coat belts have glue applied and abrasive granules sprinkled on top. Closed-coat abrasives have glue on the belt, and then the abrasive applied, and then another coat of a bonding adhesive applied. Closed-coat typically costs more to produce and is generally considered a higher-performance product. You can tell an open- from a closed-coat belt simply by looking at them. Open-coat has less abrasive on the surface to reduce clogging from sticky materials or simply to reduce cost. An open-coat, cheaper abrasive is highly desirable in specific applications, even though you might think you will get more out of a closed-coat abrasive. An open-coat usually has 50 percent to 70 percent surface coverage. A closed-coat has more than 70 percent surface coverage and is better suited for ferrous or tough metals. As a general rule, inexpensive belts, especially AO belts, are open-coat and ceramics are closed-coat. There will be dozens of exceptions to this, depending on the engineered application. Open-coat belts work best when the material being ground or sanded sticks to the belt and starts to clog it up. Plastics, most woods, and G10 materials can quickly load a belt up and kill it. If you have an open-coat belt, this gives that sticky material somewhere to go, ultimately giving you better abrasive engagement in the material. I always use cheap, AO, open-coat belts on wood, nonferrous metals, and phenolics. In most things knifemaking, it is a rare case where the cheapest might be the best one to use, but don't overlook the savings to be gained here. If you want to ruin your day, grab your new, expensive ceramic belt and grind some plastic or other high-pressure laminate with it. The belt will load up quickly, and this will kill it. You can try to remove the sticky junk using a rubber block—which you should have and use often when grinding sticky material—but, chances are, it won't save the expensive, closed-coat ceramic belt.

Bonding

Abrasive belts use different types of bonding to hold the abrasive material to the backing belt. Some bonding materials are waterproof, and some are not. The difference in technology between bonding agents is nearly as significant as the abrasive material. Super-cheap belts often use cheap glue to bond the abrasive granules. It's not always a deal breaker in using cheap belts, but make sure you don't waste time on a belt where all the abrasive flies off after a few minutes of use. Also be sure that your abrasive is waterproof if you plan on wet grinding. Some of the popular engineered AO abrasive like Norax™ and Trizact™ (gator belts) will break down quickly if they get wet. That means when you are grinding, you make a pass or two, dip in water to cool, and wipe off the water to make another pass on the grinder. It slows things down, but the finish that engineered abrasives give can be worth the extra step. Most ceramic belts shrug off water and are not affected.

Backing Material

Belt and sheet backing material varies in stiffness and water resistance. A J-Flex belt is very flexible and is often used with slack belt or small wheel attachments. The J-Flex belt will roll around contours. You definitely want some J-Flex belts in your shop, particularly for handle work. Y-weight or X-weight belts are heavy and stiff. There are several different kinds of backing material. Cloth backing is used on better quality belts, paper on cheaper. The majority of the time you will use X-, Y- or XY-weight belts. They are stiff and tough. You do want to have some J-Flex belts in tool box for times you want a flexible belt to get into a crisp plunge line or slack sand contours. There are some variations of J-Flex, but they all work the same. They flex to fit curves, and the backing material is light and bendable. The glue is also suited for the flexing action of the belt.

Grit Size Standards

To make things even more confusing, there are at least three commonly used standards for measuring grit size. They are the US-based CAMI, Micron, and FEPA scales. Most abrasives manufactured in the United States use the CAMI standard, or are just commonly called *grit.*

Engineered abrasives like the Norax™ and Trizact™ typically use the Micron basis to designate granule size. The smaller the number, like X5, the smaller the grit. Engineered abrasives in the good, better, best scheme are in the best class. Engineered abrasives usually have high-quality screening for a consistent granule size. Use these as finishing belts. They will remove metal but are primarily designed to provide a very consistent finish. Many abrasives also use FEPA, an international-based standard commonly noted by P-rating such as P100 grit. None of these standards match up exactly. It is important that you know which standard abrasive you are using when you mix belt types and brands. There are comparison charts all over the internet, and I suggest you hang a copy in your shop until you have memorized the equivalents. There are at least a dozen other grit measurements used around the world. You will generally run into just three of them in the USA. They are *grit, Pxxx grit*, and *Micron*. By far the most commonly used is plain old grit.

Other Abrasive Belt Types

Cork Belts: These belts have a thick surface of cork particles bonded to a belt backing. AO is embedded into the cork to provide a grinding surface that has some give or cushioning to it, but will still grind or polish, depending on the grit size. Cork belts are most often used as finishing belts. I routinely use one with green chrome buffing compound to give a mirror or satin finish after using a 120-grit belt. Cork belts need to be broken in before use. The cork particles are large and irregular. The high spots need to be knocked down a bit before they will give you a consistent finish. The break-in procedure is simple. Run the new cork belt at high speed and push some scrap metal into it aggressively. You will shave some of the cork particles off in the process, but you also knock down the high spots. This may take a few minutes. After that, use them as is or apply buffing compound to really speed finishing along. I keep a bar of green chrome on my grinder bench, and for nearly every blade I grind, I use the cork belt loaded with green chrome to take the finish where I want it after a 120-grit. The green chrome doesn't always stick that well, so it will have to be reapplied often. Cork belts used this way seem to last forever. I had one last for three years before the joint glue finally gave out.

Engineered Abrasives: These premium belts are designed for specific applications. They have very uniform abrasive material and can go to very small grit size. Norton Norax™ or 3M Trizact™ belts are excellent-quality belts using engineered abrasives that are as small as 5x Microns, or about 1200 SAE grit.

Engineered abrasives are exceptionally good metal finishing belts but are nearly worthless on any other material, as they release dark-gray abrasive dust that tends to stain anything other than metal.

Nonwoven: These belts are used to deburr metal edges or to provide a uniform scratch pattern. Most people are familiar with 3M-brand Scotch Brite pads, which are essentially a nonwoven abrasive. Nonwoven belts are commonly used by knifemakers to put a satin finish on knife blades, and they come in coarse, medium, fine, and extra fine. The coarse belts will actually remove steel (albeit very slowly), while the finer grits tend to polish metal. These are for metal use only. These generally cost from sixteen dollars to thirty dollars, depending on the brand and application. One of these belts will last a very long time, so just get one to start.

Leather Belts: These are just what you think they are, a loop of leather in the form of a belt. They are used by some people as power-leather strops after they have had some very fine abrasive compound added to the surface. Usually, a compound is added to the belt. This can be a paste abrasive, such as Flitz. I use a leather belt with green chrome as the final step in sharpening to, micro polish the edge and remove any remaining burr. Leather belts, by nature, stretch unevenly and will wobble all over the grinder wheel. It's the nature of the beast. Don't leave a leather belt under tension in your grinder, or it will keep stretching to the point of failure.

Felt belts: These are belts made from the same material as felt, and they are fairly thick at approximately a quarter-inch thick. These almost always have buffing compound applied to them ,and are used for polishing metal. These are expensive and hard to find. This is old-school technology and has largely been replaced by other abrasives or processes.

Now, the Question Is, "Then What Belt Should I Use?"

The answer is, "It depends." Every knifemaker will develop a belt progression that works for them. I'll share with you what works for me, but if you ask ten knifemakers about their belt progression, you'll get fifteen different answers.

I usually grind fixed-blade knives from thick stock (in the .180 to .2-plus range), so I start with a coarse-grit belt and do about 80 percent of my stock removal using it. I begin with a forty-grit ceramic belt to do the heavy lifting. I grind at full speed initially. I use a 3,400 RPM grinder, and I push hard. I want it gone. Mistakes are easy to fix here, and I remove as much metal as I can. When I have 80 percent to 90 percent of the metal removed, I switch to a 120-grit ceramic or zirc belt and slow the grinder down quite a bit. I shape the blade to 90–95 percent of what I want it to end up being. I make sure and remove every bit of forty-grit grinding marks, as I usually take blades to a high mirror polish. Even if you don't grind to a high polish, you always want to remove every bit of the last grit marks.

When I'm done with the 120-grit, I switch to 100x engineered belts. I make sure and grind away every bit of the 120-grit marks and finalize all metal removal with this belt. I want all the grind lines in place and edge thickness of the blade right where it needs to be when I am done with this belt. The remaining belts I follow this 100x with are all just to improve the finish. The next Norax™ belt I use is a 65x, and, again, a bit slower on the grinder. Mistakes here are frustrating, and a slower grinder makes smaller mistakes. A slower grinder also means less heat buildup. The finer the grit, the more heat it produces. All previous grit marks must be removed. You will not spend a lot of time on the remaining belts, but skipping one will add time to get a consistent finish. I am not trying to remove metal at this point; I am improving the finish as the grit gets smaller and smaller. If I want a satin finish, I stop with the 65x Norax™. I then typically progress to 45x, 16x, and finally a 5x if am going for a full mirror polish. These work out to a 240-, 600-, 800-, and 1,300-grit, respectively. I finish with just a minute or two under a sewn cotton buff wheel with green chrome to give the blade a little color. If you pay attention to the details, you will have a high mirror finish at this point.

Alternatively, I will grind to 120-grit, and then switch to a cork belt with green chrome if my grind lines are exactly where I want them. I can take the finish to whatever level I want using a cork loaded with chrome. It's faster and cheaper. It's also messy, but knifemaking is messy.

If you are grinding thinner stock in the .100" to .140" thickness range, consider starting with a sixty-grit belt or even an eighty-grit belt. If you are grinding under .100" thickness, eighty- or one-hundred-grit will go a little slower, but you will have more control. Sharp belts will take metal off quickly, and you don't need much bigger than eighty-grit when you are grinding thin blade stock. You will probably find 120-grit is the belt you tend to use the most of. A hundred and twenty seems to be a sweet spot grit to use for touch-ups and gives you control when shaping your blade or handle.

I answered the question, "What belt should I use?" with three different answers, all of which are correct, depending on the end goal I have in mind.

The Next Question Is, "What Belts Should I Order?"

What belts you order depends somewhat on your budget. You will want metal removal belts, finishing belts, and then belts to grind and shape knife handle material. One thing to keep in mind is you can't do everything on your grinder. Regardless of what belts you choose, expect to do some hand sanding on the blade, the handle, or both. The better the finish I want on my knives, the more I find the need to hand sand them. Nothing beats old-world hand craftsmanship! Budget some funds for at least a small assortment of nine-by-eleven sheets of abrasive.

Expect to use up several belts per knife blade. In real use, you will find high-quality belts will last for more than one knife. But on the average, it is best to budget a couple of belts per knife. Most experienced knifemakers will tell you to use belts like they are free. A fresh, sharp belt is safer to use, cuts much faster, cooler, and gives you a better grind. A dull belt will grab at the knife, heat the blade quickly while grinding (burning your fingers), and makes it hard to get a clean, straight grind. When you find you are struggling with a grind, change to a fresh belt, and see if it doesn't get better.

Most new knifemakers are surprised at how many belts are needed and how much they cost. It might be easier to think of it this way: expect to spend seven-to-fifteen dollars on abrasive belts per knife. Abrasives are just part of the cost. Some belts, like the Norax™ belts seem to last forever. Some belts, such as a small-grit AO J-Flex, may wear out after one short session, and you may use multiple AO belts on one knife.

Here's a piece of advice from a guy that sells belts for a living—when you order your normal belts, get one other belt that you haven't tried before. This is especially important as you are starting out, developing your technique, and settling on a belt progression that works for the way you grind. Try each new belt out, and see how it works for you. I guarantee you will occasionally find another belt that surpasses what you have been using. The technology changes often, and your grinding style also changes as your skills improve.

Getting More Use from a Dull Belt

Occasionally, you can get a bit more use from a dull belt. The basic technique is to take advantage of the friability of abrasive material. Run the belt at full speed and push a piece of scrap metal into the belt with quite a bit of pressure. Push with more pressure than you would normally grind with. The idea is to break down the abrasive material and expose fresh, sharp edges. You don't want to press down so hard you shave off all the abrasive media. You also don't want to do this so long you wear out what little abrasive media there is left. You want to fracture the dull grit into sharper pieces, giving you more life from an otherwise dead belt. In practice, I have found engineered belts especially benefit from this technique. Not every belt benefits from this technique, as most simply wear down evenly, and there really isn't life left. It is just a technique to be aware of to try if you have a belt that appears like it should have some life left, but it has gone dull. Don't expect to double belt life using this technique, but it might help you out in a pinch someday.

Safety

Belts on a grinder throw abrasive grit and dust, along with small bits of whatever they are grinding. Always wear safety glasses and a respirator if your machine is running. If you grind long enough, you will have a belt break and slap you. I promise it will scare the ever-loving-bejeebers out of you. When it happens, take a break or take the rest of the day off. You won't grind all that well with the shakes, trust me. If you are really lucky, you will only get slapped once, and it will be a small grit, and at slow speed. That usually isn't how it happens, though. It always seems to be at high speed, with a big-grit belt that will scratch you up pretty good as it slaps you a couple times. I've had several belts break over the years I've been making knives. You need to know it is going to happen and be ready for it. I always wear safety glasses and a respirator, so that has deflected the broken belts from slapping me in the face very hard. If you have a damaged belt, don't use it. The few dollars you save by using a damaged belt are not worth the scare (or pain) it will give you if it breaks on you. How often will this happen to you? Not all that often. Maybe one in a 1,000 belts break. But when that first one pops on you, it will definitely have your attention and respect after that.

Only you will be able to determine what belts will serve you best. A basic progression of rough-grit ceramic, followed by fine ceramic, followed by a series of polishing belts is a good place to start, regardless of your technique or final finishing style. Proper attention to the belts you use will improve not only your speed of production, but also your quality. Good belts and good belt selection are an important key to next-level knifemaking.

CHAPTER 6

Blown-Burner Basics

Geoff Keyes

MANY KNIFEMAKERS SOON get to a point where they become weary of charcoal and a pile of bricks as their primary heat source. From there, they often look into building a propane forge. This chapter will give considerations and design specifications for building your own blown forge burner. I like blown burners. They are brute force and dirt simple (just like me), so if you are looking for Venturi advice, you needs go elsewhere.

Safety Warnings

Building and operating a burner like the one described below is dangerous. It can burn you (since hot is what it does). It can create explosions of various sizes. You are responsible for your safety, the safety of your shop, and the safety of everyone around you. Properly built, properly used, and properly maintained, a blown burner is safe to use. Use appropriate caution.

Further Safety Warnings

If you ignore safety, you won't live long enough to be a next-level knifemaker. Here are a few more safety considerations before we get down to this forge burner business.

Regardless of your burner setup, if you smell gas, shut down and find the leak. Propane is heavier than air, and it can fill up a building, which can ignite and do a lot of damage. I have a big tank of propane (150 gallons) outside the shop, not inside. I always turn the gas off and let the gas in the manifold burn out when I am done forging. That way, nothing is pressurized when I'm not around. I don't put Teflon tape on the threads of the burner parts, but the burner isn't pressurized, so it has never been a problem for me. The gas connections should all be checked frequently. If you find that you've got a leak, then you absolutely must seal it up.

Propane forges produce a lot of CO (carbon monoxide). Don't use a propane forge in an enclosed space without providing for an exhaust fan. If your work space is small or enclosed, a CO monitor is prudent. I work in a big space, and my hot shop has a high ceiling and isn't particularly airtight, so I've forgotten about these kinds of precautions. Thanks for reminding me.

You can build the burner in galvanized pipe, *so long as* the injector nipple and the reducer are black iron. If the galvanized pipe gets hot, it lets off zinc smoke, which will make you sick. Zinc smoke has long-term effects (see welder's disease on the internet) and has been known to kill.

The Basic Blown Burner

Now that we're past the safety lessons, I can talk about what you really want to know: how to build a blown forge burner. This type of burner has been around in one form or another as long as I have been making knives, since the mid-1980s. The only innovation on my part is the use of reducer bushings. The advantage of using bushings is that there's no fabrication to do, as all of the parts are available off the shelf.

The burner is pretty basic. It's got two legs—one for the fan, one for the gas. As far as I can tell, the only critical part is the reducer at the injector end. Without a little bit of back pressure, the flame is weak and hard to control.

I like to build the burner in either one-and-a-quarter-inch or one-and-a-half-inch pipe. One inch is too small, as it's hard to get enough air through the system to get a good burn. I've never had a forge that seemed to need a two-inch burner.

A Basic Parts List

(1) Elbow
(1) T
(1) Reducer
(2) Four-inch nipples
(1) Eight-inch nipple
(1) Nipple (A single pipe size smaller)
Bushings (as needed)
(1) Needle valve
(1) Floor flange

The bushings help you size down from the one-and-a-quarter or one-and-half-inch pipe to the .250 size of the needle valve. If you are lucky, you might be able to find a .250 to one-and-a-quarter-inch in a single piece. Most often, you need two bushings. I get my needle valves at a BBQ supplier online, though sometimes I can find them at hardware stores. These are also available at www.hightemptools.com, and occasionally on eBay. The round flange is simple to mate to the floor flange—some nuts and bolts and a couple of holes drilled, and you are done.

The other essential item is a blower. The range you are looking for is sixty-to-a-hundred CFM. I use a one-hundred CFM fan for my forges (I bought five of them the last time Surplus Center had them), and it's really too much air. Using the one-hundred CFM fan, I have to choke my vertical forge down about 70 to 80 percent, and even my welding forge only runs at about 50 percent airflow.

The Burner Parts

The Burner In Two Different Configurations

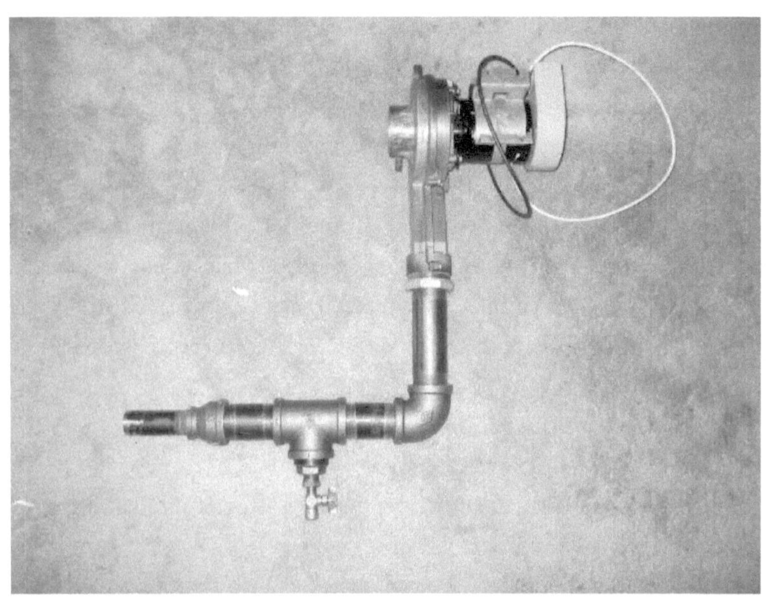

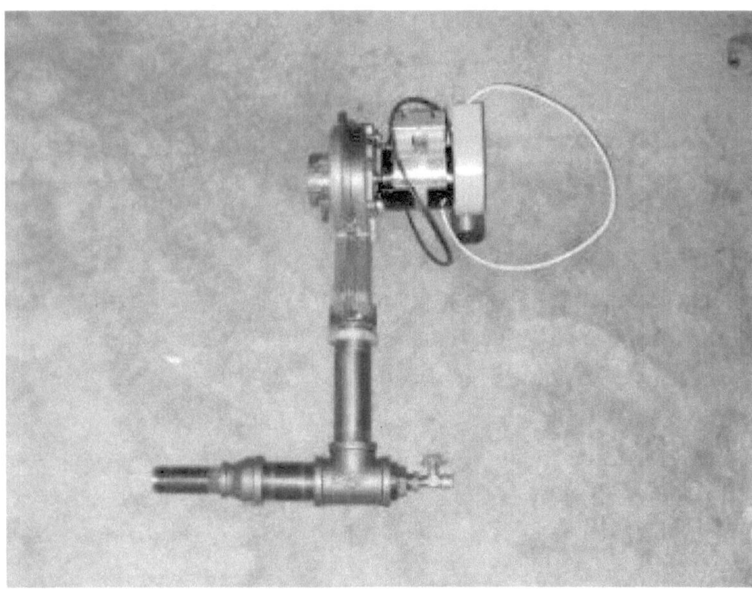

I have used both of these, and I can't say that I ever noticed a difference. When I was starting out, I was told that the elbow promoted swirl and fuel/air mixing. I think having the fuel being injected into the air stream at 90 degrees to the flow creates plenty of mixing.

Some folks put a gate valve between the fan and the gas inlet to adjust the airflow in the burner. I use a bit of magnetic sign material over the intake on the fan. It does the same thing.

To operate this burner is pretty simple. I have all three of my forges connected to a black iron manifold, and each forge has a quarter-turn shutoff valve (in case you need to kill the forge fast) between the manifold and the needle valve. The steps may vary a little if you're connected directly to the propane tank.

Step 1: Pressurize the manifold (turn the gas tank on).

Step 2: Turn on the blower.

Step 3: Open the quarter-turn valve between the manifold and the burner.

Step 4: Light the plumber's torch.

Step 5: Open the needle valve to let the gas into the burner.

Step 6: Light the forge.

When I first started, we used to ball up a piece of newspaper and stuff that in the forge, and then turn on the gas and air. This resulted in a *whomp*, and a ball of flaming paper would shoot out of the forge, which always scared the new guys. Cool! Now I use a plumber's torch. By lighting it first, you avoid any gas buildup (and the big *whomp*) as the forge lights.

Troubleshooting Your Forge Burner

If the forge pops and goes out, add a bit more gas or shut some of the air down.

If the forge has big, billowy flames coming out of it, turn the gas down.

Once you've found the operating mix for your forge, you can adjust the fire by opening and closing the air control, and by adjusting the gas flow with the needle valve. Most of the time, you want just a bit of blue-green flame out the door of the forge. That means that all of the air is being burned in the forge (a reducing atmosphere), and the excess fuel is lighting as it hits the outside air.

I have found two ways to control the temperature with this burner. For my vertical forge, I set the air (allowing about 20 percent flow) and vary the needle valve up and down. With my HT forge, I want to be able to run at very low (for the burner) temps, in the 1,450 to 1,550 range. To get that, I run the line pressure up to eight-to-ten PSI, just crack open the needle valve, and then fine-tune with the airflow. I have gotten stable temps as low as 1,380 Fahrenheit, which is pretty low.

One more consideration is counterintuitive. I have had people build this burner, and then come back and say, "I tried a test run, and it doesn't work." The burner will not hold a flame in open air. It needs to be inside a forge in order for it to work. Most of the Venturi burners will burn on a test bench, and I think that people expect the same behavior in the blown burner. If you want to test your setup, build a brick box around the end of the burner, or use a roll of Kaowool. That should do the trick.

Editor's Note

While the focus of this chapter is blown-burner construction, many successful smiths use naturally aspirated Venturi burners. Michael Porter's book, *Gas Burners for Forges, Furnaces, and Kilns*, is the seminal work on the subject. I (Jason) have built several Porter burners, including my welding forge. I can run my welding forge with a three-quarter-inch Porter burner running at ten-to-twelve PSI.

CHAPTER 7

Introduction to Anvils

Geoff Keyes

Anvils: Where, Why, and How

MOST MAKERS BEGIN their journey into the craft of bladesmithing making do with what equipment they have. The right sort of tools to make knives are expensive and often difficult to find. One of the first large purchases and great early needs for those who wish to forge blades is a suitable hammering surface. The process of finding a usable anvil can be quite daunting.

Do I Need an Anvil?

The first question you'll have to decide is if you need an anvil or not. If you want to forge blades, or other steel things, then, yes, you need an anvil. On the other hand, if you are primarily interested in stock-removal knives, an anvil isn't required. But do you need a "real" anvil, or could you do what you want with something else? As it turns out, there are lots of ways to get the functionality of an anvil without the cost and trouble.

What Is an Anvil?

An anvil is essentially a large bottom tool. The top tool is your hammer most of the time, or some other struck tool like a punch or a fuller. The anvil has several different surfaces built into it, such as the horn and the step, and sharp edges and corners if your anvil still has any. An anvil also has a tool holder (the square hole), called a *hardy hole*, and it may have a smaller, round hold to assist you in punching operations, called a *Pritchel hole.*

Anvil Physics

Hammers will not rebound on a surface that is soft. As an example, imagine hitting your hammer on a rubber mat. The soft mat will absorb the power of the hit. While all steel is likely harder than a rubber mat, soft steel is more susceptible to plastic deformation, which means the atoms can slide around each other very easily. When the hammer strikes soft steel, the hammer's kinetic energy is absorbed by the soft-steel atoms moving relative to each other, creating heat and a dent. Hard steel does not deform as easily, so instead of the anvil face deforming, making the hammer lose kinetic energy, there's no other place for the energy to go but back to the hammer. Having both the hammer face and anvil face hard makes forging more efficient due to these properties.

If something interrupts the force of the hammer strike, the anvil is much less efficient than it could be. If there's a crack in the heel, or a broken horn, or a broken waist joint, the pieces will vibrate against one another and dampen out the energy of your blow. You will have to completely lift the hammer off of the surface over and over, with no rebound force helping you, and will wear out your arm. You will also accomplish less work with each blow, adding to your frustration and making forging more of a chore instead of more fun.

In addition, an anvil that isn't connected to its block will bounce, which also steals energy from your hammer blow. If you strike the anvil on the horn, or on the heel, you should notice much less rebound, and a *clonky* noise. This is because those parts are not supported as well by the mass of the anvil and are flexing under impact.

The engineers at Nazel (a builder of power hammers) believed that a twenty-to-one ratio of anvil to hammer weight was ideal for a power hammer to be efficient. I'm not sure how that relates to hand hammers, but it is something to keep in mind. Too much hammer, or an anvil that is too light or not attached to its block, is going to waste energy.

However, given that anvils are often expensive and difficult to come by, we have to make do with what we can get. More weight is better, but a small anvil that has most of its mass under the striking surface will work better than a larger, but more distributed, piece of steel.

What this means is, if you have a piece of plate one-inch thick and six-inches square, you will get more work done hammering on the edge of the plate than you will on the flat of the plate. The edge puts more mass under your hammer. A six-by-six-by-twelve steel block weighs about 130 pounds. On end, this is a good weight for a bladesmith's anvil. On the other hand, a 130-pound London pattern anvil only has about 60 percent of its weight under the sweet spot, making it a less-useful tool. But, to be clear, *any anvil is better than no anvil at all.*

What Should I Pay for a Used Anvil?

Whether or not to buy a used anvil is a difficult question. In the long-ago times, when wild anvils roamed the earth in packs, we used to say that anvils cost one-to-two dollars a pound. I paid about $2.25 a pound for my first anvil, and that was a pretty good deal then. Once you get past five or six dollars a pound for a used anvil, you're into new anvil territory, and maybe that is where you should spend your money. You'll discover that there are tool prices, and there are collector prices. In a collector market, the prices are very high, more than a poor bladesmith can (or should) afford. Just because an anvil is 200 years old does not make it a lost treasure. The success of the TV show *Forged in Fire* has greatly increased the market demand for anvils and forging tools, and therefore, anvil prices have significantly increased in the past five years.

When you are looking for an anvil at first, the temptation is to pay any price for the first one that comes available in your area, just because anvils are so hard to find. Resist this impulse. However, if you find something that's not perfect, but is usable, and the price is good, it's reasonable to get it and use it for now. A less-than-perfect tool can always be modified, put to another use (I have seen pictures of battered anvils used as the anvil for a power hammer), or given to the next guy who needs a hand up. Having an anvil, even a beat-up one, gives you some time to keep looking for a good one at a good price. You will ultimately have to decide for yourself whether the anvil you find is good enough, or whether the price is too much or too little. Getting started in bladesmithing is never going to be cheap, but spending way too much on an anvil just to have a "real" anvil isn't the way I would go.

Where Do I Find an Anvil?

First and foremost, anvils are where you find them. Look in junk stores, flea markets, garage sales, Craigslist, and Facebook marketplace. If there are smiths in your area (and we are like spiders—we are everywhere, you just don't see us) contact them and ask if they have one they could sell, or if they know of one that might be available. Tell everyone you know that you are looking for an anvil, and you never know where one will turn up.

How Do I Test an Anvil?

A good anvil returns energy to your hammer stroke. It does this by having a hard face and mass beneath the hammer. An anvil with a soft face will still work, but it won't return much (or any) energy to your blow. You can test an anvil with either a ball bearing or a light hammer blow. The "sweet spot" on an anvil is the area of the face that is directly over the center of the base.

You should ask before testing the anvil, as many owners will be angry if you start hammering on their anvil without asking first. Once you've received permission, take the ball bearing, hold it about twelve inches above the center mass of the anvil, and drop it. On a top-quality anvil, the ball should rebound nearly as high as the drop point. You can do the same thing with a hammer by holding the hammer in two fingers about twelve inches above the sweet spot of the anvil and letting it fall *while* holding on with your fingers. Just let the head pivot down and strike the anvil face. The hammer should rebound almost back to the same position.

If the hammer or bearing only rebounds a bit (see Fisher anvils, below), or if it just lies there, that is a bad sign. If the anvil thunks, or buzzes, those are both bad things. This poor anvil is junk and should be left where you found it. See "Can I Repair This Anvil?" below.

Having said that, a broken heel or horn isn't always the end of the world. If you can remove the cracked part, say with a Sawzall and a metal blade, even a partial anvil can be used for a long time. It is the vibration of the broken part that causes problems. A great many early-nineteenth-century anvils are found without a horn or heel. This is less about anvils being intentionally damaged during the Civil War (a story told over and over) and more to do with anvils being made in small, discrete pieces. Those weld joints can fail over time. If the face is good, a damaged anvil is still a good tool, just more limited.

Anvils, New and Used

There are a number of modern anvil makers that should not be confused with the makers of anvil-shaped objects (ASO) sold by certain purveyors of cheap tools. These ASO will not hold up to the stresses of forging. Don't buy one, even as a stopgap until you find something better.

New anvils start around six dollars a pound.

Potential sources of new anvils include:

- http://www.blackiron.us/anvils.html
- http://www.blacksmithsdepot.com/
- http://www.incandescent-iron.com/
- http://nimbaanvils.com/
- http://fontaninianvilandtool.com/
- http://oldworldanvils.com/anvils/index.html
- http://bigbluhammer.com/hand-tools/anvils/blacksmith-anvil
- www.euroanvils.net/
- http://www.hoffmansforge.com/my-work/anvils/
- http://www.blksmth.com/Refflinghaus_Anvils.htm
- http://www.texasfarriersupply.com/index.php
- https://usaknifemaker.com/
- https://www.hollandanvil.com/

Old Anvils

Vintage anvils are out there, and most of them still have some life left. Some common brands are:

- Brooks
- Hay Budden
- Peter Wright
- Fisher
- Trenton

These are all top-quality anvils, or at least they were when they were made. If they have been treated badly, that should reduce the value. Damage should—but does not always—reduce the price, but there's a difference between collector and tool prices.

Vulcan / Arm and Hammer

Vulcan and A&H anvils are often considered a second-tier products. The top plates are thin and brittle and often chip. On the other hand, any anvil can be better than no anvil at all. If you find a Vulcan or Arm and Hammer, and if the price is right and it's not too beat up, you should not pass them by just because of the brand.

Anvils by Brand

I like Fisher anvils, as the first anvil I ever bought was a 200-pound Fisher, which I still own. Fishers were made with a welded face. By design, Fishers don't ring, which, in the hold of a ship or a small shop, is very nice. They don't have quite the rebound of one of the other top-grade anvils, but they are still some of the best American-made anvils. My Fisher also has closed cleats on the foot, which makes bolting to a block easy.

The rest of the anvils in the above list are top-notch, with the exception of Vulcan. That said, I would take a pretty clean Vulcan over a battered-and-abused Brooks every day.

Can I Repair This Anvil?

Whether or not you can repair an anvil depends on what you mean by "repair." Small chips and dents can be ground out or worked around. Cracks and major delaminations, probably not. It is very difficult to get a modern welder (stick, MIG, or TIG) to penetrate deep enough to re-weld a top plate or to weld a whole new plate to an old body. Heat-treating a new plate is also going to be an issue.

Most anvil repairs ultimately fail. The first way they fail is an insufficient bond between the top plate (the hard part) and the body. This causes vibration between the hard plate and the body, killing the rebound. The second type of failure is leaving the top plate soft. The welding process heats the steel past the tempering level of the top plate. The plate is left soft, and the all-important rebound is deadened. This same softening happens to anvils that have undergone a shop fire.

You could re-harden an anvil, in theory, but in practice, it's quite difficult to do. First, you have to heat an anvil up to quenching temperature (around 1,500°F) and heat it evenly. Second, you need to be able to move the 1,500°F anvil to your quench medium. Third, you need to be able to cool it fast enough to make the top steel hard, without the heat in the mass of the anvil drawing the anvil into a soft state. Fisher anvils were quenched in an artificial waterfall, pouring thousands of gallons of water over the anvils. It's very hard to do on a small scale.

There are stories out there that there are particular "hard facing" welding rods that are deposited as hard material. This requires the body of the anvil to be preheated to 400 Fahrenheit, and then pass after pass of hard rod laid down, and then machined to shape. It would be very time consuming to do (think many dollars).

Can I Build My Own Anvil?

Building anvils has been done by many blacksmiths. I know of at least one person who has cast a custom anvil, but he works for a company that does this kind of thing as a business. It's expensive and time-consuming. I have seen a forum post elsewhere of a maker who found a slab of four-inch-thick steel, cut out an anvil shape, machined all of the surfaces and hard surfaced the piece. I don't think he saved any money doing it. I think it probably cost more than simply buying an anvil.

Anvil Substitutes

So you can't find (or can't afford) a "real" anvil. What should you do? If we deconstruct an anvil, what do we have?

1. A hammering surface
2. A horn (a drawing surface)
3. A hardy hole
4. A Pritchel hole

Those are the things that jump out, but there are a few others.

1. A step
2. Edges—some sharp, some radiused
3. A heel
4. Some known lengths and measurements
5. Mass

As a bladesmith, not all of these are as useful as others. I rarely use the horn for my work. A hardy is useful for holding all sorts of tools, but I don't punch holes all that much. Knowing that the face is *X* inches across and *Y* inches long means that you don't need a ruler—measurements are built in. I don't have need of the heel, or a step, but good edges are handy.

1. A block anvil. Mine is about five by six-and-a-half by twenty-nine inches. I got lucky, but you don't need all of the length that I have.
2. A second block, set on its side, that I use to hold different sorts of tooling. Primarily, guillotine tools.
3. A swedge block. It sits on its side most of the time. I use the holes as hardy holes. Various cutoff and bending tools fit it. With help (I need to build a small crane), I can set it on edge to use the forming shapes.

4. All of this sits on a piece of one-inch plate, so it can be moved as a piece. The plate also adds weight, which keeps the whole thing in place. I can get a pinch bar under it and put it on rollers, if I need to move it.
5. Down the center is a hammer rack, so my most-used tools are right where I need them.

That's what I have done. What you do depends on what you can find and how you work.

Railroad Track Anvils

Railroad tracks have been used for makeshift anvils ever since someone first cut the end off of a length of track. Railroad anvils fall into the category of "better than nothing." The biggest problem with track is the web between the rail and foot. This web is very thin, and so it vibrates and flexes. You may not see it, but you sure can feel it once you've used a better surface. I have seen people weld plates under the rail in an attempt to shore up the top. Vibration and less-than-perfect welds make this problematic. I have seen people try filling the space under the plates with junk (nuts and bolts and pieces of scrap), but this amplifies the vibration issue and makes it worse. I saw one filled with lead once. The anvil was heavy, but it was also dead, worse than it started, not to mention the environmental issues with melting and pouring lead.

Although railroad track anvils are not ideal, they can be made to work. Take a piece of railroad track, smooth off one end, and bolt the rail to a stump, on end. The end of the rail is your anvil.

Sharpen the top edge of the web, which gives you an integral cutoff tool.

Take a second short piece of track, and bolt that horizontally to your stump to use as a drawing surface.

Weld a receiver to the foot of the vertical track. A piece of square tube will do, though you could build something better supported and bigger. You can then build some tools that will fit in the receiver and reach over to your anvil to act as third hand tools.

That is most of the functionality of an anvil. Add a tool rack to the stump, and you've got a nice "portable" work station.

I found this idea on the web. I would not have built the welded horn, partly because of vibration problems, and because it would hit me in an uncomfortable spot. But notice the hardy hole. It would be easy to build a cutoff tool, bottom fullers, and all kinds of tools that would reach from the hardy to striking face. A short piece of rail could be fitted horizontally as a drawing surface, and, as I suggested, sharpening the web would provide you with an integral cutoff tool. If that were bolted to a post or a stump on the foot side, I think this would be perfect.

A general blacksmith needs most of the features offered by a London pattern anvil. A bladesmith does not—at least, not all of the time. I almost never need a horn, so my setup has a removable drawing tool. Having two edges where I can forge tapers (and which are close together) is important to me, so a small, square forging surface with some mass under it is what I have. A longer surface for straightening a piece is handy, but it doesn't need to be an anvil. A long piece of half-inch plate would do the job. Most anvils, prior to about 1,500, were small, just a couple of square inches of surface. A lot of things were forged on these little anvils—knives, swords, armor, household items, pretty much anything and everything that was made with a hammer. You may find that with a bit of thought you can build yourself everything you thought you needed when you began looking for a "real anvil.

In Conclusion

The single most important tool in your kit is *your brain.* A smith is a problem solver. My first teacher, a fine smith named Jerry Culberson, used to forge with two rocks, a small one as a hammer and a big for the anvil. Were they good tools? No, they were not. Did they get the job done? Pretty much. With a bit of thought, pretty much any forging problem can be overcome with makeshift tools. Do you want to do that every day? No, you don't. But that is one of the joys of being a smith. Making your own tools can be quite satisfying, as long as it doesn't get in the way of your primary mission. Do you want to be a tool maker, or do you want to make knives?

An anvil is just a tool. Find the right one for the work you are doing, change it, improve it, use it, and move on. Don't get hung up on the tools. They are just the way all of those knives in your head become real objects.

CHAPTER 8

Introduction to Knife Steel

Larrin Thomas

THE WORLD OF knife steels can be intimidating at first glance. There are so many steel types, names, numbers, and compositions, and so many properties to keep track of like toughness, strength, hardness, and wear resistance. When you combine technical knowledge about steel with the "simple" task of learning to make a knife, learning about steel can seem a task too big to handle. In this chapter, I will introduce the major categories of steels and describe which steels fit into each category. I will also give an overview of steel and knife properties to help you understand which qualities we are looking for in our raw material and finished product. To wrap it up, I have a simplified ranking of different knife steels so that the reader will have a starting point for selecting steel for different applications.

Basic Steel Properties

Toughness

Toughness is the property that gives steel resistance to fracture, cracking, or breakage. A brittle, low toughness piece of steel will fracture rather than bending. Toughness tests are performed with impact testers, where the steel is struck with a heavy blow so that it breaks. The energy absorbed by the steel is measured, and the more energy the steel requires to fracture, the tougher it is. When a knife edge is chipping, the damage is the result of insufficient toughness for the given edge geometry and task.

Flexing, Bending, Strength, and Hardness

Heat treatment is used to increase the steel's strength and hardness. Strength is the resistance of a material to being deformed. When a soft steel is flexed, it stays bent, and when a soft edge is flexed, it rolls. Hard steel will flex and return to its original shape—both when bent and when flexed on the knife's edge. Hardness is an easy measure of strength, which is partly why it is such a common measure of knife steel. Hardness measurement involves a small indenter that is pressed into the steel at a fixed load. The steel's response to that indenter indicates its hardness. The harder the steel, the smaller the indent that is left in the steel after the test.

Flexing of steel works under a different set of properties than bending and staying bent. Hardened steel that flexes and then returns straight moves by stretching and compressing the bonds between iron atoms. The bonds between atoms can be thought of as tiny springs, stretching and compressing as necessary. Therefore, strengthening the steel through heat treatment does not affect flexing, because the strength of the iron-iron bonds does not change with heat treatment. However, the degree to which the steel can flex before being permanently bent is controlled by its strength.

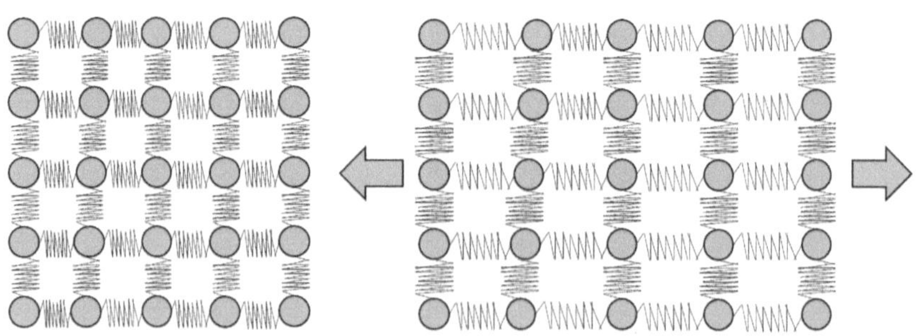

The amount of force necessary to flex the steel isn't controlled by its heat treatment or strength, but rather by its geometry. Bigger pieces of steel are more difficult to bend. In the simple equation to predict the load required to deflect a rectangular bar, thickness is cubed (t^3), while width is not. Therefore, thickness is much more important than width for making a knife difficult to bend. While knife edges are not rectangular, they follow a similar principle, in that thicker edges are more difficult to bend than thinner edges.

If a piece of steel is clamped to the table and bent by pushing it toward the floor, the top of the piece experiences a *tensile*, or "pulling" force, while the bottom experiences *compression*, or "pushing" force. Steel is much more likely to break in tension than in compression. The thicker the piece of steel, the higher the tensile stress at the surface. This is partly why flexible fillet knives can be bent 90 degrees without breaking, because the thin steel experiences less tensile stress. Similar things happen with edges. A thin edge is easier to bend, but is also less likely to fracture because of how thin it is. Higher strength is required to prevent the edge from rolling because it is thinner. However, flexing of the edge with a thin cross section cannot be prevented.

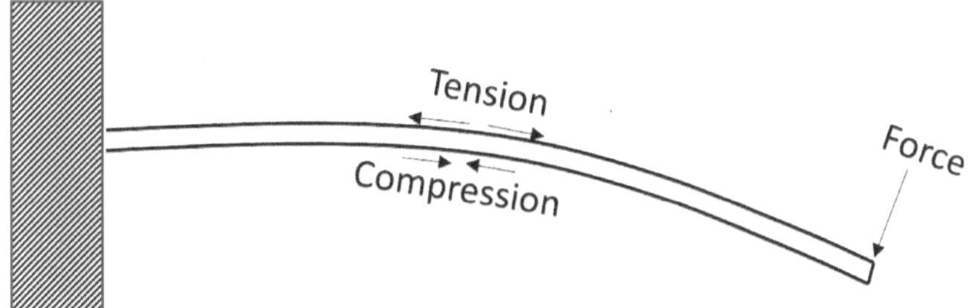

Effect of Hardness on Other Properties

Strength and hardness also indirectly affect other knife properties. For custom knives, the typical hardness range is between fifty-eight and sixty-two on the Rockwell scale, abbreviated RC. Anything below 58 RC can be considered low hardness, and higher than 61 or 62 RC can be considered high hardness. This does not mean that steel should not be outside of the 58 to 68 RC bounds, but some relative numbers will help in understanding the rest of the information presented here. Higher hardness usually means lower toughness. The very hard steel is more brittle, and therefore, easier to fracture. A high hardness knife edge is more easily chipped. Harder steel is also more wear resistant. Or in other words, the harder a material is, the more difficult it is to gouge or scratch. This higher wear resistance means the steel is more difficult to grind or finish for the knifemaker. It also means the steel experiences less wear in cutting and will have better edge retention. However, there are other factors that affect toughness and wear resistance. See these graphs comparing toughness (higher is better) and wear resistance (lower is better) versus hardness for different steels:

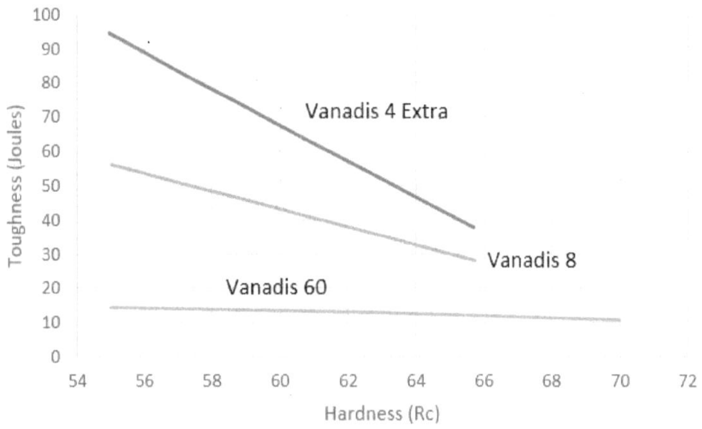

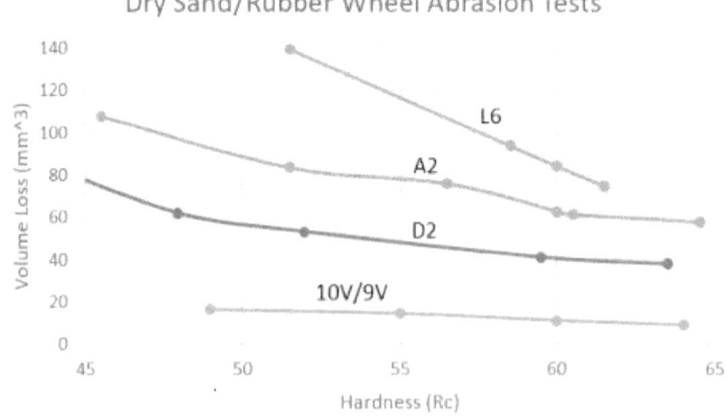

You can see that Vanadis 4 Extra is tougher at 64 RC than Vanadis 60, even if it is heat-treated down to 56 RC. You can also see that L6 steel is less abrasion resistant at sixty RC than D2 is at 48 RC. Heat treatment can certainly change properties of steel, but it does not mean that a steel with poor wear resistance or poor toughness can suddenly become like something else. The difference between these different steels comes down to the alloy carbides in each. Carbides are hard particles in steel, formed between carbon and other elements. Because they are so hard, they contribute to wear resistance but reduce toughness.

Carbides and Wear Resistance

There are several different carbide types, the simplest of which is cementite or iron carbide (Fe_3C). Iron carbides are the softest of the major carbide types and contribute the least to wear resistance. At the other end of the spectrum are vanadium (VC) and niobium carbides (NbC), which are much harder than steel. In the middle are chromium carbides such as those formed in stainless steel ($Cr_{23}C_6$ and Cr_7C_3), and molybdenum (Mo_6C) and tungsten carbides (W_6C), formed in high-speed steels. Other types in the table include nitrides, particles formed with nitrogen instead of carbon, formed with either chromium (CrN) or vanadium (VN). The $(Cr,V)_7C_3$ refers to chromium carbides that are enriched in vanadium, which increases the hardness of the chromium carbide; that carbide type is common in stainless steels with large vanadium additions. The harder the carbide type, the more it contributes to wear resistance and edge retention for a given amount. One percent of vanadium carbide is roughly equivalent to 5 percent iron carbide in terms of contribution to edge retention. The hardness of each carbide is given in Vickers (Hv), which is a different scale than that familiar to knifemakers, Rockwell C; most of the carbides are too hard to be measured with Rockwell. One thousand Hv is roughly equal to 69 RC.

Carbide	Hardness (Hv)
Fe_3C	1,000
$Cr_{23}C_6$	1,200
$(Mo,W)_6C$	1,400
Cr_7C_3	1,500
CrN	1,700
$(Cr,V)_7C_3$	1,950
NbC	2,600
VC	2,800
VN	2,800

Carbides and Toughness

In terms of toughness, however, the carbide type/hardness is less important than the carbide size and volume fraction. Cracks easily initiate at large carbides because they are such brittle particles. The cracks either form around the carbide or crack the carbide itself, and cracks can grow from carbide to carbide because that is the path of least resistance. The larger the particle, the lower the stress required to initiate the crack. Therefore, a larger amount of carbide particles leads to lower toughness, and large carbide particles lead to lower toughness. In the image below, a crack formed within a large carbide on the right side of the image, and then grew along other brittle carbides as it traveled left.

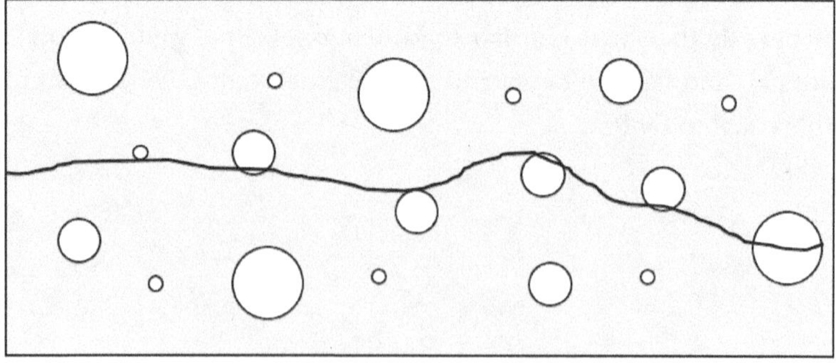

In the toughness chart comparing Vanadis 4 Extra, Vanadis 8, and Vanadis 60, there's a significant difference in carbide volume fraction. Vanadis 4 has about 9 percent carbide volume, Vanadis 8 has 15 percent, and Vanadis 60 has 25 percent. The difference in carbide volume is what makes Vanadis 60 much less tough than Vanadis 4. In a chart below, you can see a range of steels with different carbide volume fractions, each heat-treated to approximately 60 RC, where there's a clear trend demonstrating the effect of carbides on toughness.

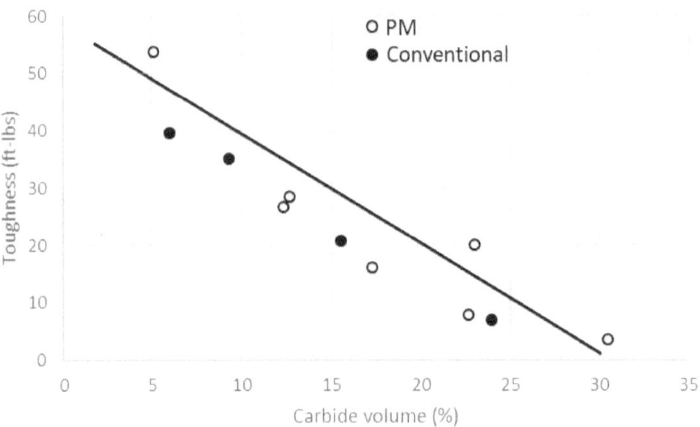

Steelmaking

Producing knife steel typically starts with the melting process, utilizing steel scrap and various alloys. The steel is melted by a process such as induction, and very high temperatures are required. The steel is then poured into a mold, where it slowly cools and solidifies. The cast steel is then hot rolled to final dimensions. This final hot-rolling step typically reduces the steel by many times, such as a 500:1 reduction. The hot rolling puts the steel into the desired dimensions for final use, but it also refines the microstructure, reducing the carbide size.

While a steel data sheet often gives a single composition for steel, such as 1.45 percent carbon, 5.2 percent chromium, and so on, the steel is rarely at that exact composition. Due to variability in steel scrap, loss of alloy and carbon during the melting process, and other factors, there's always a range of composition. This range of composition usually does not greatly affect the final properties and heat treatment, but in some cases, there can be variability within each melt of each steel type. For example, if a particular melt of steel was low in the range for carbon content for that steel type, the final hardness may be 1–2 RC lower than the midpoint composition. There's also some range in impurities like sulfur or phosphorous which reduce toughness in the final steel. The impurity level depends on the process used for steel production, among other factors. Receiving steel composition information from the steel producer for the given heat of steel that is being purchased can allow the comparison of composition from batch to batch.

Powder Metallurgy Steel

One method by which the carbide size is kept small is called *powder metallurgy*. With typical steelmaking, there's a large ingot of molten steel which slowly cools. The slow cooling allows the growth of carbides to large sizes that are detrimental to toughness. With powder metallurgy, a stream of molten steel is passed through a gas spray that solidifies the steel nearly instantaneously. Each powder particle is like its own ingot that cooled down very rapidly. The powder steel is then turned into a solid ingot under pressure and high temperature. The powder metallurgy process can significantly improve the toughness of steel for a given volume fraction of carbide. Powder metallurgy isn't necessary for every steel. High-alloy steels have carbides that form in the liquid steel as it cools; diffusion of elements and growth of carbides are very fast in the liquid. Low-alloy steels and carbon steels have carbides that form at lower temperatures, when the steel is solid and managing their size is much easier with forging and heat-treating.

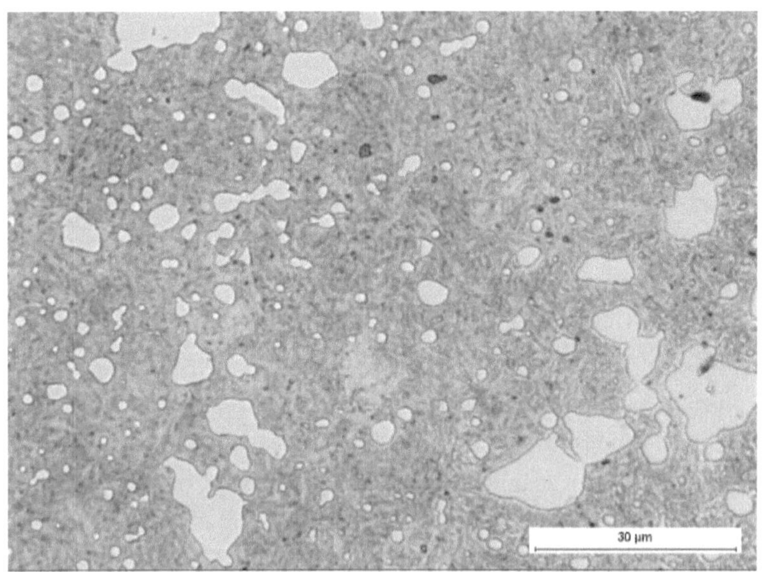

Conventional 154CM with large carbides

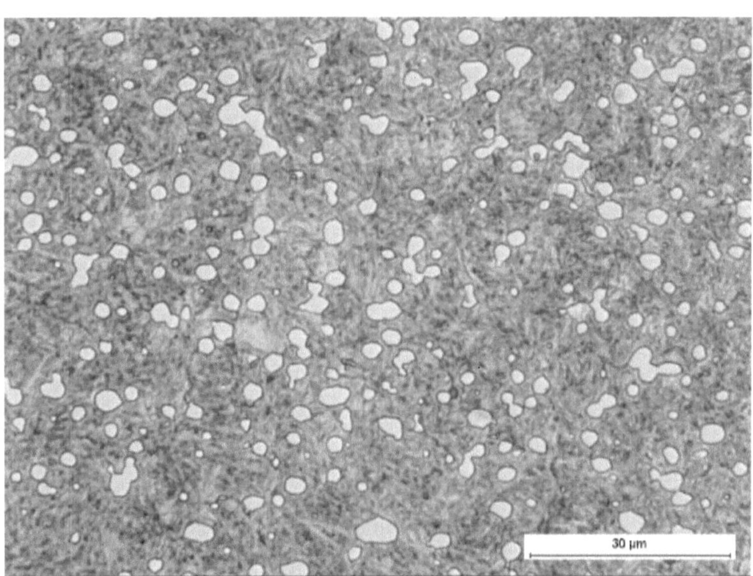

Powder metallurgy 154CM with small and uniform carbides
Used with permission from Sandvik

Grinding, Sharpening, and Polishing

Ease in grinding, finishing, and sharpening is roughly the opposite of edge retention and wear resistance. Almost all knifemaking operations require abrasives for wearing of steel, so it makes sense that higher-wear resistance would make finishing and sharpening more difficult. For knives that are display pieces, requiring very high finishes, or for knife users that prefer ease of sharpening rather than edge retention, higher-wear resistance may not always be desired.

Toughness-Wear Resistance Balance

For knives where maximum performance is desired, the primary tradeoff is between toughness and edge retention. Increasing one usually leads to a decrease in the other. Higher edge retention requires more carbide, which reduces toughness, or requires higher hardness, which reduces toughness. However, because toughness is primarily controlled by size and volume fraction of carbides, while edge retention is helped by high carbide hardness, some combinations are better than others. A smaller-volume fraction of harder carbide can lead to a better combination of toughness and hardness. This is the principle that is used in vanadium-alloyed steel. 3V powder metallurgy steel has a small amount (~5 percent) of very hard vanadium carbide for excellent toughness, while still having good wear resistance. 10V powder metallurgy steel has a large amount (~18 percent) of vanadium carbide for excellent wear resistance and good toughness. CPM-154, a powder metallurgy stainless steel, also has about 18 percent carbide, but instead has chromium carbides. With a similar carbide volume, the toughness is roughly equal to 10V. However, because the chromium carbides are much softer than vanadium carbide, the wear resistance is significantly less for CPM-154 compared to 10V.

Cutting Ability and Sharpness

Sharpness is defined in part by the energy required for initiating a cut. If you imagine pressing a knife into a soft piece of rubber, a dull knife requires more force being pressed into the rubber, and it must press into the rubber to a greater degree until the cut starts. A very sharp knife would require very little force and would hardly deform the rubber at all before the cut starts.

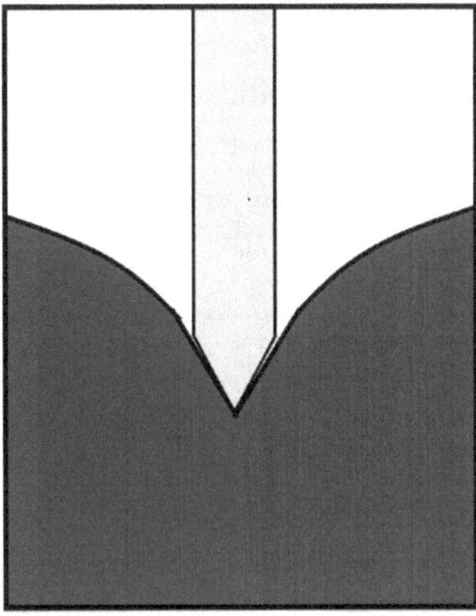

Geometrically, the main factor that controls sharpness is the width or radius of the very tip of the edge. As a knife is worn, the radius increases from being nearly triangular to being rounded and dull. When sharpening to higher sharpness, moving to finer grits isn't as much about removing scratches and smoothing the edge as it is about allowing one to make the edge width smaller and smaller.

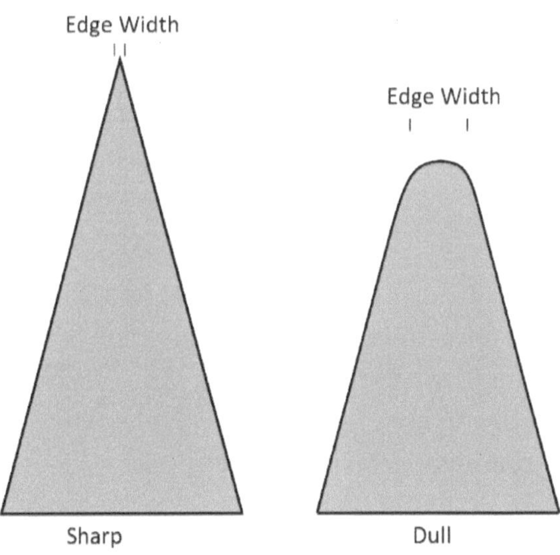

Cutting ability is the energy required for making a complete cut, rather than just initiating one. Cutting ability is influenced by sharpness, yes, but also by the geometry of the edge as a whole. One important factor is the angle at which the edge is sharpened. A more obtuse angle (56°) isn't as good at cutting as a more acute angle edge (20°).

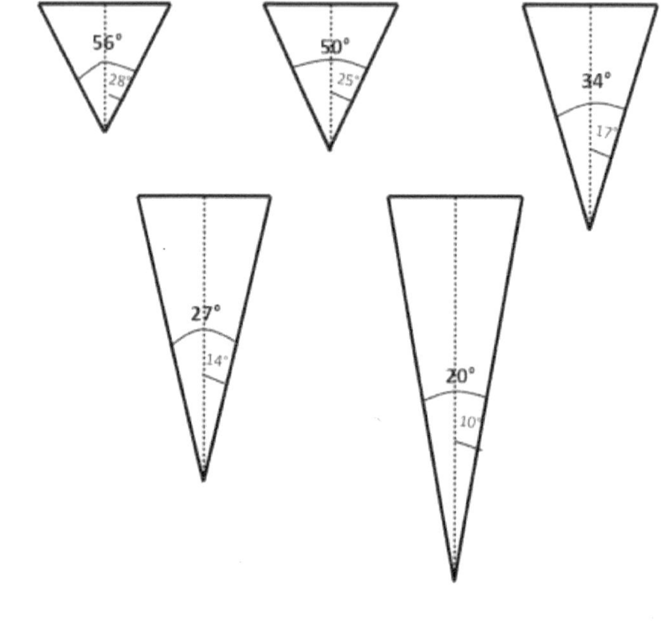

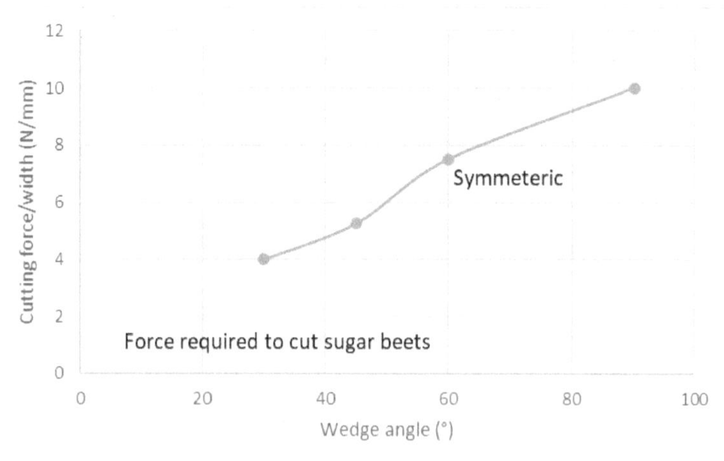

Another important factor is the thickness "behind the edge." The thinner the edge is behind the primary edge bevel, the better the cutting ability, even when sharpened to the same angle.

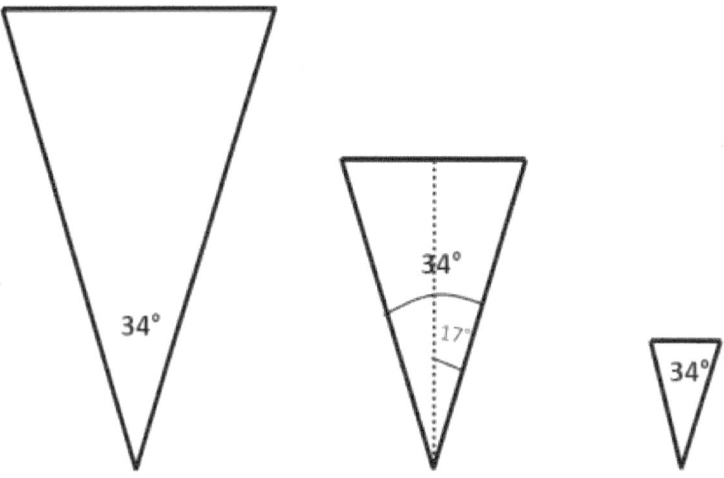

Edge Retention

Improving cutting ability also improves edge retention. Some believe that a thinner edge has better cutting ability, but a thicker edge lasts longer, but that isn't seen experientially. Below, I have a chart showing total cardstock cut in a CATRA test with different edge angles. CATRA is a measure of slicing edge retention. The knife cuts 5 percent silica-impregnated cardstock at a fixed load, slicing distance, and number of cuts. More cardstock cut means the knife had better edge retention. You can see that a knife sharpened to 20° (10° per side) cut nearly 1,000mm of cardstock, while at 50° it cut less than 200mm.

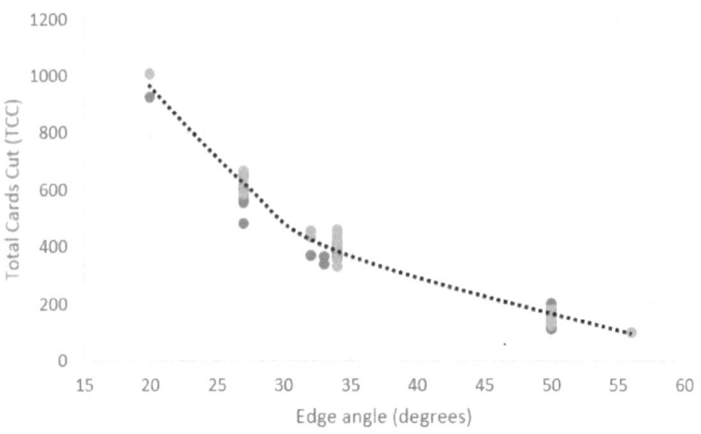

Ease in Sharpening

Ease in sharpening is controlled by several factors including hardness, wear resistance, geometry, and difficulty of deburring. Lower hardness steel is more difficult to sharpen to high levels of sharpness, and leads to rougher edges. Low-wear resistance steel is easy to grind away. Deburring is more difficult with soft steels. Higher hardness is better for high sharpness. Thinner behind the edge means that the bevels are smaller, and less material needs to be removed for sharpening.

Edge Stability

The exception to the above edge-retention discussion is with hard cutting or chopping tasks where chipping or rolling is the dominant edge-loss mechanism. This kind of edge damage is particularly likely when the edges are optimized for cutting, i.e. very thin bevels with very acute edges. Thinner edges are prone to rolling or chipping, and therefore, steel choice and heat treatment must be optimized around avoiding those failures. To avoid rolling, high hardness is necessary, but high hardness decreases toughness. Therefore, steel should be selected with high toughness, which usually means small carbides and a small-volume fraction of them. Large carbides also present problems for very high sharpness edges, as the carbides can be larger than the edge radius itself. A very sharp edge is well under one Micron, so with large carbides, there's "carbide pullout" leaving small holes in the edge. Below I have a comparison of conventionally produced

154CM compared with powder metallurgy CPM-154, where carbide pullout is evident in the conventional steel, but not the powder metallurgy version:

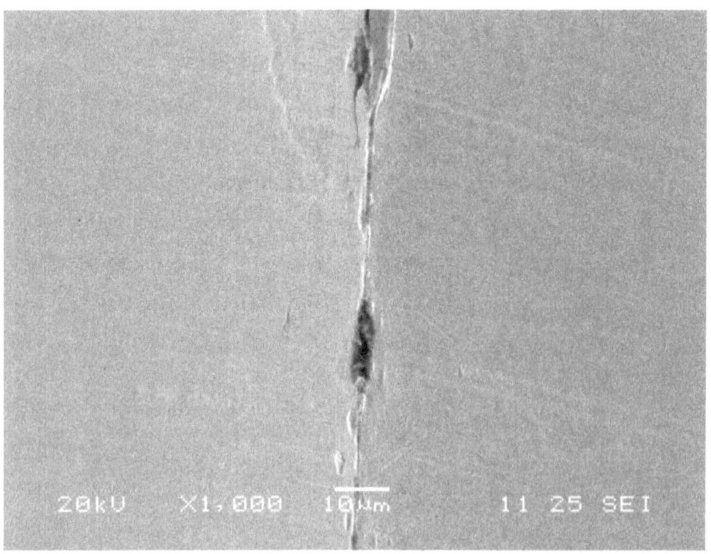

Conventional 154CM with gaps in the edge indicating carbide pullout

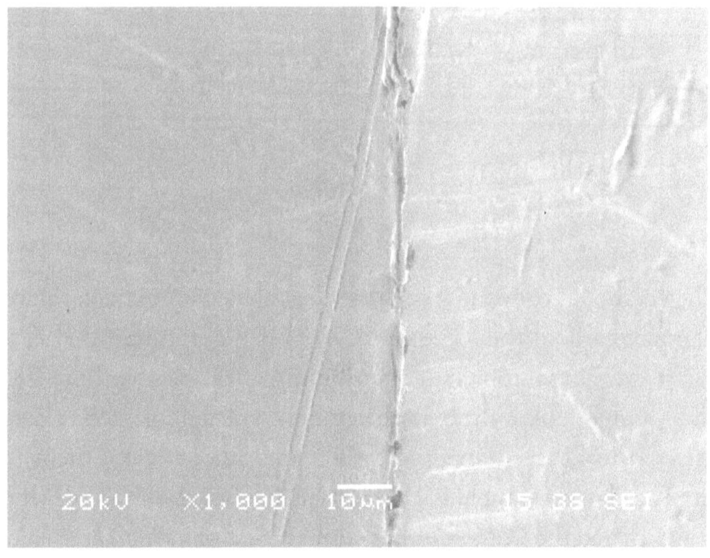

Powder metallurgy CPM-154 with a consistent edge

Corrosion Resistance

Stainless steels are designed for better resistance to rusting and corrosion when compared to simple carbon steels. Stainless steels are alloyed with chromium, which forms a transparent, passive film of chromium oxide that prevents further corrosion. Without a passive film, rust forms, which tends to flake off—and corrosion of the steel continues. More chromium means that the passive film is more complete on the steel surface to better prevent corrosion. There's no fixed cutoff where a certain amount of chromium is enough to prevent corrosion, and the corrosion also depends on the environment. Sometimes 11 percent or 12 percent chromium is given as the cutoff point, after which a steel is called "stainless," though there are many stainless steels with more chromium than that.

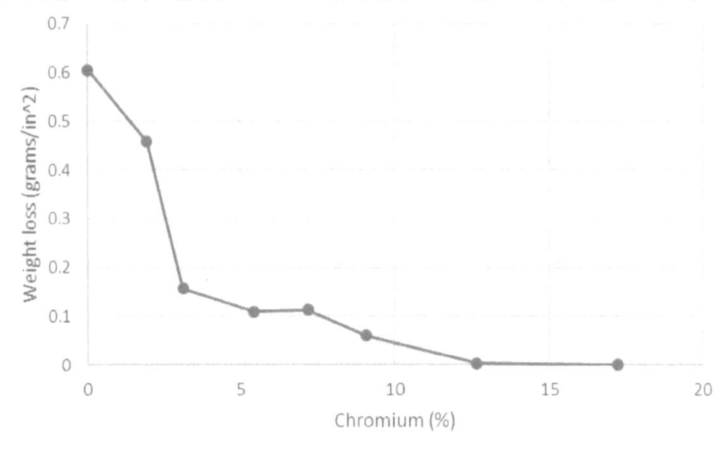

When carbon is added to a stainless steel, then chromium carbides form, and the more carbon, the more carbides. When chromium is tied up into carbides, it isn't "in solution" for contributing to the passive film. Therefore, you cannot simply look at the bulk chromium content of the steel to determine its relative corrosion resistance, as carbon and other alloying elements also affect it. The classic example is D2 steel, which has about 12 percent chromium, but isn't considered a stainless steel because of its high carbon content of 1.5 percent. The amount of chromium in solution can be estimated with sophisticated software or measured with electron microscopy when combined with composition measurement equipment. Other elements such as nitrogen, molybdenum, and tungsten also contribute to corrosion resistance. Those elements strengthen and support the chromium oxide film, but don't replace it.

Another important factor for corrosion is the final finish level to which the steel is polished. A knife with a coarse finish has many tiny crevices where rust can more easily form. Highly finished steel is less prone to rusting and corrosion.

Hardenability

Hardenability is a measure of how fast a steel needs to be quenched to achieve full hardness. This is different than the maximum hardness the steel can reach. A steel can have high hardenability but still only be possible to heat treat to relatively low hardness. Low hardenability steels will form soft phases like ferrite or pearlite, rather than the desired high-hardness martensite. Water-hardening steels need a water quench or very fast oil quench to achieve full hardness. Oil-hardening steels can reach full hardness with a slow oil quench. Air-hardening steels can be left in air, after austenitizing, and reach full hardness.

Categorizing Knife Steels

Below are simple introductions to the different types of knife steels. While it is beyond the scope of this chapter to include all possible steels, effort has been made not to include anything that doesn't at least have some current availability in the United States.

Carbon Steels

Carbon steels are those steels that are alloyed only with carbon (C), manganese (Mn), and silicon (Si), and are labeled 10XX, where XX refers to the carbon content, i.e. 1095 has 0.95 percent carbon. Higher carbon content means that they can be heat-treated to higher hardness. Above about 0.75 percent carbon, there's retained carbide after heat-treating, which contributes to wear resistance. More carbon content gives the potential for more carbide formation. Despite only being named after the carbon content, these steels vary somewhat in

Mn content, which controls hardenability. 1095 requires a water quench or a very fast oil, while 1084 can more easily be hardened in oil. Carbon steels are well-suited for forging because their low alloy means they are less likely to crack when forged at low temperatures or when cooling to room temperature. They can be heat-treated with a forge because their C-Mn design means that only short hold times are required at high temperature prior to quenching. Their low hardenability means they can be normalized and annealed easily without a controlled furnace. The higher-carbon steels have higher wear resistance, and the lower-carbon steels have superior toughness.

Steel	C (%)	Mn (%)	Si (%)
1050	0.5	0.75	
1060	0.6	0.75	
1084	0.84	0.75	
1095	0.95	0.40	
W1	0.70-1.50	0.25	0.25

Low-Alloy Steels

Low-alloy steels are those steels that include different alloying elements such as Mn, Cr, Mo, and V. When too much alloy is added, then the steels are grouped into the *high alloy* category, but the line between the two categories is fuzzy. I have included the tool steels W2, L6, S5, and O1 in the *low-alloy* category. These low-alloy steels have a range of suitability for forging and heat-treating with a forge or torch, as some may have hardenability that is too high, or long required soak times for hardening. Alloy elements in parenthesis () means that it is an optional addition. These steels, like carbon steels, have relatively low wear resistance, with CruForgeV, 52100, and O1 being the best in that respect. Also, these three steels can achieve high hardness. 5160, 8670, 15N20, S5, and L6 are good choices for high-toughness applications.

Steel	C (%)	Mn (%)	Si (%)	Cr (%)	Mo (%)	V (%)	W (%)	Ni (%)
5160	0.6	0.9	0.25	0.8				
8670	0.7	0.5	0.25	0.4				
15N20	0.75	0.4	0.1					2
52100	1	0.3	0.3	1.5				
W2	0.60- 1.40	0.3	0.3			0.2		
80CrV2	0.8	0.5	0.3	0.5		0.2		
L6	0.7	0.5	0.3	0.75	(0.25)			1.5
O1	0.9	1.0	0.3	0.5			0.5	
Cru ForgeV	1.05	0.75		0.5		0.75		
S5	0.55	0.8	2		0.4			

High-Alloy and Tool Steels

High-alloy steel, also called tool steel, is a very broad category that includes a wide range of available choices. I have not included the Si or Mn content of these steels, as nearly all of them have some amount of both, but it isn't really a differentiating aspect between them. This category includes many modern powder metallurgy tool steels as well. I have labeled each steel as either PM (powder metallurgy) or ingot (conventional steelmaking). These steels are air-hardening, so they have high hardenability, and they typically require high temperature hardening treatments. Therefore, they are poor choices for use in forging and are not advised for those who don't have furnaces for heat treatment. I have also grouped the steels called *high-speed tool steels* within this category. These high-alloy steels are so complex that estimating properties just by looking at the composition is difficult or impossible. The rankings included at the end of this chapter are better for estimating properties.

Steel	Process	C (%)	Cr (%)	Mo (%)	V (%)	W (%)	Co (%)	Ni (%)
S7	Ingot	0.5	3.25	1.4				
A2	Ingot	1.0	5	1	0.2			
D2	Ingot/ PM	1.5	12	1	1			
M2	Ingot	0.85	4	5	2	6.4		
M4	Ingot/ PM	1.4	4	5	4	5.5		
Rex 45	PM	1.3	4	5	3	6	8	
Rex 121	PM	3.4	4	5	9.5	10	9	
3V	PM	0.8	7.5	1.3	2.75			
4V/Va- nadis 4E	PM	1.35	5	3	4			
10V	PM	2.45	5.25	1.3	9.75			
15V	PM	3.4	5.25	1.3	14.5			
CruWear/ Z-Wear	Ingot/ PM	1.1	7.5	1.6	2.4	1.15		
Vanadis 8	PM	2.3	4.8	3.6	8			
Z-Tuff	PM	0.7	7.5	2	1			1.5
K390	PM	2.47	4.2	3.8	9	1	2	
Caldie	Ingot	0.7	5	2.3	0.5			

Stainless Steels

Stainless steels are those steels that are stainless, more properly described as *resistant to corrosion*. They have different levels of corrosion resistance based on the chromium content, carbon content, and other alloy additions. They are a subset of high-alloy steels that have higher corrosion resistance. Cronidur 30 is made with a special process called *pressurized electroslag remelting*, which is what PESR means below.

Steel	Process	C (%)	Cr (%)	Mo (%)	V (%)	W (%)	Co (%)	Nb (%)	N (%)
420HC	Ingot	0.45	13						
Cronidur 30	PESR	0.3	15	1					0.4
AEB-L/13C26	Ingot	0.68	12.9						
19C27	Ingot	0.95	13.5						
440C	Ingot	1.05	17	0.5					
Vanax	PM	0.36	18.2	1.1	3.5				1.55
S30V	PM	1.45	14	2	4				
S35VN	PM	1.4	14	2	4			0.5	
N690	Ingot	1.07	17.3	1.1	0.1		1.5		
BG-42	Ingot	1.15	14.5	4	1.2				
154CM/ ATS-34	Ingot/PM	1.05	14	4					
Elmax	PM	1.7	18	1	3				
20CV/ M390	PM	1.9	20	1	4	0.6			
XHP	PM	1.6	16	0.8	0.45				
S90V	PM	2.3	14	1	9				
S60V	PM	2.15	17	0.4	5.5				
S110V	PM	2.8	15.25	2.25	9		2.5	3	
S125V	PM	3.3	14	2.5	12				

Rating Steel Properties

Using a combination of reported information from steel companies and independent researchers, relative rankings of steels can be made in terms of toughness, wear resistance, and corrosion resistance. Not every steel in the chart above is included, as I don't have sufficient information on all of them. Several of the carbon and alloy steels are missing, though those steels typically have low carbide volume and wear resistance. The included carbon and alloy steels provide a rough guide for the properties of the others.

Toughness numbers have all been normalized to the Crucible Charpy c-notch values given in the previous chart, versus carbide volume. I used toughness values reported by Crucible, Carpenter, Uddeholm, and some I have tested myself. The toughness numbers that were not available are based on the steel's carbide volume using the Crucible chart, as well as comparisons with similar steels. Carbide size information isn't widely available, so predictions cannot be made based on carbide size. There are other factors that control toughness that I have largely not covered that are not included in the ratings; however, using carbide volume gives a baseline of how high the toughness *could be.* There may be some steels that are lower in toughness than their carbide volume indicates, but it provides a rough guide.

Toughness (ft-lbs) = -1.902*carbide + 59

Wear-resistance rankings are based on the carbide type and volume fraction to account for different carbide hardness. I used experimentally reported carbide numbers for all of the steels, and if I could not find experimental numbers, the steel isn't included in the table. The reported number is a predicted amount of cardstock cut (mm) in a standard CATRA test, with a knife sharpened to 15 degrees per side. CRC refers to any chromium carbide type, whether Cr_7C_3 or $Cr_{23}C_6$. CrVC refers to steels with vanadium-enriched chromium carbide. MC refers to either vanadium carbides (VC) or niobium carbides (NbC). M_6C refers to either Mo, W, or Mo/W carbides. VN refers to vanadium nitrides, and CrN refers to chromium nitrides.

$$\text{TCC (mm)} = -157 + 15.8*\text{Hardness (RC)} - 17.8*\text{EdgeAngle}(^\circ) + 11.2*\text{CRC}(\%) + 14.6*\text{CrVC}(\%) + 26.2*\text{MC}(\%) + 9.5*M_6C(\%) + 20.9*\text{VN}(\%) + 19.4*\text{CrN}(\%)$$

Corrosion resistance is estimated from the chromium, molybdenum, and tungsten in solution, calculated using software. I calculated a "chromium equivalent" using an equation I developed based on reported corrosion resistance experiments. The higher the number, the better the corrosion resistance.

$$Cr_{eq} = Cr + 0.8(Mo + 0.5W)$$

Steel	Fe_3C	CRC	CrVC	MC	M_6C	VN	CrN	Total Carbide	Edge Reten-tion	Cr-eq	Tough-ness
8670	0							0	225	0.4	90
5160	0							0	225	0.8	85
AEB-L/13C26		6						6	324	12.4	80
3V				5.1				5.1	391	8.4	70
420		3						3	212	13.0	60
CPM CruWear			5.9	3.4				9.3	448	8.6	60
Cronidur 30							4.5	4.5	329	15.2	50
4V/Vanadis 4E				9				9	524	6.2	50
52100	6							6	303	1.1	40
A2		6						8	324	4.7	40
19C27		8						8	347	11.1	40
(CPM) M4				5.8	5			10.8	488	7.3	32
Vanadis 8				15				15	682	5.9	31
O1	3							3	288	0.7	30
1095	3							3	304	0.0	30
Vanax						13		13	513	18.3	24
S35VN			10.5	3.5				14	502	11.2	24
S30V			10.5	4				14.5	515	11.3	23
D2		15.5						15.5	446	7.1	23
10V				17.5				17.5	747	5.3	23
M2				2.2	12			14.2	460	7.5	20
Elmax			16	2				18	543	11.8	20
CPM-154								17.5	453	0.0	20
XHP		22						22	503	9.9	19
S90V			13	9				22	667	13.5	19
20CV/M390			17.5	2.5				20	578	13.6	19
440C		12						16	376	12.3	16

Steel	Fe_3C	CRC	CrVC	MC	M_6C	VN	CrN	Total Carbide	Edge Reten-tion	Cr-eq	Tough-ness
N690		16						16	420	12.5	16
154CM/ ATS-34		17.5						17.5	453	12.4	16
S60V			21.5	2.1				23.6	626	11.4	12
S110V			13	11				24	735	15.3	10
15V				23				23	891	5.3	9
S125V			16	12.5				28.5	818	13.4	6
Rex 121				35				35	1316	6.8	4

Using this information, along with the descriptions of the different alloy types, steels can be selected for specific applications, depending on the desired properties. I have provided a few generic recommendations for different types of knives. None of these are hard-and-fast rules. Many steels can be made to work for a wide range of knives, but heat treatment, edge geometry, and so on will need to be adjusted to accommodate the properties of the steel. Even with optimal steel choices, there's a design loop around optimization. The optimized edge geometry is controlled by the intended use, steel, and heat treatment, and each is dependent on the others. As more optimal targets are found for one aspect, this, in turn, may affect the other properties. If a steel is found that can handle a higher hardness with similar toughness, that may allow a thinner edge geometry, for example.

Large Chopping Knives

These knives typically have somewhat thicker edge geometry to accommodate heavy shock and side loads. They must be able to resist both deformation and fracture. For chopping, there's little contribution from wear resistance or edge retention, and that is therefore a less-necessary property. With large knives, the ease in sharpening is also important because of the time involved, another reason why low wear resistance is desirable. Therefore, high-toughness steels with good ease in sharpening like 5160, L6, 8670, S5, S7, Cronidur 30, and AEB-L are good choices for chopping knives. Using S7, Cronidur 30, or AEB-L if air hardening is required. Use AEB-L if stainless properties are desired, and Cronidur 30 if extreme corrosion resistance is required.

High Edge Retention

High edge retention is necessary for knives that will see a lot of slicing of abrasive materials. The edge retention ranking makes this selection process relatively simple. However, there are cases where ease in sharpening, finishing, or toughness requirements may restrict the steel selection to simply the very good, rather than the extreme end of the edge-retention spectrum. The very high vanadium grades with extreme edge retention like 15V, Rex 121, or S125V can also be expensive or difficult to obtain. The point of "good enough" edge retention likely depends on the knife and the intended customer.

High Edge Stability

As discussed in the edge stability section, knives that are intended to maximize cutting ability need very thin edge geometry, and such thin edge geometry requires both high hardness and toughness. Carbon and alloy steels that are capable of high hardness like 1095, O1, and 52100 are excellent choices. Stainless steels are less capable of very high hardness, though AEB-L has a very fine microstructure and can achieve hardness of about 63 RC, which is enough for many knives.

High Corrosion Resistance

Knives that will see very corrosive environments, such as around salt water, require a steel with high Cr-eq. If high toughness is required, then Cronidur 30 is the best choice. S110V is better for high wear resistance and slicing-edge retention. Vanax is a more general-use choice, with edge retention and toughness in between those two options.

General-Use Knives

General-use knives are both the easiest and most difficult to select steels for. They are easy in that many steels fit in the middle somewhere and are difficult in that it is hard to predict how a given person will use a knife. I personally prefer knives that are easier to sharpen and high in toughness, while other people prefer a knife that is higher in edge retention. For steels that are similar in properties, other factors may be more important, like cost, ease in heat-treating, working, or finishing, or the perceived value of the steel by customers.

The topic of steel has filled many books, and this chapter only scratches the surface. Rather than looking at a single work as the be-all-end-all of steel research, use each source to independently point you toward a thorough understanding of the steel types that you work with. Dive deep into your chosen steels, without being consumed by the breadth of steel choices available.

CHAPTER 9

The Basics of Heat-Treating

Larrin Thomas

ONE OF THE challenges of any knifemaker is ensuring that your chosen knife steel is heat-treated properly. The internet is full of information and "secret recipes" for heat-treating almost any steel known to man. While you would think that such a pool of easily accessible knowledge would be a great benefit, the truth is that there's so much information out there that it is hard to sort out the good science from the bad. How do you know who to trust, or which authority to follow, especially when various authority figures are in direct conflict with one another when it comes to how to properly heat treat steel? Ultimately, you'll have to decide for yourself who to follow. The goal of this chapter is to outline the scientific basics of the heat-treating process, in order that you may improve your heat-treating processes, and in order to help you sort out the flood of information on the internet.

Introduction to Heat-Treating

Below is a basic schematic showing the process of heat-treating. Temperature is on the Y-axis, and progress through time is on the X-axis. At time zero, we have our steel, as delivered by the steel company or supplier. It is annealed, is very soft for ease in drilling and machining, and is ready for heat-treating.

We then heat it to a high temperature called the *austenitizing* temperature, which prepares us for quenching. The austenitizing temperature is sometimes called the *hardening temperature.* The quench is rapid cooling to room temperature, and can be performed in water, oil, or even air, depending on the steel in question. There's an optional "cold" treatment, that, depending on temperature, can also be called a *subzero* or *cryogenic treatment.* After that, there's tempering, which is a relatively low-temperature process that somewhat reduces the steel hardness so that the steel isn't brittle. In between tempering steps, the steel must be cooled to room temperature. After tempering is complete, the heat treatment is done, and the steel is ready to go. In this chapter, I will describe each of these processes in more detail, so you understand what each step accomplishes. We'll also discuss how to dial in your heat-treatment process to optimize the final knife's properties.

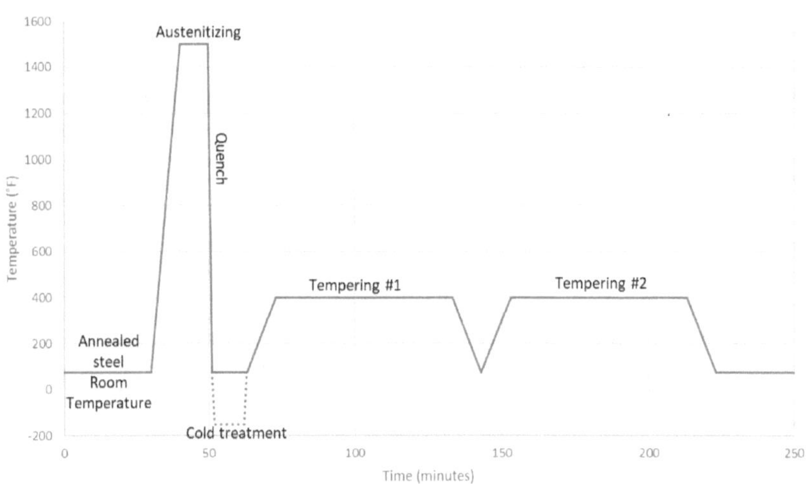

Should You Heat Treat Yourself?

There are several factors that dictate whether heat treatment should be done in your own shop. One is cost. If you are a hobbyist knifemaker who will only ever make a handful of knives, then the cost of the equipment for heat-treating would exceed the cost of paying for outside heat-treating. Another is time. If you are making a high volume of knives per month, or if you're building in large batches, then it may not make sense to heat treat them all yourself. The biggest advantage to heat-treating knives yourself is complete control over the heat-treatment process, allowing custom designed heat treatments for each steel and knife. If quick turnaround times are required, then sending out blades for heat treatment may not be possible. If you do your own heat treatment, many times you can turn around a blade in a day. For those who are forging their knives, heat-treating in your own shop is more necessary. At the very least, the steel must be put in a position for the outside heat treater to properly harden it. The more consistent the normalizing and annealing of the steel prior to sending it to the heat treater, the more consistent the results will be. Since the initial preparation of the steel up to that point cannot be avoided, it is best to simply perform the entire process within the maker's shop.

Some will try to convince you that heat-treating is too hard or technical for you to do yourself. Heat-treating isn't difficult. If you can sharpen a knife, you have already learned a skill that is more difficult than heat-treating. Some knifemakers or knife companies are known for their great heat treatment. But what is a good heat treatment? What makes one better than another? How do we change steel properties with heat-treating?

Equipment Required for Heat-Treating

Heat-treating, in its simplest form, can be performed with a forge and a bucket of water. That method is only suited for very simple, low-alloy steels. Even then, it is extremely difficult to have repeatable, consistent results when heat-treating in a forge. Other people can provide you with instructions for heat-treating in that way, but I will not. I promote heat-treating with a PID-controlled furnace, where heat treatments can be dialed in and performed the same way each time, regardless of the level of light available, or how you feel that day.

The primary piece of equipment necessary for heat-treating is the furnace itself. The two most popular brands are Paragon and Evenheat. Both have their fans, and there doesn't appear to be a clear winner. The key features of these ovens are digitally controlled temperatures and an electric heat source that reaches a high temperature range, above 2,000°F.

For steels that require high hardening temperatures such as tool steels and stainless steels, heat-treating foil is necessary to prevent decarburization (loss of carbon) and scale formation. Heat-treat foil comes in two primary varieties: 309 and 321. The 309 can go to higher temperatures, and is therefore more flexible. No paper, kerosene, baby powder, or so on is necessary for putting in the foil along with the steel. The foil works by itself. For steels with low hardening temperatures (<1,600°F), you can get by without foil, though a better option is anti-scale coating that allows one to quench directly into oil without removing foil first.

Steels with low hardenability like water-hardening steels need to be quenched either in water or a very fast oil, like Parks 50. Water is more likely to lead to quench cracking. Oil-hardening steels can use a slower oil, like AAA. Air-hardening steels and stainless steels can be hardened just in still air. However, *plate quenching* is popular, and it cools the steel faster and helps maintain straightness. This process involves putting the steel in between two plates of aluminum, and the heat is drawn out by conduction. One-inch-thick plates work well.

Cold-temperature treatments can be performed with dry ice or liquid nitrogen. Storing liquid nitrogen requires a special insulated vessel called a *dewa*r. Cold-temperature treatments are optional, though I will describe to what extent these treatments are necessary later in this chapter.

Tempering can be performed in either your primary furnace, or with a kitchen oven or toaster oven. If you use your furnace, you have to let it cool down after the initial austentizing heat before you can temper your blades, as the tempering temperature range is much lower. If you are using a kitchen oven, it is worth buying an oven thermometer to check the accuracy of the temperature setting and also to see how large the temperature swings are.

You will also need some welding gloves, tongs, and other miscellaneous supplies. You'll be handling hot steel, pulling it out of a hot oven, and putting it quickly into oil that may catch fire. Personal protection is a must.

A Rockwell hardness tester is also highly desirable to be able to check heat treatments and ensure they are working as intended. Without a hardness tester, it is best to either pay for hardness testing such as at a machining or welding shop, or to find a knifemaker friend who has one and is willing to check samples.

Steel

When you buy a bar of steel, it usually comes annealed. This is a soft condition, for ease in machining so that it can be drilled, cut, and ground. In this condition, at room temperature, under high magnification, we have something that looks like this schematic:

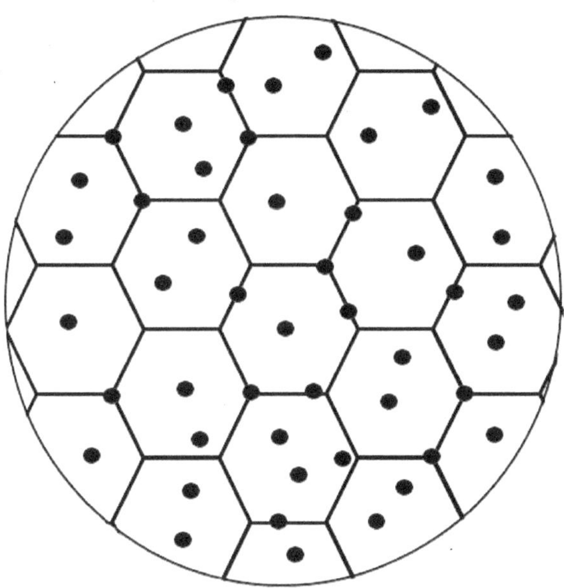

The black circles represent carbides, which are hard particles in the steel. In a steel with only iron and carbon, these carbides are called *cementite* and are made up of one carbon atom for every iron atom, often given as Fe_3C. In the annealed condition, almost all of the carbon is bound up in cementite carbides, and almost none of it is "in solution" in the steel itself. This is a big reason why annealed steel is so soft—because carbon is the best strengthening element in steel. If we get the carbon out of "solution," then the steel is soft, and it can be machined. At an even smaller scale, the steel in between the carbides is made up of countless iron atoms that are all packed together and bonded with metallic bonds.

The iron atoms in steel are in a regular arrangement that repeats. If we take the smallest representation of the way the atoms are packed together using the cube in the image above, we get the *unit cell* of this atomic arrangement. For annealed steel, this is known as *body-centered cubic* (BCC), which has an atom in the center of each cube, and each cube has one-eighth of an atom shared between all of the surrounding unit cells. This BCC arrangement is an iron phase called *ferrite.* A phase refers to the state the steel is in. Just like water, this can be liquid, solid, or gas.

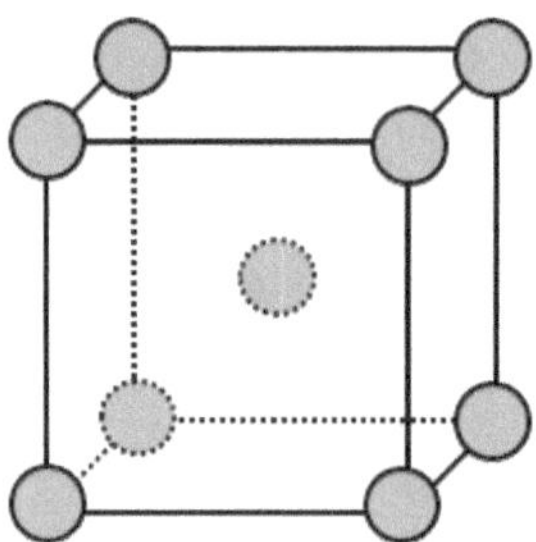

Knowing about these atomic arrangements isn't purely trivia; the steel can change its arrangement, and that will lead to different properties. At high temperature, the steel transforms to a new phase called *face-centered cubic* (FCC), which is so different than BCC iron that the steel isn't even magnetic anymore. The FCC phase is called *austenite.*

The schematic of the steel with carbides in it also includes hexagons, which represent the grain boundaries in steel. All of those atoms in their close-packed arrangement are all parallel with each other, until they reach another "crystal" that is oriented a different way. Grain boundaries are the transition between different orientations of atoms.

At high temperature, grains tend to grow. The larger grains consume the smaller grains, and the larger grains continue to increase in size. The steel doesn't like those boundaries and wants to get rid of them, and it does that by growing its own grains. Many aspects of heat treatment and steel processing are related to keeping the grain size small. Small grains mean better properties, in general.

At high temperature, when the steel transforms from BCC to FCC, the carbides also dissolve, whether partially or totally, and the carbon enters solution. FCC can accommodate relatively large amounts of carbon, unlike BCC, which is limited to about 0.02 percent. The carbon atom is much smaller than iron atoms, and fits in between the iron atoms at high temperature. When steel is rapidly quenched from high temperature, the carbon atoms are trapped in between the iron atoms, and when the steel attempts to transform back to BCC at low temperature, the carbon distorts the atomic structure, making the steel very strong. This makes the structure tetragonal rather than cubic, which is a phase called *martensite.*

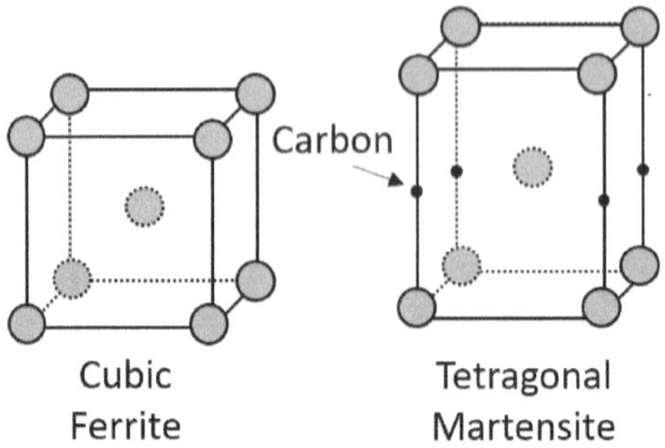

The more carbon was in solution in FCC at high temperature, the more carbon is present in the martensite, and the stronger the steel is. Higher austenitizing temperatures means that more carbide is dissolved, leaving more carbon in solution for higher hardness. Strength is often measured with a hardness test, usually with the Rockwell C (RC) scale in knives. The higher the hardness, the higher the strength. Strength is a measure of how much load is required to deform the material. In other words, after bending a piece of steel, it stays bent. Very strong steel can be bent a significant amount and return straight. Very soft steel cannot bend very far without staying bent. A typical range for knives is 52–66 RC, with the lower values being more common in consumer knives, where they are concerned about people breaking them. The graph below shows how hardenability varies with carbon content.

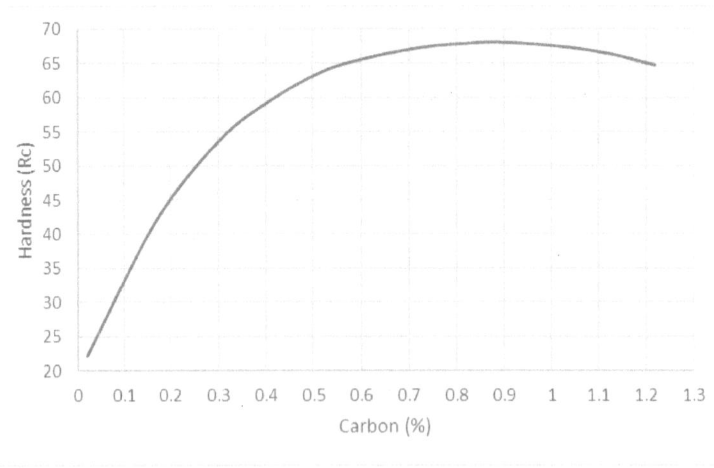

After quenching, the steel is tempered because as-quenched steel is very brittle. Tempering involves holding the steel at a relatively low temperature (300°F –1,200°F) for one-to-two hours. Tempering decreases the strength somewhat while increasing toughness. The two graphs below show a typical tempering curve for L6 steel, with toughness and hardness as opposing properties. Toughness increases and hardness decreases as tempering temperature increases.

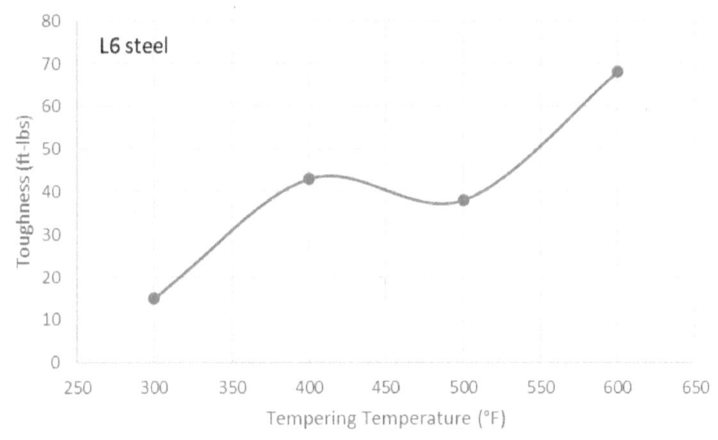

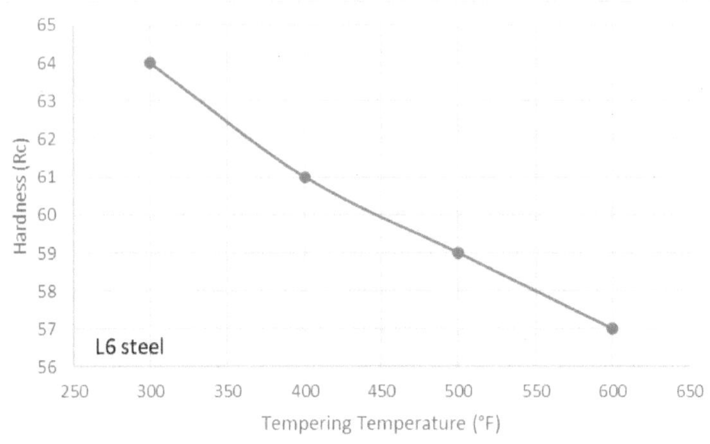

The Steel Data Sheet

The starting point for heat-treating any steel is the data sheet. Data sheets can vary some in the information that they contain, but almost all of them contain recommended temperatures for each heat treatment process. I will be giving some example temperatures in this chapter, but not providing exact temperatures for a list of steels; those temperatures come from the data sheet.

When starting with annealed material from the steel supplier, the starting point is typically hardening. The hardening temperature is labeled as the austenitizing temperature because the steel will be transformed from ferrite (BCC) to austenite (FCC). Sometimes, a single temperature is recommended, though often it is a range, and a holding time is also given. When a range is given in a data sheet, an easy starting point is to simply pick halfway between and to soak for the recommended amount. Sometimes, it says to soak for some amount for the "first inch" and to add more time for each additional inch. You should not divide this soak time by the thickness of the steel (i.e., thirty minutes for the first inch does not become 225 seconds for one-eighth-inch steel). After inserting the steel into the furnace and closing the door, the temperature will have dropped. Start the timer on the soak after the furnace has returned to the specified temperature. The soak time doesn't have to be ± one second; there's some leeway in the soak time. Temperature is more important than time, and the difference between twenty-eight and thirty-two minutes for a target of thirty minutes is relatively small.

There are also usually "preheating" temperatures listed, which are lower than the final austenitizing temperature. The preheating step is optional, though it may reduce warping or distortion. With multiple furnaces, it is possible to preheat it in one furnace and transfer to another at the final austenitizing temperature. With one furnace, it requires that you ramp from the preheating temperature to austenitizing, which occurs more slowly. This may increase the chance of decarburization (loss of carbon), scale formation, and grain growth, to some extent.

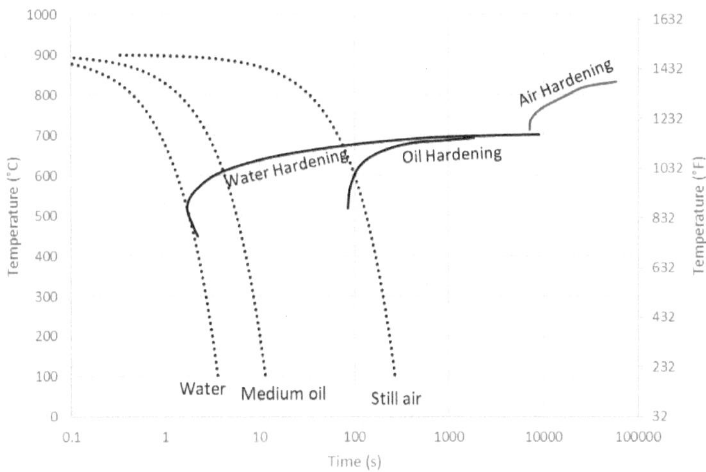

The above chart is a *continuous cooling transformation* (CCT) diagram which show how fast a steel must be quenched to form hard martensite without forming softer pearlite. The solid lines represent the start of pearlite formation, which is softer than martensite and therefore the formation of pearlite reduces the overall hardness of the steel. At high temperatures, the time required for pearlite formation is long, and reaches the shortest time at an intermediate temperature around 500°C (925°F). The *critical cooling rate* is the rate that is necessary to form 100 percent martensite. A very high required critical cooling rate would mean that a water quench is necessary. Three steels are shown in the figure, a water-hardening steel such as 1095 or W1, an oil-hardening such as O1, and an air-hardening steel such as D2.

When the steel is pulled out of the furnace with tongs, the steel should be quenched quickly out of the oven. However, there are at least a few seconds before the quench must occur, even with water-hardening steels. In the CCT diagram, you can see that there's quite some time before transformation starts in still air. The rate of transformation to soft phases rather than martensite is the slowest at high temperature, which gives a little bit of time. You don't have to be superhuman to make it to the quench in time.

If quenching into oil or water, the blade can be moved up and down as if cutting into the oil to prevent a vapor jacket forming, but must not be moved side to side, which can lead to warping of the blade. The steel can be pulled out at a relatively low temperature and straightened before it fully cools. One must be careful with straightening, however, as when the steel has fully hardened and then cracking becomes much more likely.

For some steels and heat treatments, the transformation to full martensite isn't complete even at room temperature, and some amount of austenite is "retained." In those cases, cold treatments can be performed to complete the transformation. These are most effective directly after quenching to room temperature. While dry ice or liquid nitrogen are best, even a household freezer makes a difference. Here is hardness and retained austenite versus austenitizing temperature for AEB-L, where you can see that the hardness is higher and the retained austenite lower when using the freezer:

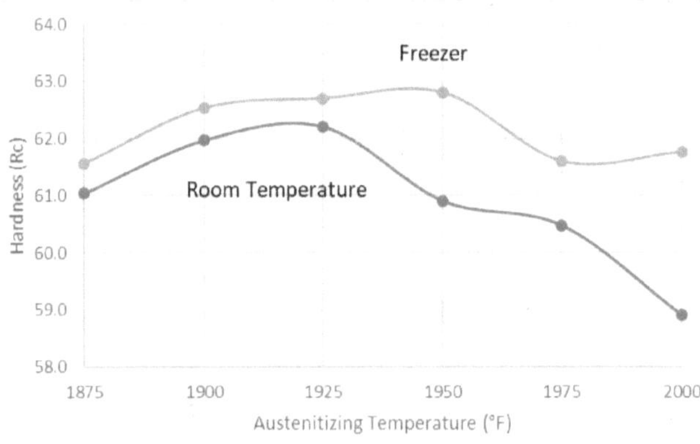

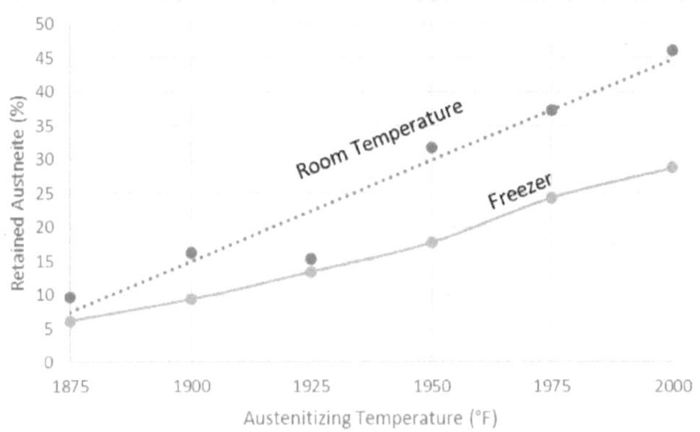

Cold treatments are necessary for achieving maximum hardness with high-alloy steels. However, even if maximum hardness isn't required or desirable, there are benefits to reducing retained austenite. If a blade has high retained austenite, even when at the same hardness as a similar knife with little or no retained austenite, the strength of the steel is reduced. The "yield stress," or point at which deformation begins and the steel "stays bent," is lower for a given hardness when there's a large percentage of retained austenite. Also, when stress is applied to steel with retained austenite, it transforms to martensite, which is untempered. That untempered martensite is brittle and can lead to lower toughness. Therefore, cold treatments are recommended to minimize retained austenite. If dry ice or liquid nitrogen are not available, then use the lower end of the austenitizing range and use the freezer instead.

Finding the Optimal Temperatures

A plot of hardness versus austenitizing temperature such as the one for AEB-L above is highly beneficial, and can be generated by anyone with a heat-treating setup. Using 10°F or 25°F increments for austenitizing temperature and then measuring the hardness allows one to find peak hardness and to see if the furnace is offset from the reported values in the data sheet. The peak hardness obtained with room temperature quenching is a good starting point for optimal heat treatment, as above that there's excess retained austenite. Heat-treating greatly above that temperature often also leads to grain growth and excessive carbon in solution, both of which lead to a reduction in toughness. For carbon and low-alloy steels, the peak hardness with a room temperature quench should be viewed as the maximum possible austenitizing temperature, as brittle behavior is likely above that austenitizing temperature. In some cases using a lower austenitizing temperature may be beneficial for enhancing toughness, particularly with carbon and low-alloy steels. With high-alloy steel, it's often possible to use a somewhat higher temperature in combination with a cold treatment to get more hardness, without too much loss in toughness.

In terms of tempering, 400°F is the starting point for many materials. You can use as low as 300°F when higher hardness is desired. Much higher than 400°F and you're in danger of reaching the *tempered martensite embrittlement* range where both hardness and toughness are reduced, leading to a poor toughness-wear resistance balance. You can see an example of this in the L6 tempering curve earlier in this chapter, where the 500°F toughness was lower than 400°F toughness. If higher toughness than is obtained with 400°F is desired, it's better to reduce hardness through a reduction in austenitizing temperature instead. Many tool steels have recommended tempering temperatures in the 950°F –1,100°F range rather than the 300°F –400°F range. This is known as "secondary hardening," where the hardness increases with higher tempering temperatures. Tempering in that range makes the steel less sensitive to overheating in grinding, as the steel can be heated to nearly the tempering temperature without being overtempered. However, there's some evidence to indicate that the lower tempering range is better, even with steels that are recommended to use the high temperature range. In a study on Z-Wear (CPM CruWear), knifemaker Warren Krywko and I compared 400°F and 1,000°F tempering, and we found that the 400°F temper led to better toughness with the same hardness:

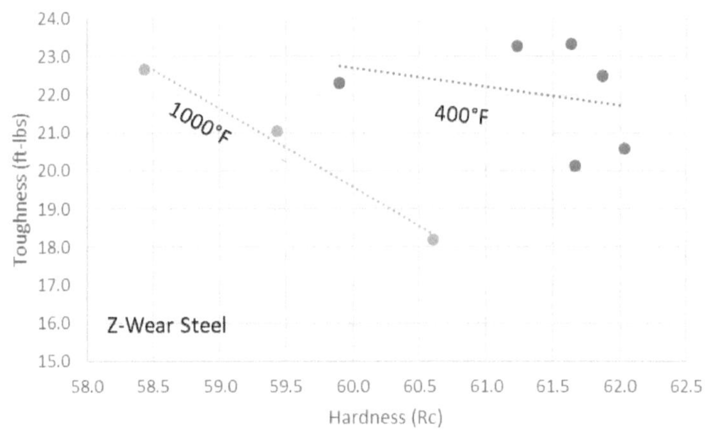

With tempering, like austenitizing, temperature is more important than time. Typically, one-to-two hours per tempering treatment are recommended. Double tempering, where the steel is cooled to room temperature between tempering treatments, is also recommended. The steel has to be overtempered by several hours to see any significant drop in hardness versus a standard double temper for two hours each.

Maximizing Hardness with Heat Treatment

If the goal is to maximize hardness of steel, it is necessary to use cold-temperature treatments to convert retained austenite. This also allows the use of higher austenitizing temperatures for more carbon in solution. High-austenitizing temperatures, cold-temperature treatments, plus low tempering temperatures leads to maximum hardness and strength. Of course, high hardness also means poorer toughness.

Maximum Corrosion Resistance

Stainless steels have chromium locked up in carbides rather than in solution to contribute to corrosion resistance. Higher austenitizing temperatures means more carbide dissolves putting more chromium in solution. Tempering above about 700°F also leads to a reduction in corrosion resistance, so lower tempering temperatures are preferred.

Maximum Toughness

In general, higher toughness is achieved at lower hardness. For a given hardness, it's possible to achieve that value through a variety of austenitizing-tempering temperature combinations. A higher austenitizing temperature can be used to allow a higher tempering temperature. Or a lower austenitizing temperature in combination with a lower tempering temperature can be used. It's usually best to reduce the austenitizing temperature and temper down to the same hardness. Lower austenitizing temperatures means less grain growth, less carbon in solution, and less likely to reach the tempered martensite embrittlement range by overtempering to the desired hardness. Below, I have plots showing the effect of grain size and carbon in solution versus toughness, and a plot showing the toughness of K390 tool steel with different austenitizing temperatures where it was tempered to the same hardness for each. Lower austenitizing also means less carbide is dissolved, and more carbide is bad for toughness, but this effect is usually drowned out by grain growth and carbon in solution. Furthermore, when austenitizing, it is the smallest carbides that dissolve first, leaving the largest carbides, which are most deleterious for toughness.

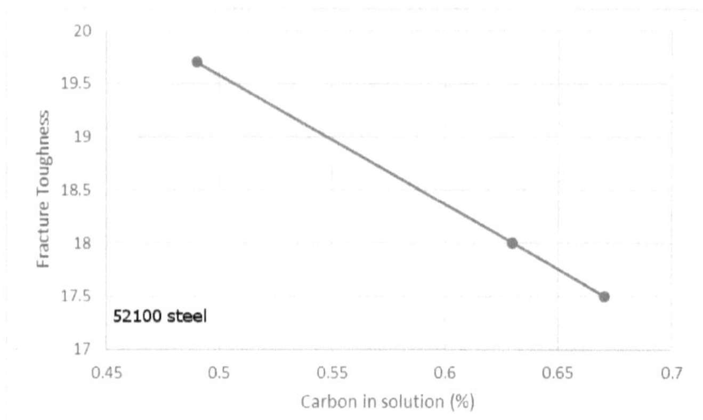
20
19.5
19
18.5
18
17.5
17
Fracture Toughness
52100 steel
0.45
0.5
0.55
0.6
0.65
0.7
Carbon in solution (%)

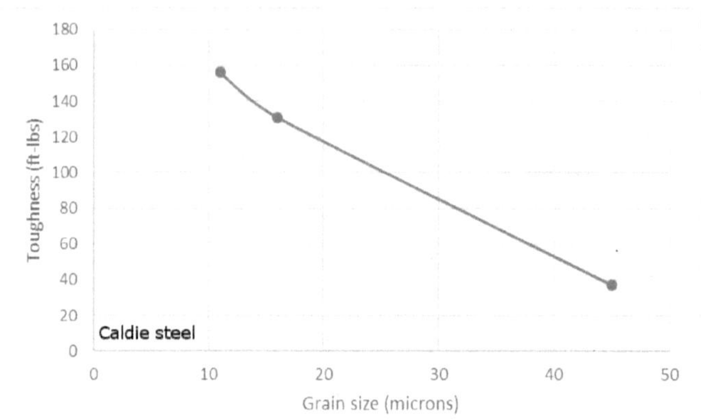
180
160
140
120
100
80
60
40
20
0
Toughness (ft-lbs)
Caldie steel
0
10
20
30
40
50
Grain size (microns)

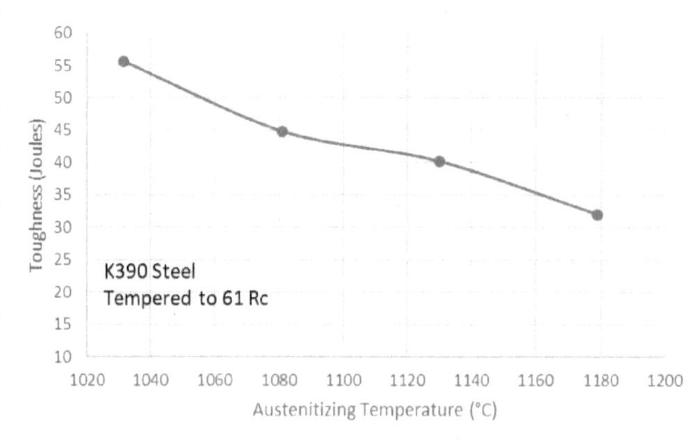
60
55
50
45
40
35
30
25
20
15
10
Toughness (Joules)
K390 Steel
Tempered to 61 Rc
1020
1040
1060
1080
1100
1120
1140
1160
1180
1200
Austenitizing Temperature (°C)

Ease in Sharpening

Lower-hardness steel is more difficult to sharpen to high levels of sharpness, and leads to "rougher" edges. Low-wear resistance steel is easy to grind away, though that's controlled more by the steel's carbides than by heat treatment. Deburring is made more difficult by high fractions of retained austenite and in soft steels. Therefore, to maximize ease in sharpening, the steel needs to have low retained austenite, either with reduced austenitizing temperatures or cold treatments. Higher hardness is better for high sharpness. The exception is high wear resistance steels where high hardness can lead to poor grindability for difficulties in sharpening.

Edge Retention

Edge retention for a given steel is primarily increased by using higher hardness. When the hardness has already been selected for the application, the edge retention can be increased slightly by using a lower austenitizing temperature and tempering at a lower temperature to reach the same hardness. The lower austenitizing temperature means less carbide is dissolved so there's more carbide to contribute to wear resistance.

Balancing Properties

In summary, lower austenitizing temperatures are usually better unless a greater hardness or corrosion resistance is needed. There's a point when the austenitizing temperature may be too low. This is especially apparent when there's a steep drop in hardness, which indicates either the steel didn't reach full austenite (some ferrite left over) or that insufficient carbide is being dissolved to put carbon in solution.

Most steels have some hardness beyond which there's a dramatic reduction in toughness. It can be tempting to take a steel that is very tough at 58 or 60 RC and push it to 62 or 64 RC with the assumption that its high toughness will allow it to handle that hardness. However, if austenitizing at a temperature that is too high, tempering at a temperature too low, or both, the steel could be pushed beyond its capabilities. At that point, it is better to use a steel that can use a more typical heat treatment to achieve the desired hardness. One example is 3V, which has very high toughness at 58–60 RC, but drops significantly above that hardness. At 62 RC, the "less tough" CPM CruWear has superior toughness because it has better capability for reaching high hardness. Therefore, the use of CPM CruWear would require a less extreme heat treatment, and provide superior wear resistance, compared to using the high toughness 3V. In toughness testing I performed along with Warren Krywko, 8670 achieved higher toughness than any other steel at 60 RC, but when pushed to 64 RC, it was less tough than many other steels even when at the same hardness.

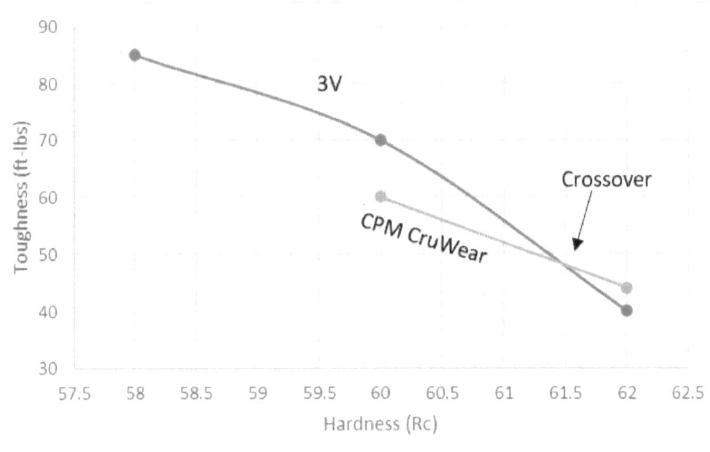

Testing Steel and Knives

Steel can be tested somewhat independently of knives. Measuring hardness is one good example. Corrosion tests can be performed on either knives or polished steel specimens, such as putting them in saltwater or the dishwasher. Small specimens can be created using different heat treatments and hit with a hammer to get a feel for the changes in toughness. If more hammer blows are necessary to break the specimen, that likely means better toughness. It requires some experimentation to find a good specimen size and to get a feel for how they break.

Eventually, testing of knives is necessary to understand what the steel can do. Stress tests for knives need to be devised to ensure the knife is performing as designed. The most obvious is to simply use the knife for its intended purpose. If it is a kitchen knife, cut a bunch of vegetables. If it's a straight razor, then shave with it. If it's a chopper, then chop some two-by-fours. More extreme tests can be performed to ensure the knife still performs even when pushed harder than normal. Some chop into very hard woods or antler, or even cutting into a soft metal like brass, and twisting out of the cut. If the edge comes out unscathed, then it will probably survive any normal situation the knife sees. If the edge survives, it may be possible to go for even thinner geometry. If the edge chips, then either heat treat for higher toughness or select another steel. If the edge rolls, then heat treat to a higher hardness. Once the limit is found, then the knifemaker can be assured that performance has been maximized. Sometimes, it's surprising what a knife with a very thin edge can handle. Finding the point of "good enough" is very difficult, because no one can predict the behavior of any given user. Consumer knives are made overly thick and with soft steel so that no one can break them. The beauty of custom or handmade knives is that they can be made to a higher standard with much better cutting performance.

Forging Process and Post-Forging Heat Treatments

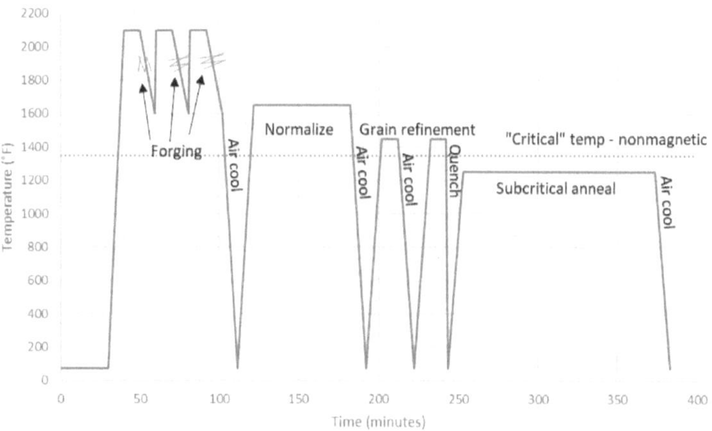

Forging

As with other aspects of working steel, it's best to use the recommended forging temperatures provided in data sheets and heat treater's guides. Forging temperatures that are too high can lead to excessive grain growth, while forging temperatures that are too low can lead to cracking. A typical forging temperature for 1095 or 52100 is 2,100°F (1,150°C), and the minimum temperature between 1,500°F –1,700°F depending on the steel. With high-alloy tool steels and stainless steels some bladesmiths are tempted to go to a higher temperature to make the steel easier to work, but this can lead to hot shortness where the steel becomes brittle and is more difficult to work. That is why following the recommended forging temperatures is best.

Normalizing

After forging is complete, it's time for normalizing. Normalizing isn't the same as grain-refinement cycles. Normalizing is done at a higher temperature, such as 1,650°F for an hour followed by air cooling. After forging, there's an inconsistent microstructure of small and large grains, small and large carbides. Normalizing puts all or most of the carbide in solution and grows the grain to a consistent size, followed by formation of pearlite during slow cooling. Normalizing isn't recommended for air-hardening steels because they form martensite rather than pearlite.

Grain Refinement

Following normalizing, grain refinement cycles can be performed at a lower temperature, such as 1,350°F –1,450°F, and air-cooled. New small grains form with each heat into the austenitizing temperature range, and after two or three cycles the grain size is uniformly smaller. With too many cycles the original "new" grains are growing to the point where the grain size doesn't get any smaller. Some recommend descending temperature cycles after normalizing (i.e., 1,550°F, 1,500°F, 1,450 °F). However, that is unnecessary because the higher temperature normalizing completed the process necessary for achieving a uniform microstructure. When refining the grain size, lower temperature is better so that the new grains don't grow too rapidly. Therefore, descending temperature cycles are less effective than repeated low temperature cycles just above the austenitizing, or nonmagnetic, temperature.

Annealing

Annealing is performed to soften the steel for machining and prepare it for the final heat treatment. There are several different types of annealing, including a slow cool anneal, "cycle" anneal and "subcritical" anneal. A slow cool anneal involves heating to the low-end of the austenitization range, such as 1,450°F for 1095 or O1 for one-to-two hours, then cooling at a slow rate of 40°F –50°F/hour. This can also be performed by putting the steel in ash or vermiculite. A cycle anneal involves the use of the same austenitization process, but the steel is cooled more rapidly to a lower temperature like 1,250°F and held for four-to-six hours. A cycle anneal cannot be easily performed without a furnace. A subcritical anneal is performed without austenitization and heated to the lower temperature of 1,250°F and held for five-to-twenty hours. Subcritical annealing can be performed much more rapidly if the steel is martensitic first. One method is to quench from the final grain refinement cycle to form martensite, and then subcritical annealing can be performed in two-to-four hours. A subcritical anneal can also be performed with a forge by cycling just under nonmagnetic. Because the subcritical anneal is performed without austenitization, the final grain size developed during grain refinement is also maintained. Therefore, that is the recommended process if grain refinement is performed after normalizing, rather than in the final austenitization process with triple quenching, described in the next section.

There are some reports of carbon and alloy steels that have been annealed to such a great extent that they aren't easily heat-treated. With time at temperature the carbides of steel slowly grow, and with excessively long annealing times, the carbides can be so large that austenitizing is sluggish. In that case, it's recommended that the steel is normalized and annealed prior to austenitizing.

Advanced Heat-Treating

Multiple Quenching

There are some specialized heat treatments that are designed for further improving properties like toughness. One such heat treatment is the "triple quench," where the steel is heated to the austenitizing temperature and quenched multiple times. This treatment is typically performed on carbon steels and alloy steels.

The intended goal is grain refinement. The mechanism by which it works is similar to that described for "grain refinement" cycles described above, though quenched instead of air-cooled. Lower austenitizing temperatures are required to avoid grain growth and too much carbon in solution. This process doesn't always lead to an improvement in toughness. We tested heat treatments with CruForgeV where we austenitized and quenched two times from 1,450°F with the final from 1,500°F, each held for ten minutes at the austenitizing temperature. Charpy impact testing didn't reveal any clear improvement when compared with a single quench.

Prequenching

A modified version of the triple quench called "prequenching" has been studied with high-alloy steels. With high-alloy steels like D2, triple quenching has been found to lead to grain growth. However, performing the initial austenitize and quench from a lower temperature, such as 1,700°F for the prequench followed by 1,850°F for the final austenitization, leads to grain refinement in D2. These types of heat treatments have seen little study.

Austempering

Austempering is a process where bainite is formed rather than tempered martensite. The steel is austenitized as normal and then quenched to an intermediate temperature such as 500°F, usually in molten salts. The steel is then held at that temperature to form bainite. Higher hardness is obtained by holding at lower temperatures; the minimum temperature is just above the "martensite start" temperature (Ms), which can be found on a "time temperature transformation" diagram (TTT). The TTT will also show how long the steel needs to be held at the temperature to have full transformation to bainite. TTT diagrams can be found in some data sheets or a heat treater's guide. They may not be available for all steels, in that case some experimentation would be necessary. Tempering isn't required if bainite transformation is complete. However, if the transformation is incomplete than some amount of martensite will form during the final cool to room temperature. A tempering step can be added, such as at 400°F to ensure there isn't any untempered martensite. Bainite has a lower potential hardness than martensite. However, there's some evidence to indicate that bainite may be somewhat tougher than tempered martensite when at the same hardness. The toughness of bainite is less affected by high carbon in solution, and is unaffected by tempered martensite embrittlement. Therefore, when lower austenitizing temperatures are used and the TME range is avoided, the toughness of bainite and tempered martensite are very similar.

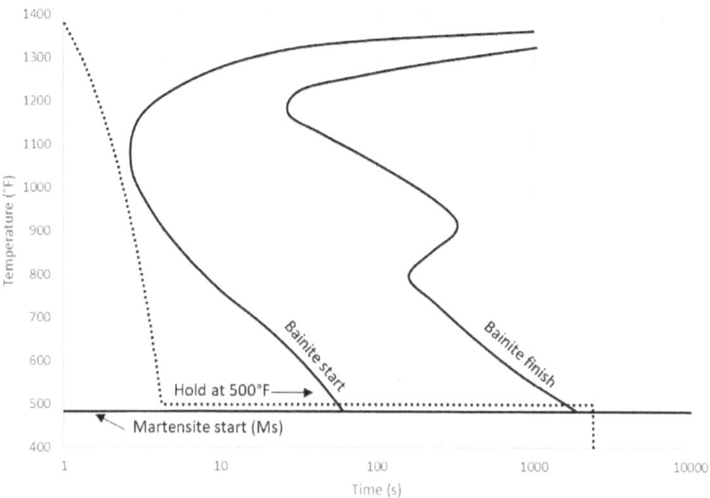

Marquenching

Marquenching, also called martempering, is a quench to an intermediate temperature followed by an air cool. Typically, it's held for a few minutes or less at a temperature around 300°F –400°F. The purpose of marquenching isn't to form bainite like austempering, though some amount of bainite may form. With quenching rapidly to room temperature, the surface cools more quickly than the core. As temperature decreases, steel shrinks slightly. This means that during quenching the surface contracts as it cools relative to the core. Furthermore, the surface transforms to martensite before the core, and martensite is a larger phase than austenite, leading to a growth of the surface. Due to these complex size changes between the surface and the core, warping or cracking can occur. Marquenching allows the steel to equalize prior to martensite formation to reduce these negative effects. This can also lead to an improvement in steel toughness in some cases.

What's Next?

Now that you've made it through this chapter, take some time to do some internet research on heat-treating the steels you use the most. Look up the data sheets for your favorite steels. Pay extra attention to the concepts you learned in this chapter as you study. By approaching your heat treatment scientifically, with precise and repeatable methods, and armed with knowledge of what is actually happening within your steel, you will continue to make better and better knives. A better heat treat makes a better knife, makes a better knifemaker.

CHAPTER 10

Professional Heat-Treating

Brad Stallsmith

HEAT-TREATING IS AN integral part of the knifemaking process. Without properly controlled manipulation of time and temperature, the finished knife will not have the desired properties: hardness, toughness, corrosion resistance, and wear resistance. Stuck roughly in the middle of the process of making a knife, heat-treating has always been an interesting and demanding part of knifemaking.

Knifemakers are in general curious and industrious individuals, so it's no surprise that many choose to perform the heat-treating of their knives themselves. Whether you choose an electric bench top kiln or furnace, or prefer a propane or coal forge, the equipment isn't difficult for the average knifemaker to find. Some forges and kilns can even be built in the knife shop. Whether purchased or built, heat-treating equipment is readily available and not terribly expensive. When it comes to heat treatment protocols and information, most steel manufacturers have heat-treating information available online. The internet also gives you ready access to the heat-treat protocols and advice of skilled knifemakers. Now more than ever before, all of the pieces of the heat-treating puzzle can come together for the knifemaker to learn and master the science of heat-treating at home.

If you are a knifemaker who heat treats your own blades and feels comfortable with the results, I applaud you and commend you for your efforts. The broader your knowledge about the heat-treating process, the better knifemaker you will be. As a professional industrial heat treater specializing in knife blades, I have also strived to learn as much about the making of a good knife to further my skills and abilities.

Some skilled knifemakers choose to heat treat their own blades, while others who are equally skilled may choose on occasion to send blades out for professional heat treatment. There's a wealth of information available to the home heat treater, including one of the other chapters in this book. In this chapter, let's focus on factors to consider when sending out your work for professional heat-treating service. There are many reasons why you may not choose to perform your own heat-treating, such as equipment issues, a new type of steel that you may not be comfortable with, and so on. Here are some things to consider as you decide whether to do heat treatment yourself or send your knives to a professional.

Time Is Money!

A major consideration in the heat-treating process is time: There never seems to be enough of it! A proper heat treatment procedure requires a significant investment of time, spread out over many hours or even several days. Heat-treating is more than just following a recipe. It's a mixture of precise timing and manipulation of exacting temperatures in sequence. This process of taking steel from soft to hard needs to continue without any breaks or delays in order to achieve the proper outcome, which is an optimally heat-treated blade. A minimum of several hours is needed from beginning to end, as even the simplest steels benefit from multiple temper cycles. The process can stretch even further depending on steel type or if a cryogenic treatment or multiple tempers are incorporated. While the maker may find time during a heat-treat cycle to do other things, such as during tempering when the blades will be in the furnace for a few hours, overall timing is critical. Heat treatment protocol calls for each step to be performed at a certain time without hesitation, so being focused and attentive to detail is crucial.

A knifemaker who wants to make progress in their skills and advance in the craft may reasonably choose to send out for professional heat treatment in order to allocate time differently. Sending your blades out to be heat-treated frees up some of your time, allowing you to concentrate on other knifemaking duties, expand your skills, or increase production. Most professional heat-treat facilities work around the clock splitting duties between three shifts. This allows for continuous, uninterrupted processing to take place without having just one person to do it all from beginning to end. Even though it's hard, tedious work, at the end of the day, the professional heat treater can go home knowing that another coworker will be finishing what he started. The single knifemaker does not have that luxury.

Let's look at an example to help you understand the numbers. You have thirty blades to heat treat and you feel comfortable processing six blades per day. At that rate it will take you a full week of heat-treating to get them all complete. Sending them to a professional gives you an entire week for other chores. If you use this time wisely, it's a lot of valuable time saved when you look at the total hours and days that you spend per month just performing the heat-treating for your knives. Let's also take a look from a monetary standpoint. We will use the same thirty blades as batch that you need to heat treat and assume those blades would take forty hours of your time over a few days to complete, same as the example above. If you put your cost as low as twenty dollars an hour to process, including equipment costs, electricity, your time, and so on then that total would be $800. This works out to $26.67 per blade. Even if you were to cut the hourly rate in half or lower the total hours by a few, the cost is still significant.

Now let's looks at the cost of heat treatment by the professional. At PHT, we currently charge $188 + return shipping/handling for thirty blades, provided the batch is all the same steel type and the knives are less than twenty inches long. This works out to around $6.75 per blade, assuming USPS medium flat-rate-box shipping. All processing is done in a highly controlled environment, including computer controlled vacuum or atmosphere hardening cycles, cryogenic treatment, proper tempering to your hardness specifications and straightening. The cost per blade will decrease with an increase in the number of blades you send, and this is standard throughout the industry. From an economic standpoint it's hard to make a case for performing your own heat-treating no matter how many blades you have. Increasing the quantity of blades that you heat treat, to lower costs, will only lead to a greater expenditure of your precious time, whereas from the pro you will get a lower cost per blade the more you send!

Sending out for heat treatment gives you time to work on other parts of your knifemaking process and saves you money in the long run, but it isn't without cost. It may take as much as a month between sending out blades and getting them back. If you don't want to be idle during that time, you need to plan ahead. The time that is freed up will only be useful if you've planned your processes to take advantage of it. If you typically profile, grind, and heat treat blades a few at a time, then finish those knives, then repeat, you may need to change your routine to take advantage of the professional heat treater. If you can tune your process to where you can profile and grind blades a dozen or more at a time, and if you plan other tasks while the blades are away from your shop, you can work more efficiently. If time is money, when you produce knives faster or with greater efficiency, you make more money.

The Tools the Pros Use

Another major consideration are the differences in the equipment and tools used to heat treat at home compared to the tools of the professional. While there are numerous sources for do-it-yourself or over-the-counter furnaces and forges for the knifemaker, and while these will certainly get the job done in terms of a hardened knife blade, home equipment has some limitations.

I began heat-treating in the early 1980s and we processed using furnaces similar to what the knifemaker can buy today. We still have a few of those furnaces in use, so I am very familiar with how they operate and perform. While I'm less familiar with forging, I do understand the process and have seen it done many times. My primary perspective is from the furnace style versus the forge style of heat-treating. Let's take a look at a few examples of the limitations of each.

Home knifemaking furnaces are generally slower to heat up because of the open, spiral element design used throughout the industry. Some furnaces may be equipped with a blower system to help speed the transfer of heat, but this is usually used only in the lower-temperature tempering units, not in a furnace used for the hardening cycle. Along with your blades, the rest of the internals of the furnace also have to heat up, thus slowing the process. If your oven takes two hours to get up to the temperature range for heat-treating stainless, for example, that's two more hours you have to plan for in the heat-treating process.

The typical home knifemaker furnace has also only a single thermocouple for controlling the temperature. The knifemaker has no way to test for the accuracy of the equipment, so he must trust in the manufacturer to supply a good thermocouple. Thermocouples are a mechanical component and may eventually break or wear out. Temperature accuracy is critical for proper heat treatment, so not having a backup to verify correct temperature presents some risk to the home knifemaker.

Atmospheric control isn't typically included in home-use furnaces. A line can be inserted to provide an inert gas such as nitrogen or argon, but since the furnace isn't air tight, this limits the ability to provide a proper atmosphere. The most common home method for atmosphere control is wrapping your blades in stainless steel foil to create a barrier against oxygen. The maker must purchase the special-use foil and make an envelope for each knife, which takes both time and money. This method is also not ideal, as small holes often occur in the foil envelopes that can reduce the effectiveness of this method by allowing for decarburization.

When considering heat-treating in a forge, your time to heat up will certainly be quicker. The primary limitation is that temperature control is done by eye, which even with experience isn't the most accurate method! While it's true that there's a major marker of temperature, as all steel goes nonmagnetic at 1,414 degrees, it takes experience to accurately judge the proper temperature for austentizing. Providing an accurate soak at temperature is also difficult. Another consideration is forge atmosphere. Without careful attention, significant scale or decarburization can form. Each of these variables eliminates an area of control or precision.

Now let's look at the tools the professional heat treater uses. The modern, commercial heat-treating facility has all the newest technologies. Thermocouples are certified and guaranteed accurate within a few degrees.

Backup thermocouples are standard, so if the first one fails, the second one can be used to complete the cycle, thus ensuring accuracy even during a failure. Over-temperature thermocouples are also employed in case of failure resulting in a runaway or overheating furnace. If the control thermocouple exceeds the temperature of the overtemperature thermocouple, then the cycle is stopped, thus saving the product from damage.

Atmosphere control is also paramount to successful metallurgy. We use pure, heat-treat-grade nitrogen for our atmosphere in our hardening furnaces. We either use a vacuum to extract the oxygen and then replace with nitrogen or force nitrogen through the furnace to purge the oxygen. These furnaces are capable of controlling the atmosphere exactly, eliminating potential problems with over carburizing or de-carburizing.

Modern furnaces use computer controlled programmers capable of heating at different rates depending on the cycle and holding an accurate temperature within a few degrees for just the right amount of time. We are also capable of quenching at different speeds to ensure hardness and proper metallurgy but still reducing warpage and possible cracking. The professional heat treater also has ready access to cryogenic and induction processing, adding another level of possible heat-treating options.

Finally, the professional brings the best testing equipment to the plate. You will know *exactly* how hard your blade is, and that your heat treat went *exactly* right. Our hardness testers are the best that money can buy because in the end, the reputation of the professional depends on reliably producing quality product. Proper metallurgy and heat treatment are evidenced by correct hardness. The other industries we serve, such as nuclear, aerospace and military, demand strict testing guidelines. We test our hardness testers daily for accuracy and also have independent outside testing done on a routine basis to ensure proper calibration. We use only certified thermocouples calibrated to within +- 1F. Our furnaces use computer programming to control the heat-treating cycles which are customizable to suit the load. Specialized fixturing and sophisticated straightening are routine. Most modern heat treaters also adhere to a quality assurance standard such as ISO. The knifemaker gets the benefit of this level of precision, resulting in more consistency and better performance from their knives.

Are You Experienced?

As a knifemaker, your hands-on experience is limited to the number of blades and different types of steel that you have heat-treated. If you're a veteran knifemaker, your total number of blades may be in the hundreds and steel types may number a dozen or so. Experience and knowledge will increase with each blade and with each new type of steel, but you will only know what those particular circumstances teach you. It's common for the knifemaker to come up with a formula that works for a particular steel/blade style and stick with it because it works. That does not mean that it couldn't be better, but the maker lacks the experience and testing equipment necessary to choose what changes to make to their heat-treat protocol to increase performance.

Experience is an area where the professional heat treater will shine. This is what we do all day, every day, most of the time 24/7. The hands-on experience and real-world knowledge increases on a daily basis. New steels are being formulated, and we will likely work with them before you do. New techniques and processes are constantly evolving. We have hundreds of different steel types in our data base. We routinely process 125–150 different orders per day. This all adds up to a vast amount of experience that the heat treater can then apply to your next order.

I have been heat-treating steel since 1981, almost thirty-seven years as of this writing. That's a long time to be at one job, but I'm not the longest-term employee at my work! There's another employee with over thirty-eight years and several with over thirty years of experience. My point is that the heat-treat industry is full of folks who have been at it for decades. Their knowledge cannot be overstated. Do something for a long time and you get very good at it!

The professional brings a vast resource of heat-treat experience that can be applied to your blades. Knife friendly heat treaters can make recommendations on hardness or different protocols to enhance performance depending on the final application of your knife. They will be familiar with the knife steels used today and will easily be able to heat treat the next new steel to hit the market. Even the professionals occasionally have deal with warpage, but they have the experience to deal with it so that your blades come back straight.

Time to Go Pro

If and when you decide to take the step and send out knives to a professional, be sure to seek out a company that is willing to listen to your requests and accommodate you if possible. Tell them about your knives and your heat-treat experience. Let them know how your knives are being used and pass along any feedback you get from your own testing or from your customers. A good heat treater will be take all of this information and apply it to your needs, helping you to become a better knifemaker.

Only you can decide if moving to the next level means going to production batches and professional heat treat. The next level for you could just as well be to go the other direction, and start building knives more intentionally one at a time. Either way, when you decide to use a professional heat-treat service, you can be absolutely certain that you are getting the best heat-treat possible. You'll save time and money to use on other tasks, which, well applied, may advance you in the art of knifemaking.

CHAPTER 11

Basic Pancake Sheath

Dave Ferry

THE MAKING OF knife sheaths probably goes just about as far back in human history as the making of knives. That chipped, sharpened rock wasn't much good if you couldn't haul it around with you, so somebody came up with a way to carry it, the first sheaths.

I believe the making of a good sheath is just as important for today's knifemaker. Particularly if like me you make using knives, your customer deserves and expects a safe way to carry their knives. I can't tell you how many knives I've sold because of my sheaths. I field the phone call all the time like, "I've been looking for a horizontal carry sheath, and yours is the best I've seen on the internet. What knives do you have for sale with a horizontal sheath?" A quality sheath not only serves your customer well, it can set you apart in the knife industry.

Most modern sheaths are made either of leather or Kydex. There's absolutely nothing wrong with Kydex sheaths, and they are very practical for certain applications. I'm not a Kydex bender, so I'm not the guy to tell you how to make a sheath from Kydex. I'm a hide pounder, and leather sheaths are what I do.

Why has leather has been used for sheaths for thousands of years? One reason is because it simply works. Leather is a special material: it's warm to the touch, it protects, it's durable, it ages well, and it can be shaped, manipulated, decorated, sewn, and made into many useful products. Knife sheaths are just one of those products that can be made with leather.

Leatherwork isn't difficult, nor does it need to be expensive. Just like knifemaking, you can have a need for kinds of tools, but I really can't think of anything that is done in leather that can't be done with a little ingenuity and cheaply. The good leather tools make things easier, and quicker, but they don't solve the impossible. You don't have that Osborne #2 edger? How about a piece of sixty-grit sandpaper wrapped around a ruler? It will take longer, and will be harder to keep as nice, but it can be done.

Let me say a few more things about tools. As a rule, just like knifemaking tools, usually the better (and occasionally more expensive) tools do actually work better, but this is *not* always the case. There are certain tools where the cheap tool works as well or better. While a long, full discourse on leather working tools is beyond the scope of this basic how-to chapter, we live in a wonderful time for finding information. If I mention a Osborne #2 edger and you don't know what I'm talking about, a quick internet search and you'll know not only what is it but also where to buy it.

I come from a ranching/cowboy background, and my sheath designs reflect that. They are all designed to carry a knife horseback, securely and safely. And I'm not talking about some rental, string, nose-to-tail trail ride either. I'm talking about crashing down some brush-covered mountain slope after some runaway leather bag posing as a cow critter. I'm talking about that cold-backed son-of-a-gun horse that can get a little humpy in the morning, or jumping a crick or… Lots of *ors* in our world, but this is the type of retention my customers need, demand, and get. It's not hard, and I'll show you how.

The pancake sheath is one of my most popular designs. It lies as flat as a pancake against the body and can be worn in several different locations on the belt. My original intent was for it to be a cross-draw-type sheath but then I started seeing people carry it in many different locations, behind the hip, small of the back, on the hip—it's pretty versatile. I sure didn't invent the pancake sheath, but I have evolved it quite a bit. I've seen variations of it for years. Heck, let's get started. Let's build a pancake sheath the way I do it.

When I sell a knife, the customer always has the opportunity to add an additional sheath for his knife to the order. I need the knife in hand to build a sheath, even one of my own knife models. All knives are a little different, and to get a decent fit, ya need the knife. In this sheath build, the customer had requested an additional pancake sheath and that's what we're gonna build for him here. Thought I'd pictorially document the steps I go through.

Here I've cut out a front and a back of a pancake-sheath pattern. I make them slightly oversized and will trim to shape and fit. Leather here is Herman Oak, veg tan leather, seven-eighths-ounce weight. A quick word about leather for sheath work. You want vegetable tanned (veg tan, veggie tan, strap leather, tooling leather, or saddle leather are all the same thing). You don't want soft chrome-tanned leather. Buy the best leather you can and stay away from belly leather. There are two American tanneries that produce what many recognize as some of the best veg tan leather in the world. These are Herman Oak and Wickett and Craig. I use leather from both. I use seven-eighths-ounce weight for the vast majority of my sheaths. If it's a larger knife nine-to-ten-inch OAL, or bigger, I start moving up in weight (thickness) of the leather to eight-to-ten ounces. I will also use the heavier leather if the sheath is gonna be carved. The lighter weight tools or stamps well, but for carving, a different process, I like the heavier weight. There are many imported less-expensive leathers out there, but if there's one thing I've learned helping lots of folks get started in the leather game, bite the bullet and get the good stuff.

I've quickly dunked both pieces in my water bucket that has a solution of water and Pro Carv in it. Pro Carv is a product made by Bee Natural that does many great things. Biggest is that it allows you to work sooner than traditional "casing" methods. Casing requires leather to be dunked in water till all the bubbles quit coming out and then wrapped in a towel or blanket and left overnight. The next morning, the cased leather is very pliable, cuttable, moldable, toolable and so on. My water container on my work bench always has Pro Carv in it. It's really a couple of minutes instead of hours. This dunking is really fast in and out. Now I'm allowing some of the color to come back. We will be making a right-hand, cross-draw sheath to be worn above the left front pocket.

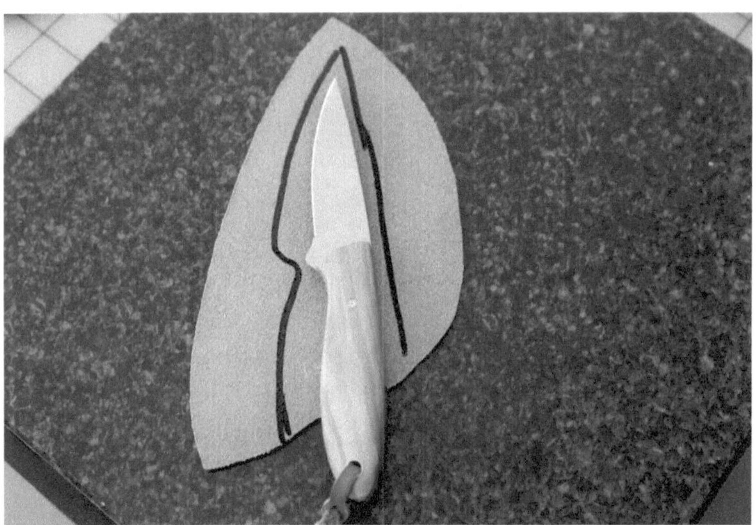

This is probably one of the most important steps and getting this right is vital for the fit and retention of the sheath. I mark with a Sharpie on the inside of the front piece the basic outline of the knife with a little extra. This is going to be the pocket that the knife will sit in when the sheath is completed. Very important to get that finger guard and the point of the welt just right. That is the widest part of the blade and it has to slide past that welt when inserting the knife. About three-eighths-inches clearance is what I'm looking for here. This is total between the top and the bottom outlines. A hair less if the handle is thin from side to side and a tad more if it's a little thicker.

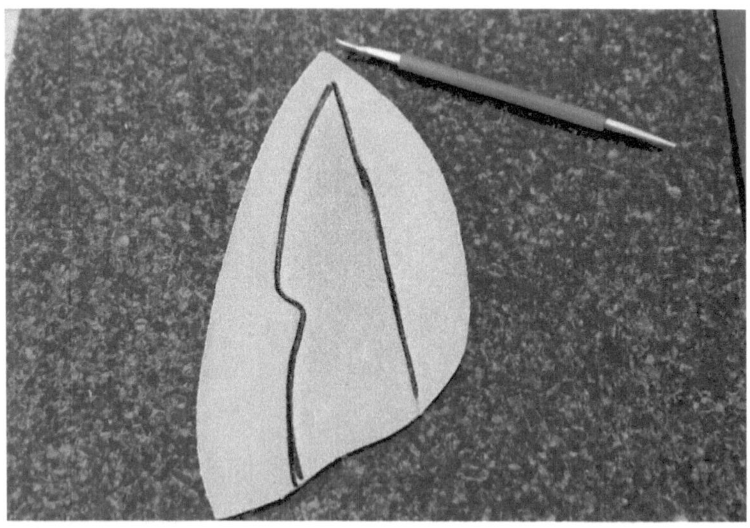

I take my pokey tool—it's actually called a modeler, and it's from Tandy—and scribe hard on the lines, three-to-four times. This transfers the lines to the other side of the leather.

So here we see the lines on the front side of the sheath. These lines are how I base trimming to fit the sheath to the knife (always looking to be as compact as possible). They also tell me where to put my stitching grooves.

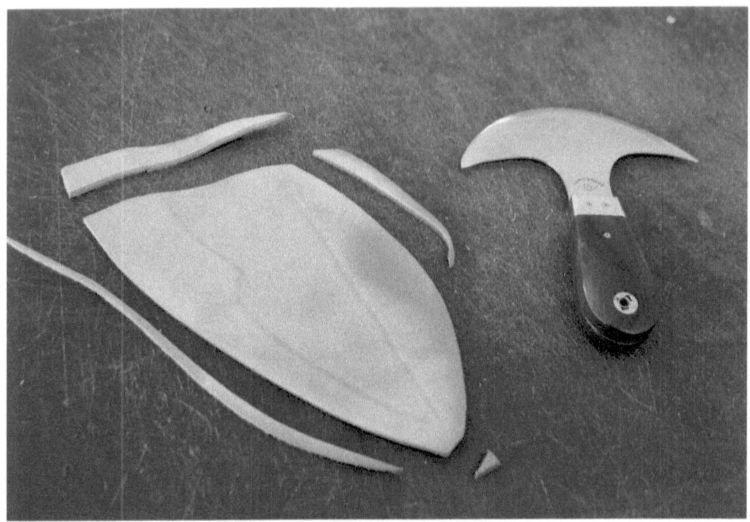

Here I'm using my round knife to trim the excess off of the front of the sheath. I do this by eye and experience, lots of experience. I haven't always got it right, but it's been quite a while since I've screwed it up. The hazard here isn't leaving enough room for your slots to fit in after you've done your stitching grooves. Round knives are a great leather-cutting tool. You start doing a lot of leatherwork and you'll want one. They've been around for centuries because they work. They are used with a push cut. A lot of good leatherwork has been done with other types of knives so if you are just starting I wouldn't hurry out to buy a round knife. Y'all want one later, though. When I started I used a Case trapper to cut leather. Worked quite well. Then started hanging out at a couple saddle-making shops and watched 'em whiz through leather with a round knife and started down that road, but that was later.

Here I'm slicking the leather down. I use a piece of lignum vitae wood with the corners rounded. Lots of folks use a piece of glass, and then it's called *glassing*. But I've gone to using this piece of wood. Slicking smooths out a lot of surface imperfections and makes the leather more uniform for stamping. I do this after I mark the lines because slicking makes it harder to scribe the lines through to the front. This is an important step that is often overlooked. It will make your work more professional looking.

Here I'm using the top piece upside down against the bottom piece to scribe the top edge. That is all the trimming the bottom piece will receive at this stage. I want to make sure too that the bottom extends past the top all the way around. Again, I know this from experience, but a guy who hasn't done it a bunch may have to do some more trimming to the top piece.

Now I've used two different groovers to get my stitching grooves marked. Both of these are Tandy products, I believe. I've had the red handled one for over thirty years, and the other one probably twelve-to-fifteen years. I keep that one set at this adjustment all the time. It's for sheaths. If I am doing something else, I have another groover that I adjust back and forth as needed for that particular project. A stitching groover cuts/inlays a shallow groove in the leather. Not only does this tell you where to stitch later, but also it inlays the stitching some, which protects the stitching from abrasion when the sheath is in use later. These tools are one of those exceptions where the cheapie works just as well as the expensive one. We've got five of these guys.

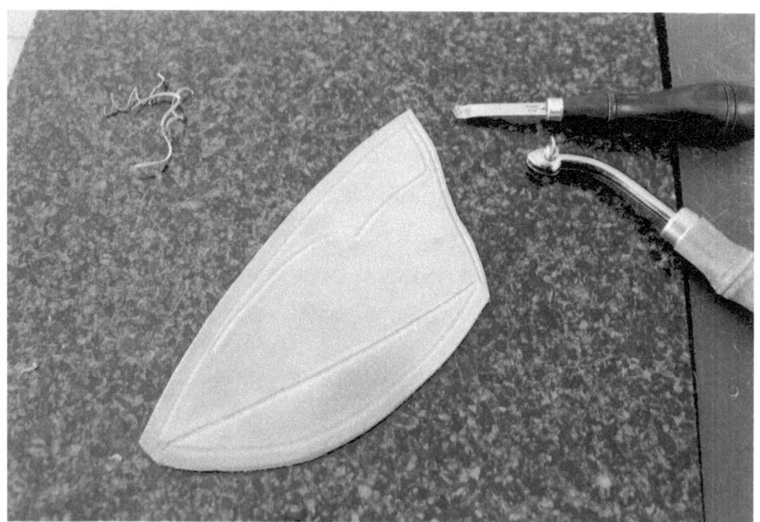

Now I've edged (both sides) and creased (just the top edge) of the front part of the sheath. I used a #1 Barry King edger for this operation. The creaser is one that Nichole bought and didn't like, so she traded me out when she stole my Osborne. I think creasing is one of those little operations that a lot of folks don't do that add just a touch of professionalism to a project. The crease is that line that isn't the stitching groove across the top of the sheath. Edging takes the corner of the leather off and makes a more rounded edge preparing it for rubbing later. I always crease first and then edge.

Now I've slicked, edged and creased the bottom side of the sheath. Again, only the top edge gets the edging and creasing as the rest of the sheath will be edged later. I'm getting ready to stamp my makers mark on the bottom of the sheath. I'm estimating and trying to get it on the pocket so it will be in between the two stitching lines when we stitch up this sheath.

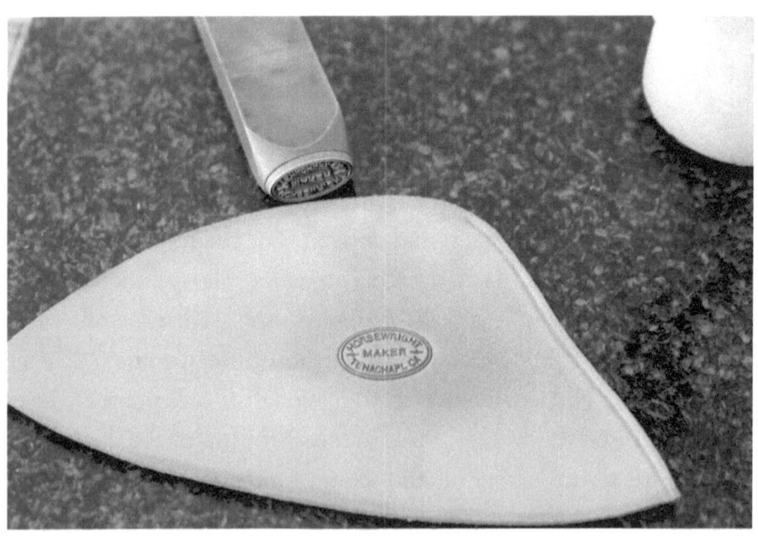

Nice clean stamp and it looks like we got 'er in the right spot. Maker's marks can be very expensive, or they can be relative inexpensive. There are lots of new options out there these days besides my old-school steel stamp, so do some research, but you should mark your work.

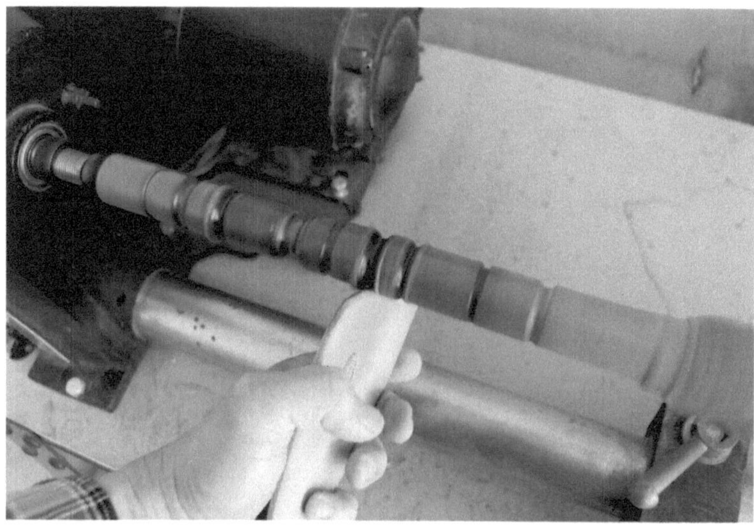

Then I take both pieces over to the lathe. I have a full-size wood turning lathe with a piece of rosewood chucked up. The rosewood has grooves of various sizes turned in it. An occasional dab of beeswax/paraffin or glycerin saddle soap keeps the leather from burning. It's an adjustable-speed lathe, and I have it set at warp speed. All I'm doing at this stage is the tops of both pieces. I don't use any gum or any other edge rubbing preparation at this stage, just the dampness that is already in the leather. If ya look close in the pic, you can see the burnishing already looking pretty good. Total time five seconds each maybe. If by the time I get to the lathe, the leather seems to dry I will redampen it with a sponge and my water/Pro Carv mix. Don't have access to a lathe or a power burnisher? Use a hardwood stick, a smooth piece of bone/antler, or a piece of canvas/denim. I use to use an awl handle that was made out of some indistinct hardwood. And lots of elbow grease.

This sheath was ordered with a basket-stamp tooling pattern. We'll get going on that now. Before tooling, you want to check your moisture content in the leather. You want the color to be back into the leather. So see how on the inside of our stitching grooves the color is pretty much back to normal? But on the left side there it looks pretty damp still. That is what I mean by wanting the color to be coming back before you stamp. If it's still too damp, a hairdryer for a minute or so will help. If it's too dry, I'll redampen the stamping area with my sponge and may use the hairdryer to get it ready to stamp. You'd find that many professional tooling benches have a hair dryer plugged in, sitting there all the time. My wife does.

Now we're starting the border stamp. I do each of these corners first and then stamp from one to the other. I'm using a stamp called a Camo border, which is the semicircular stamp. I use another tool called a *seeder* to give each corner stamp a little more visual interest. I then stamp from corner to corner completing the border stamp. Many books or videos on tooling would tell you to cut and bevel a borderline first before doing your Camo border stamp. I abandoned this practice many years ago. I found that it shortened the life span of the sheath. Particularly in hard use (remember: I make knives and sheaths for working cowboys, and they can be tough on stuff), I found that the sheaths were cracking along those cut lines. I also found that on other products too, not just sheaths, so I quit doing that.

Other instruction will tell ya to make a scribed line with a pair of dividers and then do your border stamp against that. Well, ok. Now how do you make that scribed line go away? If you look close, you will see that there's a slight line by the stitching grooves from the pokey tool? Look close in the pic with just the three corners stamped. This light line is what I use to keep the border stamp straight and uniform all the way around.

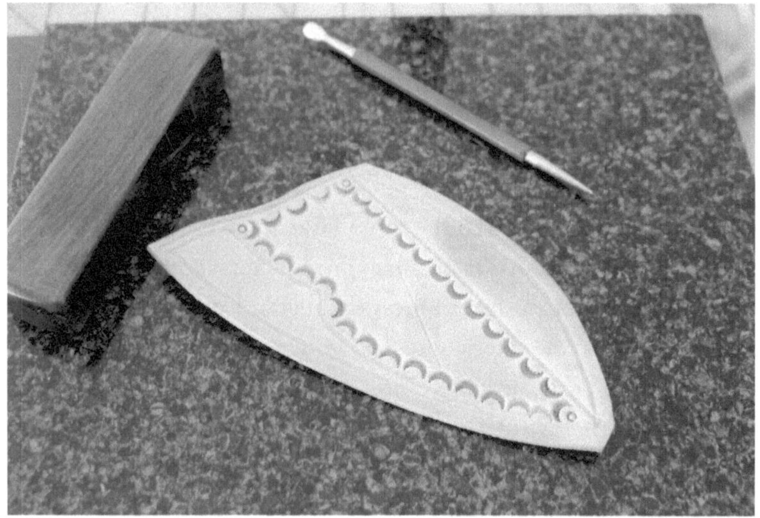

Border stamp completed and then scribing the line for the basket stamping. I know this is backward from what a lot of folks will do or what several books recommend, but it's what works for me. Basket stamping and then doing the border after just didn't work that well for me. I spent a lot of time cleaning up afterward. So I started doing the border stamp first and then the basket stamping. This isn't really a work on tooling/stamping, and there's plenty of material out there on that. One thing I would mention here is these tools: your tooling stamps is one place to spend money. Good tools make a difference in stamping, and that is for sure.

Basket stamping finished. One thing I like to do is make sure the stamping is at as a uniform depth as possible. Pretty happy with this effort. If you aren't getting a nice burnished impression in your leather like is shown here, it's either poor tools or water content in your leather, or both. A good tool should leave a nice burnished impression. Cheapie don't burnish much. If your leather is too wet, you will get a nice, deep impression but no burnish. If your leather is too dry, you will get a light, shallow impression with little burnish.

Ok, we're getting ready to add the welt. I have a welt-shape pattern that when cut out gives me a welt for 98 percent of my sheaths. The welt here is already trimmed to fit the sheath. Basically, I lay the welt on the sheath on the welt side and then use my Sharpie to mark that interior line. I'll then trim the welt and check it by laying it back on the sheath. I only put the welt on the bottom side or knife-edge side of the sheath. Then will do a little more trimming if needed. The only time I put a welt in on the top side of the sheath is if I'm making a sheath for someone else's knife with an upswept point. Then the upper welt is only about half of the top, and I skive the edge of it to zero.

Now I've glued the welt in. Skiving is thinning a piece of leather so that it fits well with other pieces. It makes a smooth transition. I've skived this edge prior to gluing, but I don't always get it right. I'm actually pushing the round knife away at the angle the center of the knife is pointing to. This oblique slicing angle then skives the welt without touching the sheath body. If I didn't have a round knife, I would peel back the welt, reskive and reglue. I've ruined too many sheaths not doing it with a round knife that I simply will not try skiving in place with any other tool, except a very specialized tool, a push skiver. Skiving the edge of the welt to zero is important for your stitching later. It prevents odd-sized stitches. If you are coming down off the welt, you'll have a couple of long stitches. If going up onto the welt, a couple of short ones. Skiving this edge to zero eliminates that and gives a nice smooth transition in the sheath from two layers to three. A walking-foot sewing machine really helps with that too but doesn't eliminate it completely. You just have to look a lot closer. Skive the edge for a finished product.

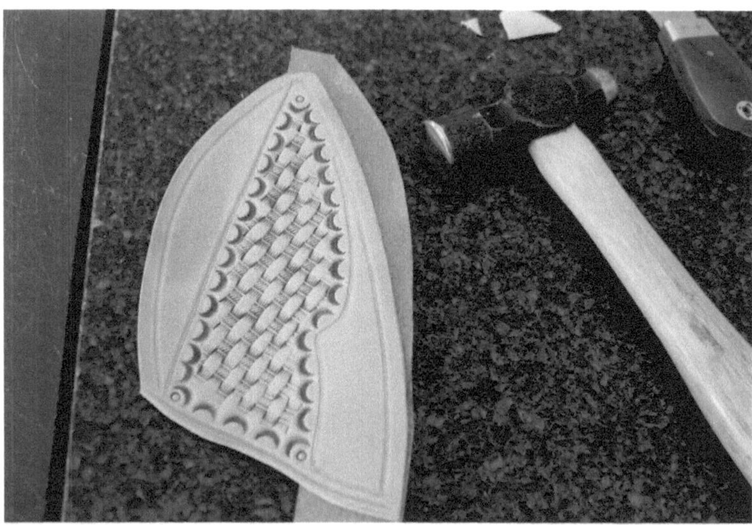

Here is the sheath with the welt glued in from the top side. I use this hammer to tap the edges to get a good bond with the glue. I keep the face of this hammer dressed clean. It's also only used for this purpose. This prevents marking up your project. You can see how the welt is just a little to the inside of the inside stitching groove. Perfect.

Ok, I've trimmed the welt and then glued up the top and bottom piece of the sheath. This pic shows the skive coming down from the welt. I use Weldwood contact cement. The kind that comes in the green can. No smell and incredible bond. Thin with water and very little gunky buildup like other contact cements. I keep it in a 99-cent-store ketchup bottle and then squirt a little into that plastic cup pictured and spread it out with that disposable foamy brush. Another thing about using this glue is that it dries very quickly. Literally, by the time you have one side glued, the other has dried. Just a few seconds. Important when you work in batches like I tend to.

Line up the top edges, make sure the bottom is sticking out all around and tap together.

Set the sheath in the sun for a few minutes. You don't want it damp when you sew. Will make marks you can't rub out. Ya can hit it with the hair dryer too.

Time to sew. I've had this machine for many years. It's a good machine, but it had a high learning curve. After about fifteen-to-twenty years, I'm kinda getting its quirks down. I've since updated to a newer machine that I like even more. A word about sewing leather. Don't have a heavy-duty leather stitcher? There are many methods of hand sewing leather. I know many a knifemaker and some sheath makers too that will spend an evening hand sewing sheaths while watching TV. Lots of info out there on different ways of sewing. A heavy-duty stitcher is a great investment for making leather sheaths. It will really speed up your production. A top-of-the-line one will cost ya about what a good two-by-seventy-two grinder will, so they aren't out of reach. There's some debate as to whether machine stitching or hand sewing is better. Done well, each method will produce a quality product that will provide years of service in the harshest of conditions. Done poorly, each one is lousy.

Another thought. Don't want to hand sew and don't have a machine? Most towns have a shoe repairman or, where I live, a saddle maker. Betcha a few bucks would get that sheath sewed up for ya.

Stitching it together. I start on the welt side where the two stitching lines come together. Back stitch the first two to lock them down and then motor on. When I come to the end here, I will back stitch two again.

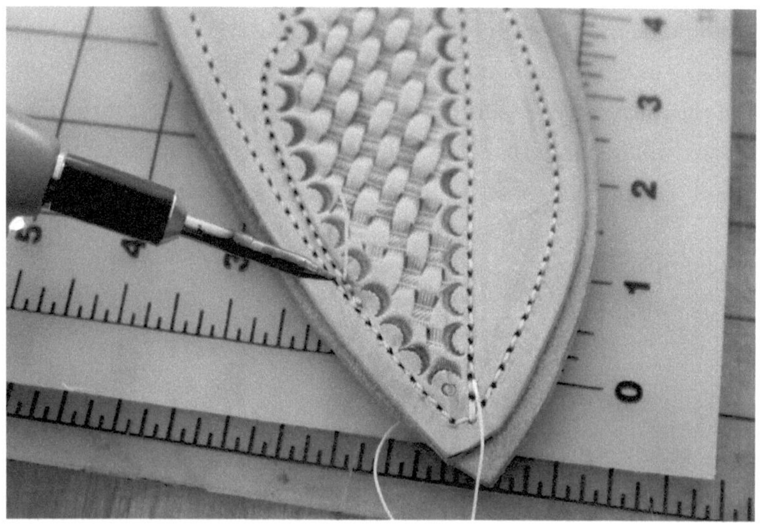

I use a fine-tipped soldering iron to melt/cut the strings flush or even down in the hole a bit. Be careful not to touch the leather, or you'll leave a burn mark.

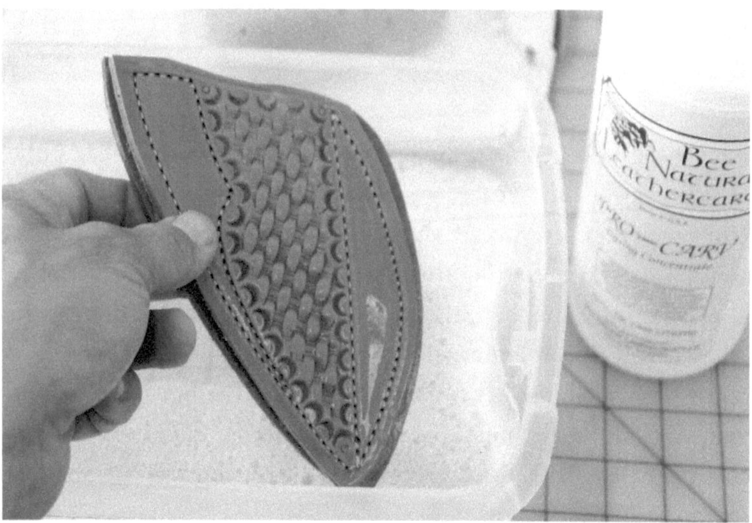

Time for wet forming. I toss the sheath into my water bucket. My water always has the Pro Carv in it. Once I started using this stuff, I have never been without it. This is a new batch of water and is still a little sudsy. Ideally, the water should be pretty warm but not very hot. I like it so I can stick my hand in without too much discomfort. If the water has been sitting for a while, I put it in the microwave for a minute or two. Anyhoo, I like to let the sheath sit in the water till it sinks. That's when I pull it out. This absorption level seems just about right for the work I still have to do to it before forming.

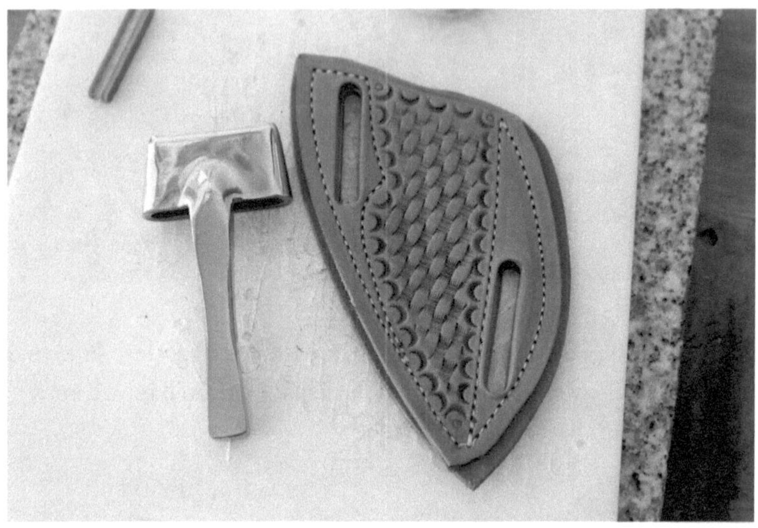

First thing I do is punch the belt slots. I use a two-inch bag punch for this. I recently got this Weaver punch, and it's far superior to the one's I've used over the years. I try to get the slots as far apart as possible and as close to parallel as possible. Getting them far apart allows the sheath to ride at an angle. The further apart they are, the closer to horizontal the sheath will ride. This sheath will ride at about a forty-five-degree cant. If you don't get the slots close to parallel, the belt will wad up under the sheath and not lay flat. Not pictured but I often put a piece of scrap leather under the sheath when punching the slots. This helps protect it from getting marred by the rough surface of the cutting board.

Now I'm trimming the excess of the bottom layer off the sheath. I don't want to move the sheath around too much on the cutting board. It can get scratched up quite a bit when wet like this. I try to hold it pretty darn steady so it doesn't move around.

I take the sheath outside and sand the edges smooth. I use a 120-grit ceramic belt for this on my six-by-forty-eight grinder. This belt is only used for leather so that it doesn't leave any stray color or dingy marks when sanding. I get all the layers even and round off the two pointy corners.

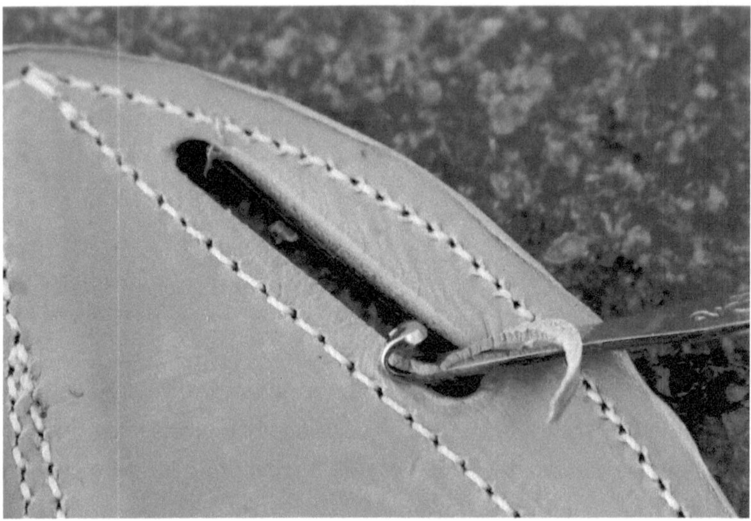

Here I'm using my bent-back tip edger to edge the inside of the slots on the bottom side. This is a # 2 JWP edger, and this is about the only thing I use it for. I will then rub the inside of the slots with a small stick that will fit in there. Then I take my lignum vitae stick and slick the bottom side getting any stray marks out. I'm rubbing out teeth marks from the sewing machine and any scratches from the cutting board and from punching the slots. These steps are very important to the finished project. Lots of folks won't rub out stray marks or edge the slots, and it shows in the quality of the finished sheath.

Next step is to edge the sheath top and bottom. I use a #3 Osborne for this, or a #4 if the sheath is made of thicker leather. I edge all the parts that I sanded. Remember the top or throat of the sheath has already been edged prior to assembly. So basically, I'm edging along the stitching. Edging will take some practice to get good at. Try to hold the cutting edge of the edger at a consistent angle all the way around the part of the sheath you're edging.

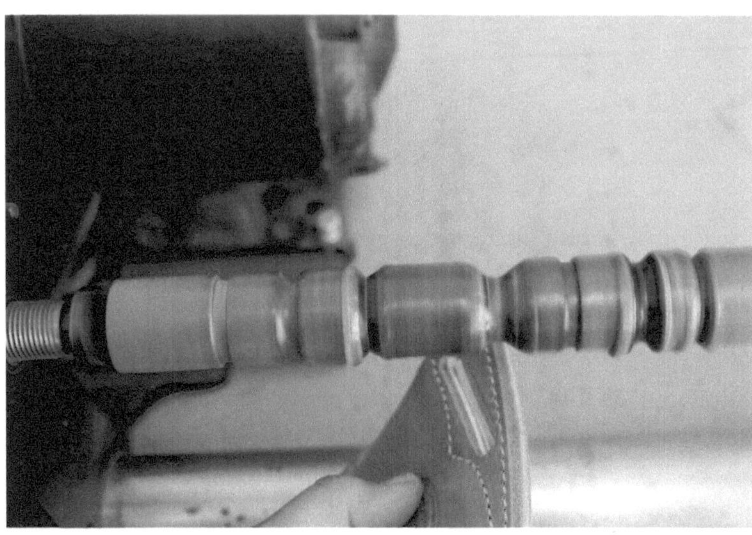

After edging, we're gonna take a trip back over to the lathe. Again, at this stage, we're not going to use any gum or agent of any kind, just the dampness already in the leather. Now we are really rounding the edges and getting the pieces of the sheath formed into one edge. Until recently, I would have gone and sanded again at four hundred grit to get some of the prep work done before rubbing. I stopped doing that when I switched rubbing products a while back, wasn't necessary anymore. I really like to think of an edge as a 3-D kind of thing. So there's a top to the edge, a middle, and a bottom. I take pains to make sure I hit all three all the way around on the sheath. That's why I use that much wider groove on the rosewood here. Allows me to get the top and bottom side well, not just the middle. I'm trying to round the three parts together.

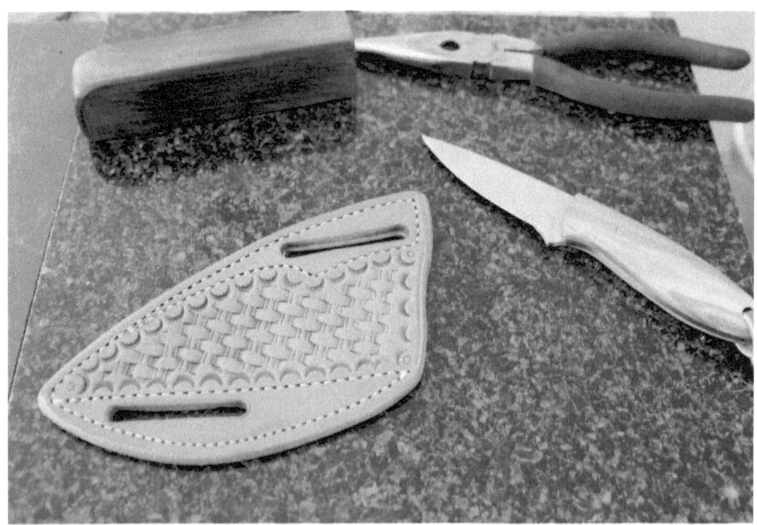

Here are the tools I use to wet form the sheath to the knife. Not pictured, I also have a rat-tailed file close by. I'll open the pocket in the sheath with the needle-nose pliers. I leave them closed for this. It's very important that the pocket of the sheath is straight when you put the knife in the first time, and I get the pliers to do this. If not straight, it's pretty easy to put the knife through the wet sheath leather, usually on the front side. Ask me how I know this. I hold the sheath kind of cupped in my left hand by the wet side of the sheath with the front of the sheath facing away from me. My hand goes over the top of the sheath and cups it from the bottom. My wrist is bent away from the sheath, and my elbow is pointing up. While this sounds awkward, it keeps you away from the front of the sheath while you're putting the knife in the damp leather. Lots of dead cow but only one left hand. So double-checking that the wet sheath is nice and straight, I start pushing the knife in. When the finger guard gets to the lump in the welt, you should start feeling some resistance. It needs to be tight but not too tight. When the knife goes past that lump on the welt, it should make an audible "clunk" when it sets into the pocket. If it's too tight and there's too much resistance, I use my pliers by opening them against the welt and the top stitch line. This should fix 'er up. If still too tight, after a couple of plier stretches, I use the rat tail file to shave a little off of the welt lump. Doesn't take much and a little tight is better than too loose. If the knife has a carbon-steel blade, I wipe it down with some WD-40 first before wet forming. If it's a stainless blade, I don't bother, but all knives get wiped down with a paper towel after being removed from the sheath.

Once the knife is in the sheath, I start wet molding. I work on the back side first, and I use my stick of lignum vitae with the rounded corners. I work on each side of the handle and a little bit on the blade from the tip to the handle. That's about it. I don't do a lot of wet molding just some, more for definition than anything else. Retention really comes with the fit of the lump on the welt, not with the wet molding. I then flip the sheath over and work on the front side. I do even less here because you don't want to squish your tooling. Just a little on each side of the handle and a light skimming from the tip of the blade up to the handle. This pic shows the sheath after the wet molding. On a tooled sheath, I would say 90 percent of the molding in on the back and 10 percent on the front. If it's a plain sheath, without tooling, probably fifty-fifty front and back.

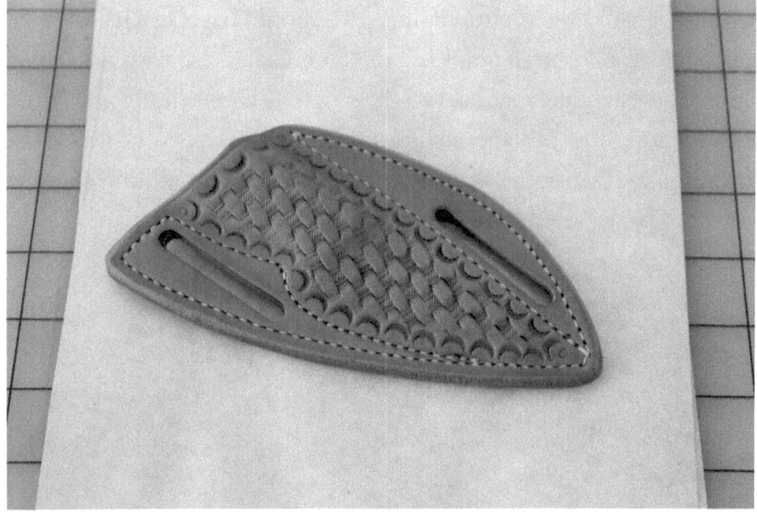

OK, now for the heresy. The standard warnings apply. Kids don't try this at home. I take the wet-molded sheath and place it on four sheets of card stock paper and here's the part that makes me an heretic bake it in the kitchen oven at 175 degrees for three hours. I know. I know. Heat and leather don't mix. But remember the title: this is how *I* do it.

1. The oven must be preheated. When an oven is coming up to temp, there are some very wide temp swings. I learned this the hard way, tempering knives. You don't want your sheath sitting in there at five hundred degrees even for a short time. So preheat your oven.
2. Four pieces of card stock keep rack marks away.

3. The lowest that our oven will go is 175 degrees.. If it went lower, I would use lower.
4. Middle rack is best. When I do a batch, I use all the racks, but if only doing a few, I only use the middle rack and middle of the racks. Not toward the edges is best.
5. At one hour, I flip the sheath onto its front side and then an hour later, I flip it back onto its back for the final hour.
6. Set a timer so you don't forget. Forget and you'll make sheath jerky. Again, ask me how I know. I once forgot and made sheath jerky out of about thirty sheaths. *Set a timer!*

I got this oven technique from an old saddlemaker who got it from an even older holster maker. I've been doing it this way for over twenty years and I've done thousands of sheaths and holsters this way. Done correctly, it produces a nice firm, hard sheath with that wet-molded definition locked into place. Done incorrectly, you make jerky.

I immediately oil the sheath with warm, 100 percent neat's-foot oil (don't use the neat's-foot compound) as soon as it comes out of the oven. I start warming the oil when the sheath has about thirty minutes yet to bake. Warming the oil allows it to penetrate the leather more evenly, and it sets quicker. It prevents splotching. I use the cheap dollar-store paintbrush shown and will get about a year out of one before I wear the bristles away. I keep this dedicated, ten-dollar crockpot and use it only for the neat's-foot oil. Use a very light coat of oil, *very* light, particularly over any tooling and around the throat.

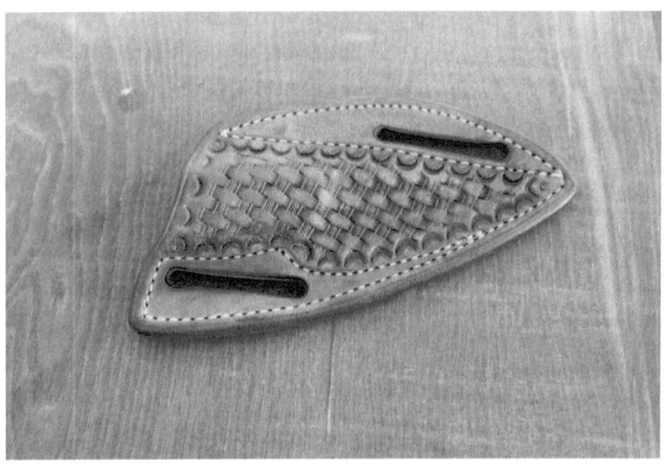

After the sheath is oiled, it goes inside and sits on the kitchen counter overnight. Won't do anything else with the sheath till the next day.

We've allowed the oil to "set" overnight, and next morning, we continue our work. Just a quick note on the oil setting. What I mean by that is the oil evens out and becomes a uniform color throughout your project. This can take several days. Don't worry if the next day you still have some unevenness in color. It'll happen. I once had one of my own holsters take about a month to even out, or set. I'd had to oil the inside of the retaining strap too, and so the top part of the holster was a little darker color than the rest of the holster for about a month. It evened out eventually. Not finishing up your sheath at this stage does not seem to make any difference in how long it takes for the oil to set. So I go ahead and finish it off. Around here always seems like there's some shipping deadline or other looming and other projects to get to.

Now we're gonna rub the edges again using the lathe. This time, I'm gonna wet the edges with Wyo Quick Slik. I get this from Barry King Leather Leather Tools. I have found this to do a better job than Gum Traganath (a traditional rubbing agent), slicker, quicker, and less messy. I've been using gum for over thirty years, and I just fired it when I found this stuff; it's that much better. In fact, I threw a partial bottle of gum away. Don't need it. On the sheath, I do all edges, 360 degrees. Last time, we left the top alone, but this final time, we're hitting them all.

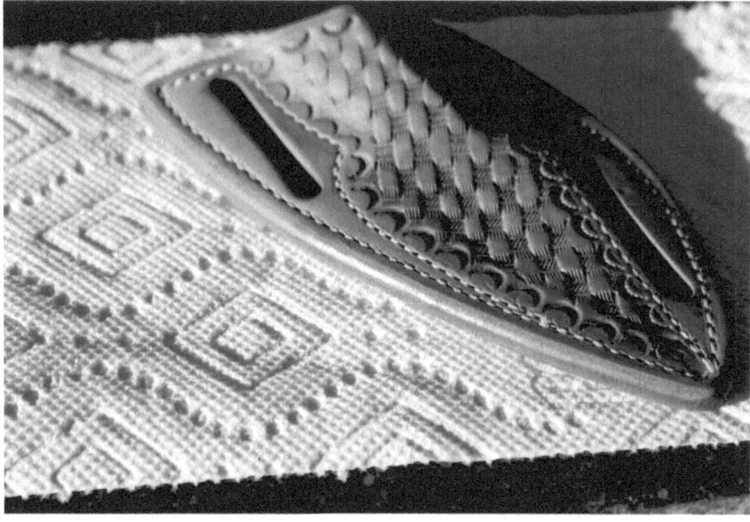

Here you can see how good that edge gets. I'm really sold on that Quick Slik stuff. You can also see that oil has not set all the way on this sheath yet. See how the welt side is a little darker. No fretting, it will set. Another note. I simply hate to dye sheaths. Over the years, I've found dyeing takes about half the life span out of a sheath. Sometimes, I can't get out of it, though. I've actually been bribed to dye a sheath black. Dye first and then oil works the best. I've found that this oil finish shown makes the leather last longer in harsh conditions. I dye other projects but not sheaths.

After rubbing the edges, it's time to apply a finish. What I do is stretch an old T-shirt tight across two fingers and then twist it, holding it that way with the rest of my hand. That is my finish applicator. There are many different leather finishes out there, and it seems everybody has their favorite. I have settled on Fiebing's Bag Kote and have used it for many years. Gives a nice satin finish. Recently, I'm trying RTC, a leather finish made by Bee Natural, the same folks that make Pro Carv. I like the Pro Carv so much I thought I'd give one of their leather finishes a try. I like it. Can't say that I like it more than Bag Kote, but I do like it. RTC takes longer to dry and is glossier than Bag Kote. When I apply the finish, I put a coat on the edges first. You will feel, after your rubbing, a definite grain to your edge. Going one way will be rough and going the opposite direction will be smooth. Go the smooth direction. You've spent some time getting those edges kinda glassy; don't rough them up putting your finish on backward. After the edges, I hold the sheath by the inside and put a coat on the top. When this has dried, I hit the edges and the top or front side of the sheath with another coat. With that T-shirt stretched tight and some finish on there (not saturated) and a light touch, you will get a nice even coat without swirl marks or streaks. After this second coat has dried, I put one coat on the backside of the sheath, and we're done. That's pretty much it from start to finish.

Here it is, all finished. I did use the RTC finish on this project, and it gives a nice look. I'm happy with it. You can see clearly how the bottom half of the sheath is still darker. It will even out over the next couple of days. You'll always want to check your fit with the knife again. Occasionally, you might have to do another plier stretch or a little more rattail filing but not often. If fitted correctly, when you put the knife in the sheath, you'll hear and feel the knife go clunk as it sits down into the pocket. You should be able to turn the sheath upside down and shake vigorously and not have the knife come out. You might want to try this over a folded-up towel on your workbench so a knife doesn't go flying if you're too loose. Before we ship a knife and sheath, we check this fit multiple times. I took this last pic, and this knife and sheath went into Nichole's office. She boxed it up and shipped it to its new owner in New York.

I have used this pattern on all shapes and sizes of knives, from bowies to small little knives like my Gordo (5.25" OAL). On very small knives, you can't get the slots far enough apart for the sheath to ride at an angle. Consequently, I modified the pattern shape and make a vertical pancake sheath for little knives. It is constructed the same way.

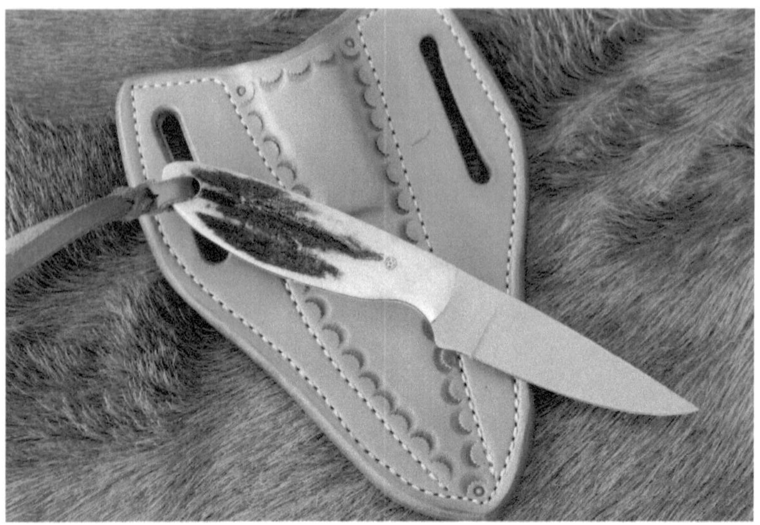

Here is a vertical pancake and its elk-handled Cowboy. The only difference here is the original shape of the sheath parts before construction.

I sure hope this information has been of help to you. While we've spoke specifically about pancake sheath, the leatherwork techniques apply to other type of sheaths as well. The importance of a good sheath can't be overstated. Make a good one and you'll sell your knives.

SECTION THREE

The Knifemaking Journey

CHAPTER 12

The Good Old Days of Knifemaking

Tom Lewis

DURING THE PROCESS of collecting chapter submissions for this book, I received this story from Tom Lewis of Carlsbad, New Mexico. He's a former Knifemakers' Guild member and an ABS Journeyman Smith. I've included it here for one reason: so that those of us who came into knifemaking in the internet age will appreciate how much information we have at our fingertips. When Tom started, not only was there no YouTube, but also there were very few books and no culture of information sharing like we have today. Tom overcame many things to rise through the ranks. We have the opportunity to move from level to level rather quickly. Don't take your position for granted. —Jason Fry

How I Got Started Making Knives

Written 2/2/2017 by Tom Lewis, for his grandchildren

As far back as I can remember, I've always liked knives. When I was very small, I remember my family visited another family in California. They had a teenage son whose room was filled with knives. I was very impressed.

My dad subscribed to lots of magazines including *Outdoor Life*, *Field and Stream*, *American Rifleman*, and several others. I read these magazines, and they had articles and ads concerning knives. When I was maybe in second or third grade, I noticed an ad in one of the magazines for a knife. The price was twenty-five cents. I sent for it, and when it arrived, it was a total piece of junk, not at all like the picture in the magazine. I think I still have that knife somewhere. It was advertised to be razor sharp, but it was so dull it wouldn't have cut butter. That was a lesson in false advertising.

My dad had a very well-equipped shop. He liked tools and was constantly buying them. I loved making things and I think I used the shop more than he did. Thinking back, I'm amazed he let me use *everything* in the shop. I taught myself a lot of skills, like welding. At home, we had a craft book that showed making a knife out of a hacksaw blade. I tried to make this knife, but I was unable to properly attach the handle.

When I was going to Phoenix College, a friend of mine, Jim Cartmill, showed me a knife his older brother had forged. I was really impressed. For the next few years, as long as I lived in Phoenix, I tried forging knives out of leaf spring steel. I used our acetylene torch to heat the blades and used a large piece of steel as an anvil. I had a hard-rock grinder that didn't work very well. I used water as a quench and a large water cooler to hold the water. We had an oak plank that I suppose came from the family's Amarillo farm, and I used it for handles. I made maybe five or six knives before we moved to Carlsbad in 1970.

Once in Carlsbad, it took a while to get my shop built. I had somewhat lost my interest in making knives and was busy hunting, caving, fishing, and so on.

I subscribed to a woodworking magazine, and one issue had an article on making knives. The process was to buy premade blades and attach the handle. I started to feel like knives again, so I made several of these kitchen knives from blanks.

Back then in magazines such as *Outdoor Life*, there would be book-club ads. You could get five free books if you agreed to buy several more books in a year's time. I filled out one of those book-club ads and checked knife books. One was *How to Make Knives* by Bob Loveless. One was the *Gun Digest Book of Knives*. I almost had second thoughts and threw the order form away, but I finally went ahead and sent it in.

It's funny how one event can really change one's interests. When the books came, I read them several times and was hooked on knife making. The book by Bob Loveless brought back my interest and taught me how to make knives. In reading the *Gun Digest Book of Knives*, I was fascinated at the different makers and the knives they made. I wanted to rise to this level of skill.

Meanwhile, I had also been accumulating knives. One of them was, I thought when I ordered it, a US Marine knife. When it came, it was a piece of junk. Also about that time, I got A. G. Russell's catalog in which he sold Morseth knives and also kits to build a Morseth knife. I really liked those knives, but they were expensive, and so were the kits. This was in the late 1970s. Years later, I spoke with A. G. Russell at a Blade Show in Atlanta and told him it was his fault I had gotten into knifemaking.

Back in the 1970s, there was only one place to buy supplies. It was owned by Bob Schrimsher. I ordered some 440C steel from him and started making knives. I started with a hard-rock grinder that wasn't very good for this purpose, then bought a cone-lock drum, which worked better.

The *Gun Digest* knife book featured a lot of well-known knifemakers, and most of them said they used Paul Bos heat-treating for their 440C steel. I wrote a letter to Paul Bos and asked some questions like how thick the blade edge should be before heat treat. Paul was nice enough to answer my letter, and since then, I have sent probably well over a thousand blades to him for heat treat.

I remember one time in 1980 when I was teaching at Puckett Elementary School. I showed one of my knives to the school custodian, Paul Estrada, and he bought it. I showed one to a fourth-grade teacher, Jay Redman, and he bought it.

That was encouraging, so next, I rented a table at a gun-and-knife show. I didn't sell a knife. I set up at a craft show. I didn't sell a knife. I went to another gun-and-knife show. I didn't sell a knife. This was discouraging, but I thought my knives were pretty good, and I was determined not to give up. Next, there was a craft show in Pecos, Texas, and I sold *two* knives. I was on my way.

When I started making knives, there was an established knifemaker in Carlsbad. I had taught both his sons at Hillcrest Elementary, and I had a good relationship with the family, but he absolutely refused to give me any help with my knifemaking. I think he thought I would take all his business away from him. He was a jerk. He would come up to me at those early knife shows and ask, "How many knives have you sold?" When I had to say, "None," he smirked.

Well, he made a big mistake, because soon I surpassed him. I started making Damascus steel, I became a member of the Knifemakers' Guild, and I achieved journeyman's status in the American Bladesmith Society. Mr. Jerk never did any of those things. One time, a friend of mine said Mr. Jerk told him he taught me to make Damascus steel. What a laugh!

Because of that experience, I have always tried to help aspiring knifemakers learn the craft.

My son Tommy and his family lived in Lubbock, Texas. I started going to gun-and-knife shows in Lubbock. At each show, I sold several knives. I put the knife profits back into the business by buying tools and machinery. I also mowed lawns on the side to raise money. I picked up pecans to buy equipment. I also was teaching at NMSU, and I was sent sample books to preview for adoption into the curriculum. I found a place I could sell these books to, so I got some more money that way.

I raised enough money to buy a square wheel grinder. This took a two-inch-by-seventy-two-inch abrasive belt. With this grinder, I really improved my knifemaking.

At a gun-and-knife show in Lubbock, I met Kent Gibson. Kent took an interest in me, bought some knives, and then, over the phone, offered to buy all the knives I had. I had thirty knives on hand. Kent offered me fifty dollars a knife for the thirty knives. I think he figured I would someday be a successful knifemaker and he could make some money by having some of my early knives. Kent also was a really nice person, and he wanted to help me out. I thought fifty dollars was a low price, but I took Kent up on his offer.

With that $1,500, I was able to buy much-needed equipment and supplies. It was good to get rid of my inventory, because the more knives I made, the better they got.

Kent was a real friend. He sent me an anvil to use. Kent found out I wanted a power hammer, and he found a hundred-pound Little Giant power hammer in Crowell, Texas, that was for sale. It was $450! That was a great buy. Kent went to Crowell, Texas, with me to get the power hammer. It was just what I needed to make Damascus.

The hundred-pound Little Giant power hammer was made in 1946. The US Air Force bought the hammer, but I don't think they did anything with it except to paint it every so often. A blacksmith shop in Crowell, Texas, bought the hammer, but it had a three-phase motor, and they didn't have three-phase power, so they didn't use it.

Jeanette had a cousin, Marian Reeves, who could make anything. Marian made a three-phase converter for me out of parts from the junk pile at a sulfur plant in Orla, Texas.

At another gun-and-knife show in Lubbock, a doctor came up, bought a couple of knives, and said, "I will send you a hundred dollars a month and some knife plans. Make one of the knives, and when you think I have paid for it, mail it to me." This arrangement went on for maybe ten years. I finally got tired of the arrangement. I no longer needed the money and some of his designs were really strange, and I didn't enjoy making them.

There was a gunsmith in Carlsbad named Gerald Hollis. Gerald was a fine craftsman. He got interested in knives, and I helped him get started. I think I learned as much from him as he learned from me.

The ABS had knifemaking classes in Washington, Arkansas. Gerald and I decided to take a one-week class on how to make Damascus steel. We towed Gerald's motorhome with his pickup truck and made the two day trip to Washington, Arkansas. This was in August 1990. It was hot, and his truck was unable to tow the motorhome and run the AC at the same time.

The instructor at the class was Master Smith Charles Ochs. He was very good. I had tried to make Damascus with my hundred-pound power hammer, but I wasn't getting the steel hot enough. When I saw how he did it, I was able to also make Damascus under supervision. I made several Damascus blades during the class and returned home knowing how to make Damascus for myself.

It was hot in the month of August in Arkansas. I drank a lot of tropical fruit punch as I worked in front of the coal forge. I sweated a lot. Once I looked at my arms and they had red sweat drops on them. This was the dye in the fruit punch that came through. The T-shirts I wore were stained with this red color, and it never did wash out.

When I got back home, I started making and selling Damascus knives along with blades of ATS-34 and wire-cable knives.

By this point, when I went to gun-and-knife shows, I usually sold several knives. There was a large pawn shop in Carlsbad called Silver Bell. Eddie Bell was the owner. I felt I had arrived as a knifemaker when, at a show, he offered to trade a gun for one of my knives. As long as Eddie was in town, he traded any gun in his store for some of my knives.

In the late 1990s, I started going to the Blade Show in Atlanta. This was the greatest knife show on earth. All the famous knifemakers were there. Setting up, I wasn't sure I could compete with all the other knifemakers, but I sold lots of knives, and after paying for gas, meals, hotel, and the table (the first year the table was $450), I still came home with lots of money.

One of my friends was Weldon Whitley. I had first met him at a knife show in Carlsbad. Weldon had lived in Jal, then moved to El Paso. Weldon was in the Knifemakers' Guild and encouraged me to apply for admission. In 2003, I was admitted as a full member in the Knifemakers' Guild.

I also was interested in the American Bladesmith Society (ABS). There were three levels in the ABS. First, apprentice smith; second, journeyman smith; third, master smith. To become an apprentice smith, all you did was start paying dues. To become a journeyman smith, you made a knife with a ten-inch blade and took it to test at a master smith's forge. You then cut through a one-inch, free-hanging hemp rope with one cut. Then you chopped through two two-by-fours, with the knife still shaving after the chopping. Then the tip of the knife was clamped in a vice, and the blade was bent ninety degrees without breaking. Then at the next Blade Show, you took that test knife and five other completed knives that a panel of master smiths examined. If they liked your work, you were awarded the journeyman smith status. I was awarded the journeyman smith status in the 2001 Blade Show. I didn't get much joy out of this, because just a short time before, our grandson, Dane Morgan Lewis, four years old, had died in a swimming pool.

As I developed my skills, I sold more knives and used the money to buy equipment. Presently, my shop is full. There's no room for more. I have seven two-inch-by-seventy-two-inch grinders, four drill presses, four band saws, a metal lathe, milling machine, a hundred-pound and twenty-five-pound Little Giant, several gas forges, a hydraulic press, and countless hand tools. Knifemaking has been good to me. I have enjoyed making knives, and the money I made allowed me to buy machinery I otherwise could never have afforded.

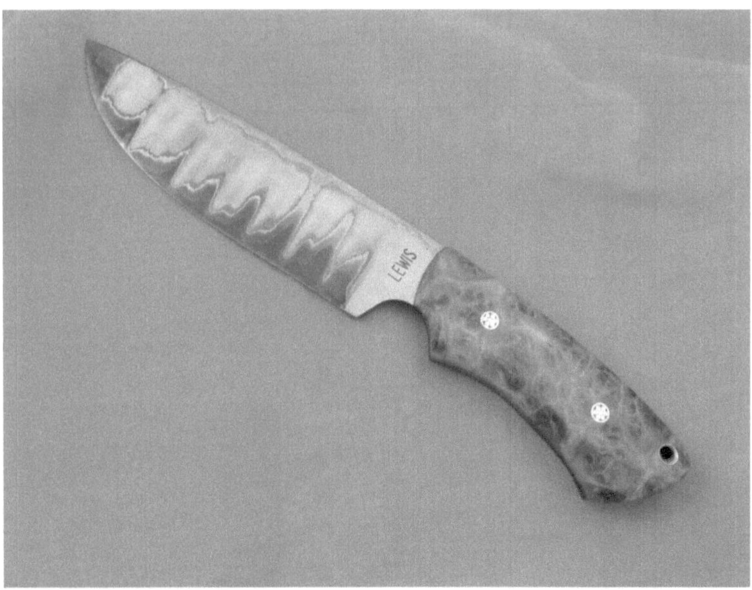

CHAPTER 13

Investing on the Front End

Bob Ohlemann

BEING A KNIFEMAKER is really cool. I know this must be true because everyone who ever asks me what I do for a living has said so. My passion for knives is intense! I've got the passion for making the knives, the passion for designing knives, the passion for researching knives, and the passion for knives made by others. Sometimes, my wife, Karen, says, "Can we talk about something other than knives?" Then we'll talk about our dogs, as there's a plenty of passion there as well. When I was asked to write this chapter to introduce others to the keys of being a successful knifemaker, I passionately said, "Yes!"

As I begin writing this chapter, I'm sitting in a motel room in Nashville, Arkansas. I've come here to spend a week in the shop of American Bladesmith Society Master Smith J. R. Cook. This is my third year apprenticing with Mr. Cook. This apprenticeship is one illustration of my philosophy on knifemaking; "Always make an effort to learn and continually desire to grow."

Education from Mentors

When I was considering getting into knifemaking in early 2014, I talked my wife into going to a knife show here in DFW. I wanted to see what the world of custom knives was all about and to meet some experienced makers who could steer me in the right direction. I met a lot of great guys at that show, and though none had any idea who I was, they all graciously shared advice with me on how to get started in knifemaking.

The one maker I met who stands out above all from that show is Johnny Stout. I didn't actually spend much time talking to Johnny, as he was busy talking to customers. On Johnny's table was a small stack of cards advertising knifemaking classes. The card read, "Five days will take five years off of your learning curve." I fairly quickly dismissed this as advertising hype. My wife picked up a card and asked Johnny some questions about the classes as I continued talking to other knifemakers.

On the drive home from the show, Karen and I talked about knives, knifemaking, and Mr. Stout's class. I was focused on plans for buying knifemaking equipment. For the cost of that class, I knew I could buy a lot of knifemaking tools. This is where I acknowledge my wife's wisdom: she said I needed to look at education as being just as important an investment as any tools. I called Johnny later that week and reserved a class slot for a few months later.

Johnny Stout's beginner knifemaking class was not overhyped. The class easily took five years off my learning curve and has been the best money I've ever spent in knifemaking. In fact, seven months after the first class, I went back and took his folder class. I absolutely would not be the knifemaker I am today without the expert knowledge Johnny shared with me in those classes.

There's nothing that will help a maker learn more than spending time in the shop of a superior knifemaker. I have dedicated myself to education. I have made it my goal to seek out hands-on training at least once a year with someone who can help improve my knifemaking. As I mentioned at the beginning of this chapter, I have spent a good deal of time in the shop of Master Smith J. R. Cook. This year, I have reserved a slot at the GRS Engraving School to learn the basics of metal engraving.

In addition to formal classes, hammer-ins and seminars are great ways to learn from highly experienced makers. Though you may not get hands-on training, these events can be huge bang for the buck. I've attended hammer-ins with as many as four ABS master smiths teaching. These men were not only a wealth of information but were also very approachable and willing to give individual advice. Even the best advice needs application, which brings me to feedback and doing something with it.

Education from Feedback

The first time I went to the Blade Show in Atlanta, I went as a spectator. I had held a table at a couple smaller shows, but this was the world's largest knife show! I had been making folders for about five months, and I carried a few with me. Keeping in mind that knifemakers are at the show to sell knives, I introduced myself to several whom I admired and, after establishing a dialogue, asked if they would be willing to look over my knives and offer suggestions. I asked them to be brutally honest, and they were. From that honest feedback, I was able to make some slight adjustments that have really helped my folders to stand out among a sea of knifemakers' work.

Getting honest feedback on your knives can be painful! Go into a request for feedback with a focus on improving your knives. If you would rather be appreciated for the hard work you've already put in, ask your mom or your cousin. If you want an honest answer, rather than "That's a good knife," you must ask for it. Thick skin is important. That's not to say all professional feedback you get is going to be useful. Understand that some makers have a bias toward certain styles or genres. For example, there are some guys out there who think the tactical market is a fad. It's important to make sure you're asking the right people to look at your knives for the audience you want to serve. While I usually focus on technical feedback from knifemakers, I also ask purveyors for their opinions, as I think they have a good pulse on the market. I'm not interested in chasing trends, but it's important to know what the market is doing and where my work fits within the overall market.

Education from Social Media

Social media is also a source of education. You can learn high-quality, accurate information about knifemaking from social media. Social media, as in an information source, isn't without risk, however, as it can be tough to filter the good advice from the bad. I have to say my early introduction to knifemaking came by way of internet forums. I spent a good deal of time not just asking questions but also searching the threads and archives for answers to the same question asked by others. Armed with even the slightest amount of background knowledge, I found that the discussion that came out of my questions would sort out who was giving solid advice and who wasn't. I also learned that the easiest solution was not always the best. Tread carefully when using social media as a knifemaking reference. As Abraham Lincoln once said, "Not everything you read on the internet is true."

Education from Professional Organizations

Another important thing to consider when getting into knifemaking is professional and educational organizations. I'm currently a member of the American Bladesmith Society, the Knifemakers' Guild, and a board member of the Texas Knifemakers' Guild (no affiliation with the international organization). These organizations all have a focus on education and invest time and money on sponsoring classes and other opportunities to help improve a knifemaker's skills.

Life Experiences That Lead to Knifemaking

Since so much of who we are is shaped by our life experiences, there's little surprise that my experiences have shaped my knifemaking as well. I grew up in the high Mojave Desert in northwest Arizona. As a young boy, cowboys and mountain men were the themes of many of my adventures. On the weekends, my friends and I would set out exploring the rugged foothills surrounding our neighborhood. We never set out without our canteens, BB guns, and knives. My first knife was a two-blade Barlow, and it was a good knife. The knife that accompanied me on most of our treks was a fixed-blade Buck clip-point hunter. That was the kind of knife a real mountain man would carry, at least in my eight-year-old mind.

Shift forward a few years (quite a few years), and I found the knife to be an indispensable piece of my military kit. For most of my military service, I found a rugged folder with a blade around three inches to be quite sufficient. In the field, a machete was often required for breaking trail or clearing fields of fire. Post 9/11, I started carrying a fixed blade during deployments. Its main use was cutting wire on ammunition crates and breaking down MRE boxes, but it was always in the back of my mind that it would be my last line of protection if everything went bad.

Those experiences shaped my view of knives as being an important part of an individual's life. However, many of the skills needed for knifemaking, I developed during my time in the military and immediately following my retirement. I didn't come to knifemaking immediately upon leaving the army. My lifelong dream upon my military retirement was to open a rod-and-chopper shop. I've always been a gearhead, but instead of the wrench-turning motor guy, I was into the fabrication side. I took all the welding and machining classes I could in high school and actually worked for a well-known race-and-chassis shop in Phoenix before I joined the army in 1988.

While in the army, in downtimes, I worked on project vehicles for myself and friends. I did a little of everything from rock-crawling Jeeps to pro-street Harleys. I put together a large shop full of tools in these endeavors (which made my military moves fairly painful as I always over the weight limit).

As soon as I retired from the army in 2008, I fulfilled my lifelong dream and opened my own shop. I moved to Texas and was open for business within six months, ready for the world to beat a path to my door so I could build the world's coolest customs. The only problem with my lifelong plan was that the economic collapse and recession coincided with my grand opening. To say times were difficult is putting it mildly. With the economy in the toilet, folks didn't have money for high-end custom vehicles.

By the time I closed the doors on my dying dream in 2014, I had been involved with some pretty cool projects, and I gained much of the experience that has helped me in knifemaking. These experiences ranged from how to organize the business, where and how to advertise, and understanding your market to skills like advanced TIG welding, CAD and CNC machining, hand-shaping metal, and even web design.

In addition, as I look back, I can point to many of my hobbies directly contributing to gaining skills that make me successful in knifemaking. My interests in art, photography, and video have all played a part. From basic art classes, I've been able to apply concepts such as balance, negative space, texture, and complimentary or contrasting colors. A photography or videography background or both can be very useful when it comes time to market your knives. I feel the most pride in my work when I receive compliments on my line, flow, proportion, and material combinations, which is a reflection on my creative skill sets.

What about Me? What Do I Have to Do with It?

I believe there are certainly things about my specific approach and beliefs that have given me an advantage in knifemaking. I subscribe to the philosophy that there's always something else to learn and do in knifemaking. There are always new interpretations, new techniques, and new styles to be learned. Taking risks and pushing the boundaries is how one develops a discernable personal style. A personal style that can easily be identified by others is treasured in knifemaking.

For me, I find creating a solid plan and following good procedures creates the consistency and productivity I strive for in the knife shop. The result is that at the end of the day, my style is recognizable. This well-planned approach most likely stems from my years of military service. My plans guide me all the way from my initial vision to the final completed product. The plan doesn't need to be completely written out; I may even have the entire plan in my head. But I enter into each knife build with a plan on exactly how I will produce it.

For me, the planning starts in the design process. Every one of my knives begins with a drawing. As I work up a drawing of a new knife model, I'm considering the steps required to get to the finished product and the order in which those steps will have to be performed. Thinking about the build process during the design phase can go a long way in preventing problems down the road. If I have a great idea but no knowledge on how to execute, then I have a couple choices: I can modify the design or learn how to perform the required task. In my process, I never perform trial and error in real time on the actual knife I want to make. I use the resources available to me to gather information, and then I do test pieces. I have produced hundreds of test pieces for everything from file work to heat-treating to anodizing. I consider test pieces part of the planning.

Procedures and routines go hand in hand with planning. If a visitor to my shop spent any real time watching me work, they might think me a bit obsessive. I have procedures for even the most mundane tasks. For example, when I pull a twist drill from the drawer, I check the size, check the cutting edge, wipe the shank, insert it into the chuck, and tighten until it just develops a bit of friction, and then I twist the drill within the jaws to ensure it's properly seated before final tightening. This procedure is repeated every time I change drills, and it ensures I don't make an easily preventable mistake.

Fine-tuning my procedures is a way of life for me. I have defined routines for everything from brushing my teeth to feeding my dogs. Because so many things in knifemaking are sequence driven, I have found developing SOPs (standard operating procedures) greatly reduces my failure rate and cuts down time requirements. Early in my knifemaking adventure, I made a lot of bulleted lists as I worked through various tasks. Often as I worked through the steps, I would scribble additional notes about looking for a better tool or asking other knifemakers about their techniques.

Failure comes in many forms in knifemaking, and while I put good effort into planning to prevent failure, I don't sweat it when it happens. There are very few skills in knifemaking that can be easily learned. A maker must accept and learn from each of his failures. Often enough, a failure in knifemaking leads me on the path to discovery if I keep an open mind. I try not to let failures weigh too heavily on my mind; instead, I focus on the new knowledge of what not to do. Many folks don't do any failure analysis and thus don't learn anything.

Equipment

Before I ever took a class, I began my knifemaking journey by planning to purchase tools. I often joke that I got into knifemaking to justify my addiction to tools. I love tools! There really is nothing like knowing that you can walk into your shop and have the tools to create almost anything.

Serious knifemaking requires a substantial investment in equipment. While it's absolutely true that you can build a good knife with fifty dollars' worth of tools, you will be limited in the type of knives you can produce and how quickly you can make them.

My equipment buying philosophy is that any tool that will make the job more efficient or accurate *and* will pay for itself within two years in either time saved or increased knife value is worth buying. I try to apply this metric to all potential purchases and not allow myself to be taken in by "cool factor." This philosophy also requires that I have a good midterm plan on where I'm going with my knifemaking. I buy tools to fill a current or upcoming need. I don't buy tools thinking that I will find a use for them later.

Another important aspect in my tool-acquisition thought process is that I prefer sole authorship. This isn't to say that I won't occasionally collaborate with another maker or an engraver, but I do prefer to make the entire knife in-house.

A key area where this sole authorship mentality will create a challenge to a new maker's budget is heat-treating. A maker can send a lot of blades to a professional heat-treating service before he covers the cost of buying a dedicated HT oven. To make matters worse, the oven is just the start of the equipment you will need once you start heat-treating your own blades. A hardness tester is mandatory if you hope to achieve accurate, repeatable results. Heat-treating foil, quenching plates, quenching oils, and other peripheral expenses all add to the price of heat-treating your own blades.

So why would a maker outlay such a large expense when a service can easily take care of it for much less? Well, as Johnny Stout explained to me when I took his beginner knifemaking class, it's about artistic flow. Stopping a project in the middle and sending a blade away for up to two weeks can seriously interrupt artistic inspiration. Add to that that most heat-treating services offer a quantity discount. This tends to force makers into a batch-production scenario to save money instead of building one knife at a time

For me, heat-treating isn't just a matter of artistic flow. Doing the work myself is also about control of the process and flexibility. This became apparent to me when I began using W2 for many of my blades. One of the most fascinating characteristics of W2 is its ability to produce a vivid hamon. Attaining a hamon requires a careful application of heat-resistant clay, tight control of heat, and a precise oil quench. The W2 steel I use comes 98 percent spherodized, which simply means that the carbides aren't evenly distributed through the steel. It will therefore not harden properly without a normalization process, in this case about twenty minutes of soak time at 1,675 degrees with a relatively slow cool down. Following the normalization process, I grind my blade to approximately 80 percent complete and then prepare it for heat-treating by applying Satanite heat-resistant mortar in a very specific pattern. It has taken many blades to determine a balance between how I apply the clay and exactly what temperature I need my blade to be when it goes into the quench oil. You simply cannot develop these types of techniques if someone else is doing your heat-treating.

Though I've gotten into some detail about heat-treating, the same equipment philosophy applies to nearly every process I perform on a knife. There have been instances when I have wanted to add a new process to my knifemaking but didn't know the best way to go about it. This is one area where having a great support network of other makers really helps. When I decided I wanted to start doing stone inlays on my knives, I was repeatedly directed to Tommy Overeynder. When I contacted Tommy and told him what I wanted to do, he said he'd be glad to help as soon as I had a pantograph mill. This again is an example where the decision-making process kicked in. I felt adding precious stone inlays to my knives would absolutely pay for the cost of buying a Deckel GK21. Additionally, the Deckel opened up other possibilities. At this writing, I have yet to produce a stone-inlayed knife, but the Deckel has already paid for itself since I was able to use it to improve artistic complexity in my knives in other ways.

I have two more points that support my philosophy about investing in tools. The first is, buy the best tools you possibly can. I hate to buy tools twice. The second point is, be safe. Know how to use all tools and equipment safely and don't take risks.

Opportunity

Being able to recognize, take advantage of, or even create opportunities has had a big impact on where I am today in knifemaking. Where that is exactly I'm not positive, but I feel like I'm at a point where I'm recognized by a good number of collectors and many of my knifemaking peers for producing a nice knife with high-quality craftsmanship. Much of this success can be attributed to being able to capitalize on opportunity.

One of the biggest things that helps me be a successful knifemaker is being retired from the military. This provides me with a pension and medical insurance, thereby reducing two big obstacles to starting a new business. My wife is very supportive and has a good career that also provides medical insurance; again, providing relief from the stresses associated with starting a new business venture that many knifemakers face.

My wife's successful career has also helped my knifemaking in another way. When she decided she liked knives enough to start collecting them, she was able to buy from many of the best knifemakers out there. She has purchased stunning pieces from no less than a dozen ABS master smiths and several makers who are regular invitees to the coveted Art Knife Invitational. This has given me a wealth of material to study firsthand. It has also opened the door to get to know these makers in a way that allows me to exchange ideas with them and get coveted feedback.

Marketing

I have a simple approach to marketing. I have defined my market, and I design and build exclusively for that market. I perform some kind of marketing task every single day.

Most of my knives go to a marketing base of collectors and will see very light to almost no use. They will be well taken care of and appreciated as a piece of practical art. That isn't a bad place to be in terms of the overall market. The downside is that this is a smaller market segment compared to the sportsmen who are looking for a great utility hunting knife. It's critical to a knifemaking business that your specific market is clearly defined and understood. What's the income of your target customer? What do they want in a knife? How often will they buy a new knife? Will they use the knife up, or will it be an heirloom?

Once you understand your market, you must design and build your knives for that market. The majority of customers in my high-end folder market would not buy a knife from me that had been water-jet cut. I need to be able to look them in the eye and tell them every piece of that knife was handcrafted by me alone. My blades are all meticulously hand finished, and I may put substantial time into a single embellishment.

Marketing every single day must become an ingrained habit! See? An exclamation point; it's that important. In this era of social media, it really isn't that hard to do. I have set up multiple marketing options and hit at least one every day. I rely heavily on a dedicated website, Facebook, Instagram, and several knife shows across the country.

CHAPTER 14

Start Quick by Learning from the Best

Mark Bartlett with Jason Fry

Finding and discerning credible information
can be as much of a skill as grinding.

MARK BARTLETT HAS been making knives for just five years, but he's already turning out incredible work, like dog-bone bowies, push daggers, and hunters with ingenious takedown mechanisms. His work is complex and of the highest quality, and yet he's relatively inexperienced. What's his secret?

The story of Mark's journey as a knifemaker begins with a call to Dwight Phillips, who was then a journeyman smith preparing for his master-smith examination. "Tell me what you already know" was Dwight's question. Mark's answer was, "I know nothing." By that time, Mark had already done the research online to know what he didn't know. The first call led to a second, which led to an invite to spend some time in Dwight's shop. Dwight was in the process of building his master-smith presentation set, with which he later passed the MS jury exam. "From the start I was able to see what that level of work looked like: dead-even plunges, the flow of the blade through the handle, and the overall high level of fit and finish," Mark said.

Never Pay a Plumber to Dig

One mistake many new would-be knifemakers make is calling an expert for a question that can be answered in a few seconds online. "Too often, new makers want to jump online and ask a thousand questions without ever doing any of the research themselves," Mark explains. "Those who have knowledge are easily and quickly turned off by someone begging for answers to questions that a quick internet search could have answered." If you want good answers to your questions, you must first begin with good questions.

Two things are worse than asking "those" questions to a master: explaining what you think you already "know" and dismissing the advice of those with legitimate knowledge. When you talk to a master, listen more than you talk. If you begin with explaining yourself, you've already started behind, because you're talking and not listening. The time of the competent is always in high demand, so make the most of it.

Another way to think about it is to "never pay a plumber to dig." Don't waste the time and effort of a master if a simple laborer could do the job, because you'll end up paying the master rate. Mark started with a self-described minute amount of knowledge, a good bit of desire, and no fear of asking questions of those who knew far more than he did about what they were doing. When approaching a master, being intimidated is easy because you're "nobody" and the master is "somebody." Mark came to the masters with respect and a willingness to listen. He was able to pick the brains of Terry Vandeventer, Van Barnett, Karl Andersen, and others, and they obliged his questions.

In times past, finding information about other knifemakers was difficult. Nowadays, many of the master knifemakers are no further away than an email or instant message, and many are active on internet forums. Just because they're easier to find doesn't mean that their time is less valuable. Approach a master with respect and a knowledgeable question, and you may find the help you seek. You may be so fortunate as to get invited over, as Mark did by Dwight. On the other hand, if you don't do your homework, ask the same old questions as every other beginner on the planet, and generally make a pest of yourself, well, good luck.

Are You in the Right Room?

A well-worn cliché in business is that "if you're the smartest man in the room, you're in the wrong room." If you're the best knifemaker that you know, you need to know more knifemakers. One of the benefits to a major knife show such as Blade, the Usual Suspects Network show, or the International Custom Cutlery Expo is the opportunity to see what others in the industry consider the "best work." If you attend a show and people are blown away by your work, good for you. On the other hand, if you attend a show and you're not blown away by somebody else's work, you need to open your eyes or attend a bigger show. Even the biggest fish in a small pond can be a pretty small fish.

Many knifemakers say that so-and-so taught them how to grind or forge, and that's why they make what they make. Mark took a slightly different approach. He spent time online looking at the works of the masters, men like Jerry Fisk, Mike Quesenberry, Bruce Bump, Mike Ruth Jr., and a host of others. He studied the takedown styles of John White and Karl Andersen. Mark was initially fascinated by the John White Legacy Dagger, and put a European-style quillon dagger in his maker's mark before he made his fourth knife. Mark says, "I knew what I wanted to make: the coffin handles, the dog bones, the takedowns. I put a MS-test-style dagger in my logo as a reminder that one day I'd have to make that dagger."

Time to Get Off the Couch

One reason for Mark's quick start was his approach to the masters. Another was his high, no-limits vision for his own work. All the information and vision in the world won't forge or grind a single knife, however. Mark knew that there would be a day when he'd have to learn to forge, beyond simply beating the steel into sort of a knife shape. When that day came, Calvin Garland was there to help. He lives just a few miles from Mark and took him in, gave him some decent steel to play with, and generally got Mark started on everything he now knows about forging.

Mark still started slowly. He had seen the quality of masterwork first-hand from Dwight and online from many others, and had moved beyond rudimentary forging thanks to Calvin. In his own shop, he spent his time at the beginning building a grinder and fixtures, working on equipping his twelve-foot-by-sixteen-foot storage building into a knife shop capable of the kind of work he wanted to turn out.

According to Mark, "Nick Wheeler always says that people think they need a shop like his to make knives like he does. Funny thing is, I still don't have a lot of tools. I've spent my money on what I feel is necessary to make a good knife: a carbide faced file guide from Bruce Bump, an arsenal of new old-stock Nicholson USA files, a good quench oil, and quality blade steel like 1095, 52100, and W2. Combine those four things with a lot of patience, a lot of stubbornness, and a little luck, and with some guidance you can make a great knife." Having a full machine shop to work with is nice, but it simply isn't necessary to produce knives of high quality.

Walk Before You Run?

You will find many who say a maker should, for example, build a hundred full-tang hunters before they try a bowie, or forge fifty choppers before attempting a dagger, as if there were some magical turning point once you hit a certain number. Maybe that advice is wise if a maker intends to learn on his or her own, but it underestimates the value of guidance. If left to your own devices to struggle along by trial and error, sure, you might not want to make a fourteen-inch bowie in your first six months. On the other hand, with the proper guidance, anything is possible. Many newer makers don't try a complex project like a dagger because they don't think they're ready, while other makers won't know they're ready until they try. If you try and fail, you've learned something more than you knew before. The next knife you make will be better as a result.

The seeds you plant are the seeds that grow. While one maker working on his hundredth consecutive full-tang hunter may watch more YouTube videos on basic forging, another will watch videos on spiral fluting handles before he's finished his tenth knife. A veteran knifemaker could easily guess which maker will be producing better work a year from now. There's certainly nothing wrong with a full-tang hunter: it's the bread-and-butter moneymaker of many an excellent knifemaker. But if you think you need to perfect the hunter before you can make anything else, you may end up spending the rest of your life learning to make and remake the same knife. It's the difference between a hundred knives' worth of experience and one knife worth of experience a hundred times.

Mark started with a few full tangs and then a hidden tang. Dwight Phillips, a master smith by this point, was making a frame handle, and so Mark, ever the good student, decided to do the same. He'd forged a blade from a roller bearing at Calvin's. He spent the time to draw out the design on paper to match the vision in his head. Eventually, that frame-handled knife, only Mark's eighth knife at the time, was published in *Blade Magazine*. Some makers build knives for many years before they're published. In Mark's case, it wasn't about the numbers or the experience; it was about the knife. Mark took his time, learned from masters, and built a knife worthy of publication before he even hit double digits!

Mark will be the first to admit that his first few complex knives were ambitious, maybe not perfect, but he *made* them. Eventually, he started building his own style of takedowns. There's no quick-and-easy way to build a takedown. "The process of building a takedown was a process of drilling, filing, fitting, refitting, and repeating until I had a knife that was as good as I could achieve," said Mark. One of the main advantages of a takedown design is that the handle and guard can be finished off of the knife. There's never a time when you're allowed to use the excuse that the knife is assembled and it's too late to take it apart and fix something. Some begin by counting the number of knives that the masses have told them to make, or using the simple number of knives as a measure of productivity. Others begin by counting the dozens of parts that come together to make a complex frame-handled knife, a different kind of productivity baseline measure.

By 2017, Mark was ready to make the John White–style dagger that inspired him so much nearly four years prior. Along with the White dagger, Mark also set out to build a takedown with no visible fasteners. Either of these by itself would be a challenge for most makers. According to Mark, "These two knives were a whole lot of headaches and a whole lot of fun. They pushed limits that I didn't even know I had."

KNIFEMAKER ~ MARK BARTLETT IMAGE ~ SHARPBYCOOP

Most knifemakers of character won't look down on another maker because he makes "only" full-tang hunters. Also, makers of character won't begrudge another man's way of making ends meet. If you want to make the same hunter a hundred times, don't let anybody tell you that you shouldn't. But whether you make one, ten, or a hundred, don't let the simplicity of a slab-handled hunter tempt you into slapping them together without attention to detail just to get them out the door quickly. Similarly, if you make one, ten, or a hundred of them, don't let the complexity of a dog-bone frame handle tempt you into cutting corners and thinking your knife is special just because it's complex.

They say that practice makes perfect, but if you practice the same mistakes over and over again, you may never improve. The best way to get better is to stop making the same mistakes, and many times, the way to do that is to slow down. Slowing down means you'll make fewer knives in the short term. You have to sacrifice speed for the sake of progress in your skills. This is an area where the hobby maker has a slight advantage: the kids won't starve if you take a little longer on a knife, and the wife can still get new shoes if you don't finish "enough" knives this month.

You have a choice to make: you could focus on how many knives you can get out the door, or you could focus on the fit, finish, and design of the knives that leave your shop. Jerry Fisk often challenges knifemakers to think about each knife in terms of where it will be a hundred years from now. Will your knife be an heirloom, having made it to the third generation? Will it be in a museum, or will it be just another broken, rusted thing tossed aside due to shoddy workmanship? Make each knife so that it will stand the test of time, so that people will look at it with reverence even a hundred years in the future. Albert Einstein once said, "I know not with what weapons World War III will be fought, but World War IV will be fought with sticks and stones." Will your knife still be around to serve when the time comes? If your knives were the only weapons left beyond sticks and stones, would they be up to the test?

Garbage In, Garbage Out, in Reverse

We've all heard the cliché "garbage in, garbage out." If you make garbage knives, you can reasonably expect garbage prices and likely a garbage career. On the other hand, if you put in good effort, get good training, pay good attention to detail, ask good questions, and get good guidance, there's a darn good chance you'll make a good knife, then a better knife, and then a still better knife. There are plenty of makers putting in the time and the effort. Reading a book like this is a step on that journey.

Another step along the way is to fill your mind with images of knives you admire and respect. You won't make beautiful knives by drawing the same three knives over and over again, or by looking at pictures of knives in the beginner forums on the internet. Focus your attention on makers who consistently crank out work you admire. Look at the Bump pistol sets, the Fisk bowies, the Quesenberry integrals, the Stout automatics, or the Barnett steampunk pieces. Pick a genre that suits your style, and dive in to the work of the masters in that area. Ask these people your questions. These are the makers whose work makes a trip to Blade Show or ICCE worthwhile. These are the people you want to be like "when you grow up" as a knifemaker.

Watch them. Learn from them. Listen. Listen some more. Ask a question, and listen some more.

Mark Bartlett says, "Those you find yourself watching constantly will be the ones you emulate. If you want to learn, learn from them. When they speak, listen. When they criticize your work, take it and move on, because chances are, they're telling you what they see in hopes that you'll not make the same mistakes they did."

Find the knives that inspire you, make those knives, and make them well.

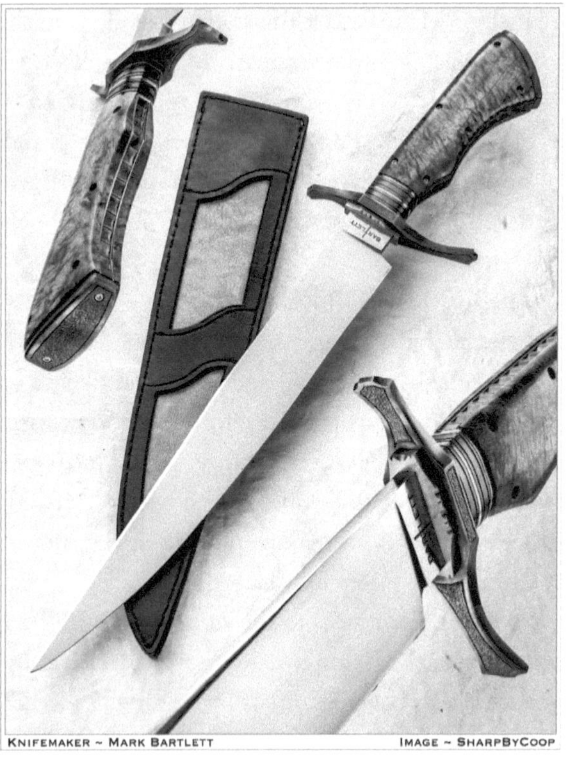

Knifemaker ~ Mark Bartlett Image ~ SharpByCoop

CHAPTER 15

Want to Make a Better Knife? Join the Club!

Jason Fry

YOU CAN LEARN more about next-level knifemaking in five minutes with the right guy than you can in a dozen hours on YouTube. Sure, you can learn *almost* everything you need from the internet, and I hope you learn plenty from this book, but there's really no replacement for talking in person with an expert. Talking directly to a master knifemaker is like the difference between googling your symptom and going to a doctor. You may feel like you will end up with the same information in the end, but only the doctor can really look you in the eye and help you. Both the doctor and the master knifemaker know the answers to questions you don't even know you need to ask.

Back when I was a beginning maker, I took thirteen knives to my very first knife show. They were the best knives I could make at the time, and I was proud of them. I sat in between a man who had made knives for sixty years and Jerry McClure, a master knifemaker. At the end of the show, I had sold only one knife, the least expensive one on my table. I was disappointed, to say the least. I called Jerry over to my table, told him it was my first show, and asked him, "Why do I have so many knives left?" The conversation that followed included advice about pricing, materials, presentation on the table, sheath work, and knife design. The whole thing didn't take fifteen minutes, but I listened intently. The next year at that show, I took fourteen knives. I'd modified many of my designs for longer handles. I'd increased the weight of the leather on my sheaths. I paid a different kind of attention to material selection and table layout. I sold nine of my fourteen knives that weekend, a very good show for any maker, and one of the best shows I've ever had. That brief conversation with Jerry changed every knife I have designed since, and I'm a better knifemaker because of it.

A Life-Changing Thirty-Second Lesson

A young man named J. D. attended a knifemaking seminar at a local university, hosted by members of the Texas Knifemakers' Guild. J. D. was eighteen but already had a top of the line grinder and an eye for what it takes to make a good knife. During the hands-on portion of the instruction, J. D. told us about his process for finishing his ricasso on a full-tang knife. It had been a struggle, with each side taking an hour or more to polish. I looked around and found a welding magnet in the shop, put a fresh four-hundred-grit belt on J. D.'s grinder, and in thirty seconds on the platen, polished each side of the ricasso of the knife that J. D. was working on to a clean finish. That brief lesson changed the trajectory of J. D.'s knife career ever so slightly, but it saved him hours and hours of polishing to get essentially the same result.

Harvey-isms

Several years ago, I was at a show seated near Harvey Dean, ABS master smith and current chairman of the ABS board of directors. Harvey and I share similar religious background and come from the same part of the country, so we hit it off pretty well. I gained three gems from Harvey over the course of that weekend, little things that changed my approach from that day forward. These are shared with Harvey's permission.

I had a forged hunter on my table for the show, one of my earliest attempts at a hidden-tang knife. I showed it to Harvey for critical feedback. He pointed out that the guard wasn't on straight. I had seen the error from the beginning and explained that it was because I'd struggled with my limited tools to get the hole fit properly in the three-eighths-inch guard stock. "Well, quit using three-eighths-inch then" was Harvey's advice. Harvey's point was about more than guard stock thickness. I had skill and equipment limitations that held back my ability to make a clean knife with that material, and so I was better served by choosing other materials until I was able to get the right equipment or develop the right skills. Every knife has choices that have to be made. Harvey challenged me to first consider my ability to use a material well, cleanly, and correctly. There's no shame in choosing a way to build a knife that's easier to get right, if the end result is a better knife. As you transition from "good" to "very good" or even to "great," consider whether your skills are up to the material you're working with. If you can only make a mediocre knife, there's no use in building a Damascus bowie with a walrus-ivory handle. On the other hand, every maker has to try walrus sometime. Make sure you choose your materials wisely based on your ability to get the knife right.

Later on, a customer came and asked Harvey what tool made the most improvement in his knife business. Harvey answered, "A riding lawnmower." Now that wasn't what the customer expected, and everybody laughed. Harvey went on to explain that when you're a full-time knifemaker, you're also likely the yard guy. He lived on a couple of acres, and the riding mower made an all-day job into a two-hour job. Being able to cut the yard faster produced more time available for knife work and therefore represented a significant increase in productivity.

Harvey Dean mows the lawn on his time-saving lawnmower.

The final Harvey lesson of that particular show was to "never miss a chance to sell a knife." I had a customer offer to buy a knife from me in the weeks before the show. I politely declined, saying that I needed the knife for my show table. At the end of the show, the knife was still on the table, unsold. There's a reason they say that "a bird in the hand is worth two in the bush," and the bladesmith knows to "strike while the iron is hot." The salesman knows to make a sale whenever and wherever a sale can be found. The bladesmith needs to remember that he's also the salesman and to take advantage of every opportunity. There are knives to be sold in many unexpected places. Since that encounter with Harvey, I have sold knives in such unexpected places as wedding showers, baby showers, church foyers, and at a Wendy's in an ice storm.

Harvey tells a story about getting a table at a run-of-the mill gun show in Waco, Texas, about twenty-five years ago. At that show, he sold a run-of-the-mill knife to a customer. That customer bought another $20,000 worth of excellent and high-priced knives from Harvey over the next twenty-five years. You think it's not worth your time to try and sell a knife every chance you get, even at a run-of-the-mill local gun show? You just never know. Never miss a chance to sell a knife.

Join the Club

There's no better way to meet other knifemakers than to join a local or national organization. You may be thinking you can meet knifemakers at a knife show, but that ignores the knifemaker's need: knifemakers primarily attend shows to do business and sell knives. A maker may help you at a show, but the quality of the help will be different than if you meet them at a hammer-in or local event where the goal of the event is to teach and to share, or if you get invited to their shop. There are those who speak critically about both local and national knifemaker organizations. Some of the criticisms are true, and some are not. I can guarantee you one thing about these groups: To avoid joining a group is to lose the benefit of the organization, even if its website may be outdated, its rules seemingly inflexible, you don't like their logo, or you don't agree with the amount of their dues, because its leaders are older than your grandpa, or any other petty reason. Even if these criticisms are the gospel truth, if you don't join, you get no benefit. One of the best ways to get better at something is to spend time with people who are better at that thing than you are. These organizations, whether you view them positively or negatively, are essentially designed for only one purpose: to make better knifemakers out of their members. If you want to be a better knifemaker, you'd best "join the club." Let's look at a few examples.

Texas Knifemakers' Guild

Texas is a state known for many things, one of which is being independent-minded. It's no surprise that a frontier-minded state that values self-sufficiency would have plenty of folks who make knives. Until 2015, Texas had not had a statewide knifemaking organization for several years. A group of makers got together and formed the Texas Knifemakers' Guild as an educational nonprofit dedicated to the perpetuation of the knifemaking craft. They host local events including hammer-ins and shop tours, most often at no charge to the attendees. Each member of the organization signs a commitment to take advantage of every opportunity both to learn and to teach, and to try to make each knife better than the previous one. They don't discriminate between methods of knifemaking, but insist on honest disclosure. Whether you grind, forge, or start with a blank, you're welcome, but you have to be up front about how the knife was made and about who did the work. The explicit goal is to accept a maker as he or she comes and to push toward greater skill and better product. Their website features a map of many of the members' locations, in order to facilitate people getting together with other makers near them. The TKG offers a knifemaker certification that requires a fit-and-finish inspection of three of a maker's knives. As the current TKG president, I believe that the TKG exists primarily to bring knifemakers together. There's exceptional, irreplaceable value in spending time with other makers, so we built an organization to facilitate those meetings. At last count, the TKG had over two hundred fifty members statewide. The TKG is far from the only example. Many other states have local knifemaking organizations, groups of people who want to help you get better at the craft. As a maker looking to move to the next level, a local group is a perfect place to initially get involved. Many of the more experienced makers in the local groups are also members of the national groups. While none of the national groups have a formal "minor league" or "farm club" type system, the local and state groups often unofficially serve this purpose.

The National Knifemakers' Guild

The oldest national knifemaking organization in the United States is the Knifemakers' Guild. Some of the best and most famous knifemakers in modern history have been guild members including Buster Warenski, Bob Loveless, Bill Moran, Jimmy Lile, Gil Hibben, Wolfgang Loerchner, Warren Osborne, and Steve Johnson. According to their website,

> The Knifemakers' Guild was established in 1970. John Applebaugh, Walter "Blackie" Collins, John Nelson Cooper, Dan Dennehy, T. M. Dowell, Chubby Hueske, Jon Kirk, R. W. Loveless, John Owens, Jim Pugh, and G. W. Stone were the founding members. In June 1970, in Tulsa, Oklahoma, the first meeting took place and Bob Loveless was elected Secretary and A.G. Russell was made Honorary President. Russell was responsible for securing a block of tables at two gun shows that year where knifemakers could sell their work and also meet each other. In 1971, the founding members met again in Houston, Texas, where more makers joined the Guild. 1972 was the first year the annual show and meeting were held in Kansas City, Missouri, where even more knifemakers came to join.

The purposes of the guild are to promote custom knives and knifemakers, to assist the knifemaker technically, to encourage ethical and professional business conduct, and to sponsor an annual knife show. The process to join includes inspection of your knives by four voting members, with an endorsement that you meet the initial quality criteria. After the signatures, the maker presents five knives to a judging panel for acceptance as a probationary member. Two years later, the maker presents another five knives to the panel. If the knives meet the Guild's high standards for fit and finish, the maker is accepted as a voting member.

For many years the guild's annual show was the best showcase of knife-making talent in the world. They're actively recruiting new members, with representatives at most every major knife show.

Masters of the Forge: American Bladesmith Society

Another long-standing knife organization is the American Bladesmith Society. The seeds of the society were sown at the 1972 Guild Show in Kansas City. Bill Moran, at that time chairman of the Knifemakers' Guild, had a dream of creating a group whose sole purpose would be the preservation and advancement of the forged blade. At that time, there were less than a dozen practicing bladesmiths in America. The number of bladesmiths was decreasing, while the number of stock-removal knifemakers was climbing dramatically.

At the 1973 Guild Show, Moran brought eight hammer-forged Damascus steel blades, the first time "modern" pattern-welded steel had been presented to the public. The knife world was amazed! Few people really understood the nature of the steel, but Bill handed out mimeographed sheets explaining not only what Damascus steel was but also basic instructions on how to make it. Even though he had rediscovered a lost art, he gave the sheets away at no cost. Moran's reintroduction of Damascus steel gave bladesmithing a much-needed shot in the arm. It was impossible to produce Damascus without forging, and immediately a significant number of knifemakers became interested in learning the art of the forged blade.

On December 4, 1976, Moran flew into the Shreveport, Louisiana, airport, where Bill Bagwell, Don Hastings, and B. R. Hughes joined him in the airport coffee shop. Out of that meeting came the original draft of the ABS bylaws, written out on lined notebook paper. Moran was elected president, Hastings treasurer, Bagwell secretary, and Hughes became the first director.

The ABS is known for its program of certification for journeyman and master smiths. It should be noted that awarding journeyman and master stamps was not a part of the original bylaws. The certification process was added later, and the first master bladesmith ratings were awarded at the New York knife show in 1981. The first master smiths were, in alphabetical order, Bill Bagwell, Jimmy Fikes, Don Fogg, Don Hastings, Bill Moran, and James Schmidt.

The first ABS hammer-in was held in 1984. Since that time, hundreds of events have been held all over the world including Canada, South America, Europe, and Africa. The ABS later established bladesmithing schools at Texarkana College, Haywood Community College, New England School of Metalwork, Southern Ohio Forge and Anvil Bladesmith School, La Forge d'Ostiches (Belgium), and Heavin Forge School (South Africa) which offer bladesmithing courses taught by experienced ABS master smiths.

The ABS boasts a membership of over sixteen hundred bladesmiths worldwide. They offer two knifemaker certifications, the journeyman and master-smith ratings. For each rating, the maker forges a knife and puts it through cutting tests, then bends the knife ninety degrees. Following a successful performance test, the smith then presents five forged blades to a jury for examination on fit and finish. While the journeyman is expected to make a clean, professional knife out of forged steel, the master is charged with making five knives without a visible flaw. The master performance test knife and a European-style quillon dagger must be made of the maker's own Damascus steel. The maker must be a member of the ABS for at least three years prior to submitting for a journeyman rating, although the waiting period is shortened to two years if the maker takes an ABS approved forging class. If you ever intend to pursue ABS certifications at some point in your future, sign up now. If you wait until your forging or fit-and-finish skills are up to par before you join, you'll still have to wait the three years, regardless of how capable you are when you join.

Harvey Dean, master smith and current president of the ABS board, sums up the organization, saying, "The ABS is all about education. Fundamentally, it's what we do. We have hammer-ins and seminars all over the country, with master makers right there to give you one on one instruction. The founders of the ABS were afraid that the art of forging would die. The ABS works to ensure that forging won't die in this generation or the next."

Two Organizations, One Show

The Knifemakers' Guild and American Bladesmith Society currently co-sponsor the International Custom Cutlery Expo. While other shows such as Blade Show may have more table holders, no other show puts more top-level talent into the same room. Each organization through its history has had its own show. It's only since 2015 that they've worked together to produce a top-quality show featuring the best the world has to offer in both forged and ground blades. The ABS hosts educational workshops in conjunction with the show, and the guild hosts its annual business meeting. The show gives awards in multiple categories from both the ABS and the guild, including best art knife, best fixed blade, best folder, and best collaboration. If you want to see the best of the best, ICCE is the place to be.

Some of you are thinking, *I can sell as many knives sitting in my recliner in my underwear with a laptop as I can at a knife show, and I don't have to buy a plane ticket, pay a table fee, or get a hotel room.* Everybody loves to sell knives at a show, but if you think that sales are the only benefit, you've missed something. Knifemakers, being mostly a humble bunch, often keep their mouths shut when they sell out. Knifemakers, being mostly a frugal bunch, tend to fuss and holler when they go to a show and don't sell anything. What that creates in the knifemaking community is an accessibility bias: we only hear the bad news. At every show, some makers sell out. At every show, some makers sell a few, and at every show, some makers don't sell any. Every single major show is that way.

A knife show has other benefits besides sales. There's no better place than a major show to pick out handle material in person, particularly stag, mammoth, or other exotics. There's no better place to see the top work of the top makers. There are plenty of pictures on the internet of excellent knives, but any teenage boy can tell you that a beautiful online picture isn't the same as holding that beautiful curvy thing in your hands. When other makers become your friends, the shows become a joyful reunion. When the show is in an interesting part of the country, the show trip becomes a vacation. When you save your receipts, the show expenses offset income on your tax return. If you think a show is the only place to sell knives, or even the best place to sell knives, you may be behind the times. If you conclude that shows aren't worth the effort, however, you're missing out on more than just potential sales.

Join or Die

A comprehensive review of every knifemaking organization worldwide is far beyond the scope of this chapter. There are organizations all over the United

States, all over the world, and with members of every skill level. The information for these groups is readily available. If you can't find one, start one, even if it begins with a few folks in your backyard. Benjamin Franklin published the famous "Join or Die" political cartoon in 1754, featuring a chopped-up snake representing the colonies. The message is just as relevant today. Unless you join, both you and the knifemaking organizations will fail to thrive. Surround yourself with other makers or fade. Join or die.

CHAPTER 16

Talking to Old Guys about Science

Ed Braun

AS YOU MOVE forward in knifemaking, the physical process of grinding a blade will at some point become relatively easy. The consistent daily application of knifemaking skills eventually becomes as much of a challenge as developing the skills in the first place. One area of skill that requires consistent attention is the area of heat-treating, specifically metallurgy. Regardless how you came into to the field of knifemaking, we all stepped into a trade that is devoted to an entire family tree of iron-based alloys. The breadth of this ferrous family tree challenges every maker to develop a long list of skills, methods, and material principles in order to consistently craft high-performance blades. All of the work put into making a blade is pointless if its heat treat is poor. Roman Landes is credited with the idea that "edge geometry determines how sharp a knife is, but heat treat determines how long it will stay sharp." Most knifemakers agree that acquiring fundamental skills is essential, be it simple grinding or developing an individual style. Even among skilled makers, however, there's a general hesitation when it comes to learning or sharing metallurgical or heat treatment information. The challenge to cultivate material science in the knife community is exasperated by complex metallurgy's emphasis on heat treatment to fully unlock all of the edge holding properties bound up in a particular steel.

It's uncommon for knifemakers to enter the trade already educated on martensitic steels. Details like how to read TTT charts and the effects of various alloying characteristics are outside typical knife-related discussion comfort zones. As such, we not only find very few knifemakers who are thoroughly versed in the science, but also we find even fewer who are able to teach it. With few competent guides to aid smiths navigate the mountain of metallurgical science, the general knifemaking community's acceptance and advocacy for the science behind turning steel into blades has been slow and arduous.

Knife science is only just now coming into a renaissance period, building on the groundwork of men such as Kevin Cashen, Tim Zowada, and Dan Marangi over the past twenty years. Because of their work, previously sensitive topics like avoiding reclaimed steel or a bias toward using industrial standard-quench oils and heat-treat formulas are now socially acceptable. Even so, there's still a lingering negative attitude toward open dialogue on heat treat and metallurgical concepts. Knifemaking on its own is a physically and mentally taxing process. Trying to undertake the conquest of the technical and scientific realm puts many knifemakers outside of their areas of expertise, and is therefore met with resistance and resentment. Metallurgy is the most difficult aspect in our work that cannot be perfected through repetition and muscle memory, and the intellectual challenge makes it the elephant in the room. Smithing communities freely share blade craft or how-to information, but often grow silent when presented questions about scientific situations.

By way of example, 1084 is often suggested as a good steel for beginners because of its easy heat-treating and strength when used for something like a camping knife. What is absent from those discussions is the role manganese (Mn) plays in both factors. As an alloying agent, Mn retards grain growth and readily facilitates carbon moving into solution, and its natural elemental properties contribute resistance to ductility and plasticity. Explaining these factors succinctly is challenging, understanding them more so; and when conversations stretch on into complicated technical aspects and include jargon, communication fails. Information overload should be considered with the same regard as a stress riser on a blade leading to a crack in quench: as a topic shifts into unfamiliar territory, the complexity and difficulty in following the discussion reaches critical mass where the recipient must either cave to their confusion or break from the conversation. When the effort to learn is overcome by the difficulty of the material, that is where and why we see negative reactions to scientific evidence in our field, and the epithet "nerd" applied to the people who promote a thorough understanding of metallurgy.

The transmission and education of many crafts relies primarily on anecdotal evidence rather than clinical, empirical data, and knifemaking is no different. Anecdotal evidence provides listeners personal, relatable, compressed, and immediate (even if temporary) answers. Learning from a mentor or from traditional narratives is relatively easy. For many of us, it's easier to grasp a story than to understand how basic alloying and heat-treating properties translate to real-world performance results. A smith bemoaning difficulties forging a piece of leaf spring may react badly when told it may be 5160H and how the problem stems from higher chromium, molybdenum, tungsten, and silicon levels than found in blade grade 5160. Their response may include references to education by noted smiths or appeals to the seniority and significance of their source to passionately defend the material because the answer they were given questioned their knowledge and competency as a smith. If the straightforward technical response is perceived as patronizing, then measures must be applied to make sure that the technical information is properly received. Breaking the situation down into informational "sound bites" that are readily identifiable, relatable, and digestible are what communicates complex concepts in fashion that most people can appreciate.

Familiarizing other smiths with metallurgy or heat treatment concepts requires you to show them that you are, first of all, on their side and empathetic, sharing a teaching moment rather than preaching. By paying attention to how the exchange evolves and taking mental notes, the same approach can be applied in similar conversations with other smiths later on. This mental archive has been my single most valuable asset as the New Jersey Steel Baron (NJSB) heat treat and steel consultant; many frequently asked questions cataloged enable me to do my job effectively. What I have personally witnessed as a result of supplying information to community members is watching them share it with their peers. The good rapport is infectious, the information is retained by the smith, and the information is then passed on to other makers. Such an organic approach ensures that science is presented in a manageable fashion, creating a paradigm for not only how the information should be discussed, but also one modified continuously without losing the original, intended message. In plain English: when information is broken down into bite-sized portions, the other person can easily share it later.

The intentional sharing of scientific metallurgy may guarantee more educated smiths, but it sadly does ensure that there won't continue to be a vocal minority that ignore metallurgical and heat treatment theory. We need not all be metallurgical experts, but it's critical to understand that there are pockets in the knifemaking community that actively, consciously persist in trying to refute the science embedded in the craft. Whether their choice is fueled by ulterior motive (i.e., marketing off a secret "magic" heat-treat method) or simply the use of antiquated sources of information, we can be assured two factors with dogmatic anti-science community members. First, they disconnect science from their relative work experience and rely strictly on performance based results as confirmation of their methods. Second, aware that their stance works against them in a debate, their recourse is often to use belligerent tactics to undermine the discussion and either use a circular argument or appeal to authority to put burden of proof on the opposition.

In the end, results are everything to a knifemaker. What the material science approach promises is both consistency and performance. As people who promote the sound, practical application of science as a path to next-level performance, it's imperative to show that questionable methods cause not only wide performance variability knife to knife, but also equally uncertain reliability and quality. Every smith operates on faith in his or her products and is governed by the confidence that he or she is getting the utmost from their methods. Despite all the effort put into making their knives, smiths who avoid the science of their craft are in essence leaving themselves open to failure.

As a metaphor, consider that we knifemakers are like steel ourselves. In order to make knifemaking second nature, it takes time and temperature in order to transform. The work of developing knifemaking skill itself hardens us, but makes us brittle. The heat of the initial learning ultimately puts us in a position where our skills reach a critical point that we can call ourselves a knifemaker. The intellectual side tempers us, taking significant time and tedious breaks in process, but makes us tough and resilient. The time commitment is one aspect that often discourages aspiring makers. By contrast, a substantial deficit in metallurgical knowledge is what makes even a skilled smith insecure about the accuracy of their work and inherent quality, making them quick to snap if pressed too hard. It's very rare that anyone seriously investigates and absorbs much technical information about metallurgy and heat treatment practices their first year as a knifemaker. Had I not had a background in research and some areas of science prior to my knife career, I would not have likely sought it out either. What was clear to me from the very beginning was the inherent inconsistency and sketchy, poorly defined procedures for "get it hot and quench." This inconsistency led me to look further into heat treatment. None of these academic efforts were successful or rewarding until several years after I began the search for knowledge and had reviewed the literature repeatedly to get it to stick.

We each take to our work with utter conviction in earnest and sincere effort, hoping our commitment and dedication shows in the form and function of our blades. The fundamental nature of most makers leads us to go great lengths and make tough decisions in order to improve our skill sets for crafting or embellishing our work. This drive should extend to learning the metallurgy and heat-treating sciences unique to our field. Even makers who outsource heat-treating to a third party benefit from knowledge of alloying qualities and characteristics imparted due to proper hardening and tempering to accompany function. If I hand three identical knives to someone in three different steels, my prime responsibility is to ensure that they should not be able to tell the difference in performance. To that point, regardless whatever parlor tricks I could employ, I will have failed as a maker if the edge isn't mated with the proper heat treatment.

A measure of the next-level bladesmith or knifemaker is versatility in employing the various steels at our disposal. I should be able to make the same knife in various steels, matching the alloying to a heat treat and edge geometry in a way that allows the engineering of the steel to shine in performance. While not rocket science, material science and physics does require planning. Ultimately, the victory begins in the preparation. Makers and customers alike can be assured that the process crafting a blade is universally applied as far as shaping, assembling, and sharpening. However, material selection should consider how the properties of the steel we select are suited to the specific task for which the knife is built. My personal specialty is kitchen knives, with lean edges and high hardness. With this in mind, it's relatively easy to select the steel, and I have a select few I prefer for their characteristics. I've worked out heat-treat schedules that each recognizes where, when, and how hardness, strength, and toughness work in concert with grind, ergonomics, and aesthetics. When you have spent as much time arguing with men who quench orange hot pieces of bed frame in used motor oil as you have spent reading and trying to understand ASM manuals, you will find how much easier it is to retain the information, and how very little patience you have for imprecise metallurgy in our field.

Two final conclusions come to mind to sum up our journey toward metallurgical knowledge. First and most importantly, as people probing the surface of martensitic materials and their use for making a knife, the fundamental sciences won't be easily grasped and retained pragmatically at first. Your metallurgical knowledge may take years to be fully integrated into your personal knifemaking gestalt. Second, knifemakers as a kind are a proud and passionate people. What matters most to us are those aspects of our work that we want to see improve.

Engaging in intellectual and scientific discussions requires a measure of patience as much as confidence. Information is leverage that can be used to move whole mountains, and in the years to follow, our industry will continue to be changed for the better as more data is shared on the ways we can manipulate our chosen medium. The change in knifemaking toward technical and scientific precision is already in motion. All we have to do is maintain the momentum so that each subsequent generation is a little smarter and has a little easier time finding the answer to the riddle of steel.

SECTION FOUR

Advanced Knife Design

CHAPTER 17

Drawn to Success

Lin Rhea

"THAT KNIFE IS real art." These are words that most makers hear from time to time. The knifemaking world includes some wonderful artists, many of whom I can only hope to imitate at some time in the future. The limit of the knifemaking art in my estimation has yet to be reached. Every time I check the various knife publications and forums, I see something new that pushes artistic boundaries.

Even considering the deep pool of talent in the knifemaking world, some makers stand out above the rest. They don't stand out because they make the most complicated knives or because they are capable of turning out work that is of such a high standard in fit and finish. The amazing thing that makes these top shelf makers stand out is that they do exceptional work *consistently.* Rarely will you see them turn out what amounts to a flop, a dud, or a boat anchor (as some of us affectionately refer to a clumsy effort at translating mental image into material object).

You can be sure that as a rule, you're just not going to see a dud out of the shop of one of this upper tier of makers. Their overall success is largely due to their consistency. Those of you who may be relatively new in the knifemaking community may feel like your ratio of boat anchor to artwork is higher than you'd like it to be. For those who'd like to improve, I make this recommendation: Draw your work. I will try to explain what I mean.

Knifemakers are often called artists, and this title implies a certain measure of abstraction. In some cases, abstract expression might work well for a maker whose primary intention is to express his or her artistic endeavor. An abstract art knife can range all the way from a cleverly designed "regular" knife to an object so far out as to barely be recognized as a knife. I would venture to say that for some of us the way a knife fits the hand is more important than perhaps what artistic impression it might leave on someone. Even makers who adopt this somewhat simplistic ergonomic approach can consistently produce some amazing works of art. After all, the concept of art itself is fleeting and very much a matter of interpretation. Given the complexity of the field of art, we will concentrate more on the practical aspects of knifemaking and not get bogged down in a discussion on exactly what elements make a knife art.

Back to the Drawing Board

One thing that I have noticed about experienced makers is that they sketch out their knife projects before they ever begin. In my opinion, this is a major step in the right direction, one of many steps toward consistently turning out end products that formerly were only seen in the mind's eye of the maker. You may think, *I already sketch out my work*, but the drawings

I'm talking about can be very exact and of great detail. There are those who might feel like the draw-then-build approach hinders their artistic flow or something. They expect to just go to their forge, heat the steel, start hammering, and let the creative juices take over. Sometimes, this approach works, but from my experience, I can say that this approach generally does not match how I produce my best work. Think about it like this. If you were going to travel to a specific destination, you would probably map it out and take a preferred route instead of just getting in your car and driving in the general direction, hoping to end up at your destination. At times, "my destination" may be a Joseph Rogers–reproduction bowie and I can't get it done to satisfaction with meandering methods. I can say for certain, when I draw and refer to my drawing in the process of construction, my knives turn out much better.

Best Bowie of the 2014 Arkansas knife show

Let's just say that we are in agreement that drawing our knives in detail before ever forging the blade will consistently improve the final results. OK, how do we go about using the drawing? I have figured out a few little tricks that make using a drawing almost foolproof. I would start by recommending purchasing a high-end drawing pad. I personally like a fourteen-by-seventeen-inch size. You can put a small knife on a big page, but you can't adequately draw a large knife on a small page. The better sketch pads have a more durable binding and won't fall apart on you. The durability of the pad will be important for more than the obvious reason that it'll live around a knifemaker's shop. Your drawings will improve the final quality your work, thus increasing the likelihood that you will want to repeat that knife again later. A good-quality drawing pad will be there for you when you decide to do that. You'll have detailed information about the knife, such as notes, model names, variations, specifics on materials, dates, customer names, and so on that can be noted on the drawings and available for future reference. Who knows? Your children may really appreciate having your drawing pad one day, even with coffee stains, so please spend a few extra dollars and get a good one.

I like to have a few drawing tools to speed up the process and make the details a little more precise, things like mechanical pencils, oval, circle, or triangle templates, French curve, straight edge or ruler, and similar tools. These tools are easily obtainable from your local hobby or drafting supply. A good eraser is a must, because you can make your changes and corrections much easier on paper than in steel. You will be surprised at how very slight tweak in a curve or a line can make a knife look so much better. This realization is a big step in developing your eye, the one you use to judge the end product while yet still on paper.

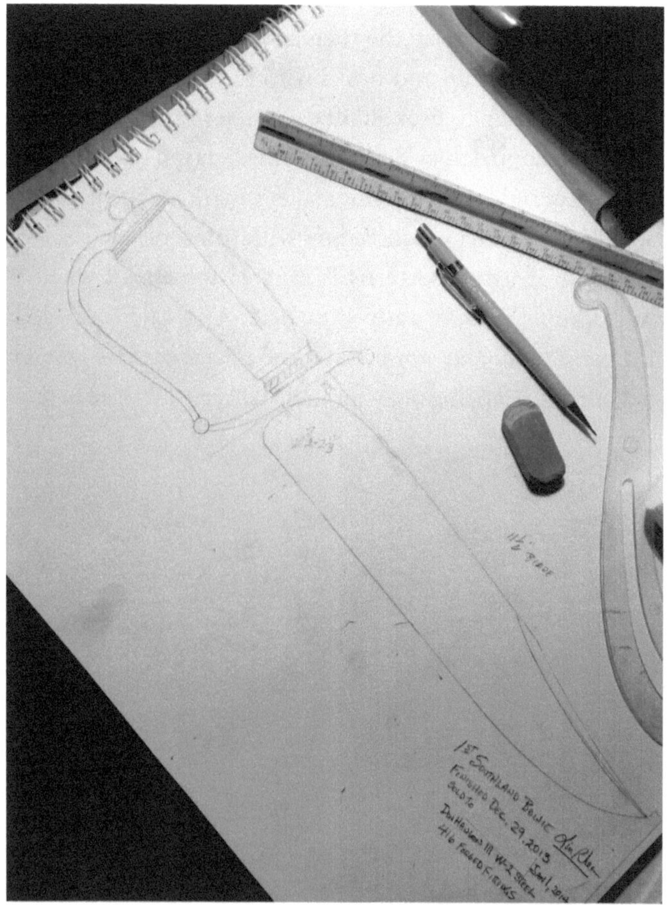

After you get your drawing finalized and you're ready now to go to the shop and forge the blade, it can be somewhat awkward to compare a hot-steel blade to a paper drawing. I make a pattern, first by laying a piece of clear Plexiglas onto the drawing and tracing the blade, tang and all, onto the Plexiglas using a felt marker. I cut and grind this to shape, then use the Plexiglas pattern to trace onto one-eighth-inch aluminum plate. After I get the aluminum pattern cut and ground, I go back to my drawing and tweak the pattern till I'm satisfied it's as close as I can get it. This aluminum pattern is the one I use as a template while forging my blade. After forging and also during the grinding stages, I refer to this pattern often. I actually hold the aluminum pattern directly over the steel blade till its profile is a copy of the pattern. To be certain all is well, I then lay the then cool blade onto the actual drawing to see if every detail lines up and works with the handle, guard, pins, and so on. I can use this principle throughout each step of the knife's construction.

By taking this approach of drawing to Plexiglas to aluminum, I can save my patterns for later use. I stamp my maker's mark on the pattern just like I do my blades so they won't get mixed up with someone else's.

The method of using patterns is especially helpful when making a frame-handled knife. A lot of early- American- and English-style knives are unique in construction, and you have to know where you're going when you start down that road. Mapping out your route will get you there in good fashion.

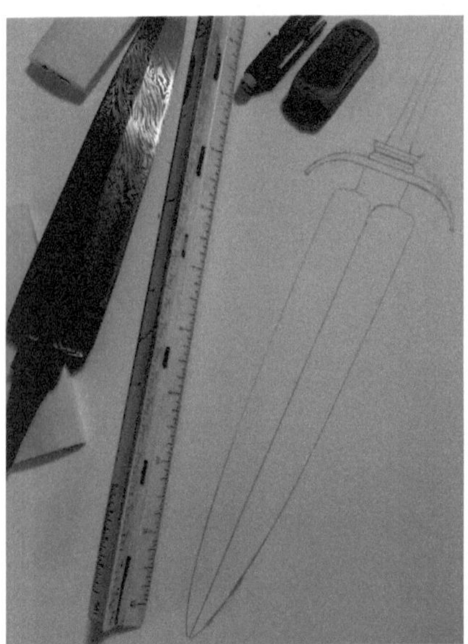

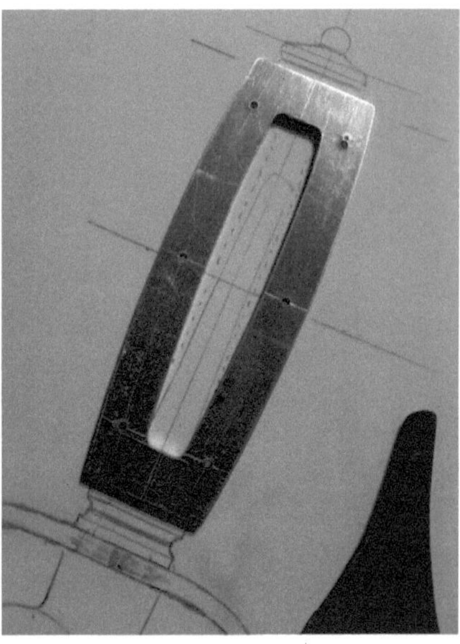

What I've offered you is a means of translating your mental image into the physical object you've imagined. While this image is still in the mind, you have all kinds of freedom to express your artistic self. The next step is to capture that image, in our case in the form of a drawing and then a metal template. After that, we apply the knifemaking methods and techniques, going step-by-step and using our patterns, to achieve the necessary amount of precision suited for the production. The degree of predictability this approach will add to your work is very satisfying, as it improves not only your work itself, but also your art-to-boat-anchor ratio. As you continue to improve, your consistent results will be noticeable immediately by yourself, by your customers, and by the knifemaking community at large.

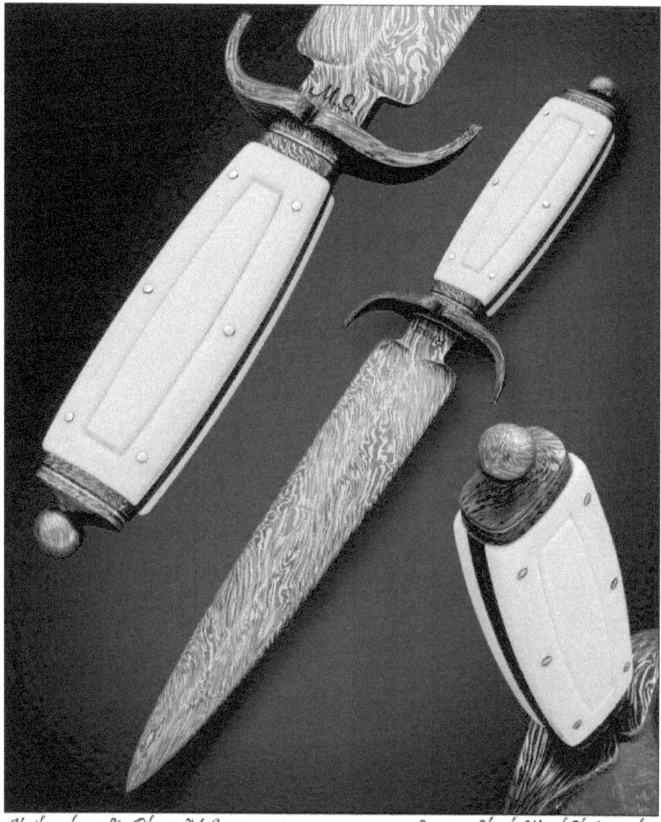

Knifemaker - Lin Rhea - M.S. *Image - Chuck Ward Photography*

Dagger Complete

CHAPTER 18

Knives as Art

Jason Fry

EVERY EXCELLENT KNIFEMAKER is an artist. We also are manufacturers, fabricators, metalworkers, woodworkers, knife salespeople, inventory specialists, the entire marketing-and-advertising department, and the yard boy, but at our core, we are artists. Our art is more like sculpture than like painting, perhaps more like architecture than pen-and-ink sketch artistry, but it's art nonetheless.

Knifemaking as Art

Every discipline has its guiding principles, and art is no different. Elements of artistic study such as line, shape, form, color, and texture are relevant to our work as knife artists. Principles of artistic composition, which are the guides by which we arrange and organize the various artistic elements, including balance, contrast, proportion, unity, and variety, come into play as well. While diving deep into art theory is beyond the scope of our effort in this book, moving to the next level in your knife work means taking the artistic side of your knifemaker brain and giving it a workout. Your knife is art, whether you approach it artistically or not. So much has been said about the elements and principles of art and beauty over the centuries that it's foolish for the knifemaker artist to remain ignorant. We can learn from other artists to make our art more pleasing to the eye, more appealing to the customer, and more likely to stand the test of time.

Five Basic Rules for Knife Design

1. The form of a knife should be suited to its function.
2. The lines of a knife should flow.
3. The elements of the knife should be in proportion to one another.
4. The elements of a knife should visually complement each other.
5. The material selections of a knife should correspond with each other and within these other rules.

Form Follows Function

Earlier chapters in this book covered this basic principle of knifemaking. The form of the knife should match its intended use.

Lines and Flow

The concepts of line and flow are difficult to describe in text, but a knife with clean lines is immediately more appealing. When you first look at a knife that catches your fancy, you don't always recognize why you like it. Those knives that have instinctive appeal most often have good flow and good use of lines. After you've read this section, go online and look at a few of the knives of Don Hanson, Jean-Louis Regel, or Wolfgang Loerchner. In this case, the picture is worth far more than the words in this chapter. Pay attention to the elements you will read about in the next few paragraphs, and the text will all start to make more sense.

The primary indicator of line and flow is the absence of harsh breaks in the visual makeup of the knife. There should be no elements of the profile that stand out or look out of place. The top line of the knife should flow in a smooth line from the tip of the knife to the butt of the handle. There's no rule that the knife needs to be straight or curved, or that there can't be multiple curves, but the line should flow. This concept also applies to the lines of guards or dropped edges relative to the profile of the handle and blade. A knife need not be simple to have clean lines.

An important consideration relative to line and flow is the height of the ricasso relative to the handle diameter. A knife with good flow is often built off of the dimensions of the ricasso. The knives with the purest lines have a ricasso that is the same height as the handle immediately behind the guard, and the ricasso lines up on both the top and bottom edges with the top and bottom edges of the handle. While there are occasional exceptions, particularly in historical knives, a knife will often appeal at a more visceral level if the handle to ricasso to blade transition is even.

There are two primary ways to assess the flow of your design. First and foremost, draw your knives before you build them. While you may not have to draw every drop-point hunter variation you build, as you progress toward more complex pieces, you must draw. Drawing a knife allows you to try different variations of lines and curves. Some use a straight edge and a French curve to aid in drawing, or an oval or circle template. Others do it all by eye. Either way, as you tweak your design with a little more curve here and a little less curve there, pay attention to how you feel about the design. When it's right, you'll know.

The second way to assess line and flow is to build a model. Using cardstock, manila folders or cereal boxes, Plexiglas, thin metal sheet, or any other number of materials, make a model of your knife that matches the outline of your finished drawing exactly. Take your model to an area that is backlit, such as in front of a window or outside against the sky. Add or remove material from the knife's profile until the silhouette of the knife is pleasing and flows cleanly.

When it comes to flow, there are no magic formulas. Your ability to draw and ultimately build a knife with good lines comes only through practice. Look at master-built knives, then draw them, then build them. As you train your eye, your eye will guide your hands as you forge and grind. As you start to make progress toward understanding the concept of flow, take a look through one of the knives' annuals. Every year, there are knives in the book with excellent lines, mediocre lines, and poor lines. As you look, learn to discriminate.

The Secret to Proportion Is Golden

There are no shortcuts to learning to design a knife with lines and flow. There are, however, guiding principles that make designing knives with good proportion much easier to accomplish. These principles come from a variety of unexpected places: human anatomy, classical art, and mathematics.

The Western world's first studies of proportion as a measure of beauty and art were recorded by the Roman author Vetruvius. Vetruvius intensely studied the proportions of the parts of the human body relative to one another. Perhaps the best graphical illustration of this concept is Leonardo DaVinci's "Vetruvian Man." Through his studies, Vetruvius was the first to describe what has become known as the "golden mean" or "golden section," the ideal ratio between parts of a whole. The basic ratio of the golden mean is 1:1.618. This ratio is close to 3:5, 5:8, and 8:13.

The golden mean can be used at many different points in a knife design. The height and width of the ricasso on a forged knife look just right when built to this proportion. On a one-inch-tall ricasso, the width is 0.61 inches. The golden ratio also works well in some situations on the knife-to-handle ratio. Given a five-inch handle, an eighth-inch blade will look just right. The golden mean can be used to define dimensions between the guard thickness and spacer thickness or between the length of the guard relative to the length of the blade.

She Sells Seashells

Another version of the golden mean was first described by Fibonacci around AD 1202. The Fibonacci sequence is made by adding numbers sequentially, where each new number is the sum of the previous two numbers. The basic sequence is:

1, 1, 2, 3, 5, 8, 13, 21, 34, 55, 89, 144, 233, 377, 610, 987, 1597

3:5 is a close approximation of the golden mean, as is 5:8 and 8:13. The further down the sequence you get, the closer the result is to 1.618. You may be thinking that you can build a knife with a thirteen inch overall length and an eight-inch blade, but what are you supposed to do with the 987? The ratio holds, regardless. If you convert to millimeters, it works. If you divide by 10, it works. If you take your handle length and multiply it by 1.618, it works. If you take your ricasso height and divide by 1.618, it works. If the guard is 1.618 times thicker than the spacer, it works.

While the golden mean is indeed golden when it comes to setting your knife's proportions, it isn't useful in every single situation the maker may encounter. Other rules of proportion may apply as well.

I'm Half the Man I Used to Be

Another way to approach proportion is to divide the unit into fractional sections, such as halves, thirds, fourths, fifths, and so on. Sometimes a blade that is the same length as the handle, with a guard in between, looks just fine. Sometimes a spacer that is one-third as thick as the guard looks great. A useful place to try fifths is the guard length proportion, with one-fifth above the spine, two-fifths through the handle, and two-fifths below the spine. This works with sixths as well.

Poorly proportioned pin placement will probably be poorly perceived by potential purchasers. If you're the type of maker who uses two pins on a full-tang knife, try placing them one-fifth of the handle length away from the ends, leaving three-fifths in the middle. Naturally, the most common method for vertical alignment of pins is to place them along the center line between the top and the bottom of the handle. As the handle typically is convex on the top line and concave on the bottom line, if you're going to miss with your pin placement, miss high. A slightly high pin won't stand out near as garishly as a slightly low one.

When considering the placement of a single pin on a stick tang with a guard, realize that you're creating an isosceles triangle between the pin and the top and bottom of the guard/handle junction. Sometimes, an equilateral triangle works better. Other times, the pin should be placed back from the guard by one-fifth or one-fourth of the distance from the guard to the end of the handle.

When considering a row of pins around the handle, such as is more common on a frame handle or coffin handle, cut your handle profile first, then scribe a line equal distance from the edge all the way around. Make your line a little deeper than you think it should go, sometimes one-third to one-half an inch, as the handle shaping will make the pins look closer to the edge than they really are. Space the pins along that line in fractional units such as halves, fourths, or fifths of the total distance between the first and last pins.

Each of these rules of proportion, whether the golden mean, the Fibonacci sequence, or dividing in fractional portions, are simply guidelines. Much like a grinding jig can initially train your hands and eyes to grind the proper angle freehand, use mathematical rules to develop your skills until your eye is trained to see proper proportions. Follow the rules carefully until you're skilled enough to break them intentionally and with good results.

Complementary Elements Complement Your Skills

They say that you can't put lipstick on a pig, but at the same time, many men appreciate the effect that the right shade of lipstick has to enhance the visual appeal of a beautiful woman. In the same way, the different design elements should be carefully thought out to complement the beauty of a knife. One cannot make an ugly knife better simply by adding more file work, any more than the lipstick helps that pig.

When it comes to design elements, many times the best design will have only one superstar. Until you get to the level where you can pull it off, consider having a single point of excellence. If you've got a great piece of handle material, maybe you don't go all file work and mirror polished bling for the blade. If you've got a great piece of Damascus, maybe you don't pull out the mammoth tooth to go with it. As you develop your skills, don't try to overwhelm your customers with too many complex elements.

Another area of attention concerns focal points, the natural areas of a design that draw the eye's attention. As you plan the knife, choose the elements so that one stands out naturally above the others. Many times a complex guard or spacer set on an otherwise clean knife can really push the design over the edge. Likewise, a bit of file work judiciously applied can make your knife stand out at a show among the tables full of three-piece hunters.

Your use of color, texture, finish, and contrast should be considered and intentional. Sometimes, all dark tones works well, as in a dark handle material and a muted etched or satin-finished blade. Other times stark contrast works well, with light and dark tones, or busy and simple textures put together on the same piece. Still other times, there's a complementary mix.

However you choose the various elements of your design, you must intentionally choose them to complement each other. Failure to consider how design elements relate to each other can result in a knife that's an artistic failure. Another error is to use every embellishment you can muster on a single piece. Even the finest of models doesn't wear everything in her wardrobe at the same time. Likewise, a knife need not have mosaic Damascus, engraving, scrimshawed ivory, file work, and inlaid jewels at the same time.

"We Are Living in a Material World, and I Am a Material Girl"

The choices that you make with regard to materials should first be relative to the function of the knife. Some folks would prefer their deer-skinning knife with durable Micarta, while others would prefer creamy ivory. The durability and suitability of the handle material should match the knife's intended function.

Handle materials come in every color under the sun. Some like the subtle texture of black canvas Micarta, and others the brightness of orange G10. Some like the greens and purples of brightly colored stabilized wood, where others prefer the muted grain of polished African blackwood. When choosing the material for your handle, consider how the handle material will contrast with or complement the blade finish, guard material and finish, and the knife's overall texture.

Another consideration is whether to choose traditional or modern materials. Some knives traditionally have certain handle materials, such as a Sambar stag-handled forged hunter or a green Micarta Loveless-style drop-point hunter. If your knife has a traditional shape to serve a traditional function, you might consider what handle materials are traditionally used for that type of knife. On the other hand, sometimes the masters can combine traditional and nontraditional materials into a single knife. Adam DesRosiers won the "Best Hunter" award at the first International Custom Cutlery Expo with a multibar twist Damascus integral hunter with black G10 handles. While you will likely best be served by choosing traditional materials for traditional knives at first, you may reach a point where something antitraditional can be made to work as an element of contrast. Consider the genre of knife you're designing. Bowies typically have certain handle materials. Kitchen knives may have other materials. Hunters and EDCs accept a wider range of materials. Match the handle material to the genre of knife you're making.

Finally, consider what the target customer likes and expects. If you're selling to an unknown customer at a knife show, maybe you should choose traditional materials. On the other hand, if you're selling to Oklahoma State or Harley Davidson fans, maybe you should go with black-and-orange G10. You should know your customers' preferences and build your knives to suit them. There will be knives that you just want to build to be different, off the wall, or outside the box, and you should build them also.

Putting It All Together

So what constitutes a perfectly designed knife? First off, the knife will do the job it was designed for, and the materials, grind, and finish will be suited to the task. The lines of the knife will be clean, with each element in proportion to the others. The material and embellishment choices will complement one another with an eye-pleasing mix of either traditional or modern elements. Finally, the perfectly designed knife will please the customer to the utmost, and happy customers buy more knives.

SECTION FIVE

Marketing, Photography, and Publication

CHAPTER 19

Next-Level Marketing

Jason Fry, Dustin Rhodes, and Erin Healy

I (JASON) MET A talented blacksmith once whose story is worth sharing. I was perusing the gift shops in a mountain tourist town when a forged bottle opener caught my eye. It was beautiful, with cleanly executed tapers and tiny, precise scrollwork. I've been making knives a long time, but I immediately recognized work of a quality that I was unable to match. Somewhere behind that bottle opener was a man or woman with serious skill. I inquired of the shopkeeper, and she gave me the gentleman's business card. It had a phone number, the man's name, and the name of his business.

I gave him a call at 7:00 p.m. The phone went straight to an old-school answering machine. I left a message, introducing myself and asking if I could stop by to meet him. I also looked him up on Facebook (377 friends) and send him a friend request and an instant message. He called back after lunch the next day, and we made a plan to meet.

The visit was wonderful! His shop was clean and well organized, and there were works in various stages of the process available to see. He had good equipment, including an impressive three-hundred-pound Peter Wright. We visited for over an hour. He brought out a lamp with exceptional forged vines and leaves twisted around the lamp stem, as well as an assortment of bottle openers and forged leaf keychains.

The young man was thirty years old and had been blacksmithing since he was fourteen. Once he decided to be a blacksmith, his mom pulled him out of high school and homeschooled him through graduation. He had taken several week-long blacksmithing courses at a nearby college, and mentioned several other smiths he described as his mentors. He sold his work through a couple of local shops, and had done a few shows over the years, some more successful than others. He had been taken advantage of on occasion, such as the store owner who paid fifteen dollars per steak turner and then sold them at fifty dollars. He'd also had a few breaks, from store owners who let him sell without even charging commission.

I left the visit with mixed feelings. The smith had amazing talent, but had a variety of situational factors working against him. He lived in an economically depressed area that was dependent on tourism for much of its income. The locals struggled to get by, which limited his local income potential. He was a member of a minority group in an area of the country where racism was a substantial downward economic force. His area was very much dominated in politics and economy by white retirees and a few local families. He was not well connected to his community. He didn't have a cell phone, although his mother had "just got a smartphone last year." He wasn't active on social media and had no website. He struggled to produce enough product to sell because he had to split firewood all winter to stay warm, and had gardening and livestock to tend in the warmer months. The beautiful lamp had taken him two weeks to build, had a $350 price tag, and had been in his inventory for four years. He had all the talent required to make it to the next level, but he won't make it without some outside intervention. At the same time, the isolation of his circumstances and lack of contact with outside influences made it unlikely that such intervention would occur.

I start with that story to make a single point: you won't become a next-level knifemaker because of next-level talent. The smith I met had plenty of talent, but he will struggle to survive because of a lack of marketing. If no one knows your name, nobody views your product on a regular basis, and if you can't be easily found by people who are looking for the kinds of product you produce, you'll struggle to make sales. Marketing isn't about being a bullhorn; it's about implementing a systematic method for applying what your customers tell you. The goal is to test, assess, and retest until you maximize your efficacy or your moneymaking potential. Then, every so often, go back to see if you're still running at peak performance. If not, conduct research, hypothesize, test, assess, retest until you implement a new plan or strategy. This way, you're not guessing; you're making decisions based on research. Your greatest sources of data are your internal operations for efficiencies and your customers' feedback for sales.

Dustin puts it this way: Congratulations on making it to the point where you can produce quality cutlery, but what do you do next? You're kind of in the same position as the talented teenage garage band that never plays outside the garage, but wonders why they can't get a leg up on gigs. At some point, you will realize that if you're going to make sales, you have to let your potential customer base know first that you exist, and next that you have product or services for sale. You can produce the finest knives in the world, but if no one knows that they are there, do they truly exist? Promoting your product is an essential part of making the sale.

Sell to the Buyers You Need

One of the critical steps to increasing your sales is to understand the audience to whom you're selling. Who is your stereotypical target buyer? Are you selling primarily to hunters and fishermen? To tactical gentlemen? To chefs or home kitchen experts? Are you trying to crack into the high-end knife-collector market? Where you advertise, how you get the word out, and what kind of product you make should be informed by your choice of target customer.

I shared this idea with the young blacksmith, who previously had approached shows from the standpoint of bringing what he had available to sell. Some shows he sold a lot, some not much. He described to me a couple of the places where his shows had been, with some pretty good insight into the target market in each area, but he had brought the same type of inventory to each show. I suggested that if he knew he was selling to locals in a depressed economy, that household items, tools, and lower price points might be the way to go, and that if he was selling to tourists at the peak of the summer rush, the tourist crowd might be more likely to buy art pieces or spend a bit more.

I once worked in a sporting goods store with a man who boasted that he could sell a Glock to a nun, and watching him work, I bet he was right. Still, with all the guns he sold, I never once saw a nun buy one. He sold guns to folks who were likely to buy guns. You may be able to force a sale once in a while in an unlikely place or to an unlikely person, but I guarantee you'll do better selling in the places your typical customer likes to shop, and to people who match the demographic and economic categories you market to. Even if you prefer to sell passively, to let the customers come to you, the location you choose to set up (both physically and online) will be a driving factor in your overall sales. If you live in a proverbial mud hut, don't have a phone, and can't be found online, then you shouldn't be surprised if you struggle to find new customers.

Erin suggests that, in the old days, a company or craftsman could put an ad in a newspaper and thereby reach all segments of their target audience at once. Small business was concentrated locally, and whether you were white, black, young, old, protestant, atheist, married, widowed, working, retired, rich, or poor, you read the newspaper. Print and local media aren't like that anymore. Your audience is fragmented, scattered all over the world, and hanging out in both likely and unlikely places online. You cannot reach every potential customer all at once, nor should you even try to do so.

It used to be that all a company ever had to do was tout its products and services ad nauseam, never going off message, never being human, never incorporating feedback from its customers. Marketing in those times was a one-way street. "We offer this, in this way. That's what we've always done, and that's what we'll continue to do. We do it 'best.' Our product is 'unique.'" Blah, blah. The only one who truly cares about you and your knives is you. While your family, friends, and fanboys will forever sing your praises, your customer fundamentally cares about only one thing: himself. He therefore cares only about your knife in relation to his life, period. He loves how your knife makes a task easier. She appreciates the craftsmanship and the colors in the handle. He just wants it to cut when a life is on the line. He wants to show it off to his friends. In the end, everything in your customer's world centers on him, not on you or your knife.

Do you need to get the message of your products and services out there? Of course, you do, but first, you just need to get inside your customer's head, figure out where his "pain points" are, and be with him as he slowly travels through the information-gathering phase about your work, and ultimately as he enters the decision-making phase to make a purchase. You need to be there when he realizes that he not only wants a knife—he wants *your* knife. There's no hard sell, no constant annoying messaging, no media barrage. Marketing is all about building a genuine relationship with your customer, offering him your best when he's ready, and nurturing the relationship so when he wants a knife for his brother, son, or wife, he comes to *you*.

Like a detective getting inside the mind of a criminal or a military strategist getting inside the mind of the enemy, you want to get inside the mind of your customer. A pain point is the reason your customer has not yet bought a knife from you, or another knife, or his fifth knife. Often the pain point is money, but not always. Does he even know custom knives exist? Why does he need a knife? Why is your knife a good fit for him? Do you share the same tastes? What does he like to do when he's not using a knife?

Some people go to the extent of naming their customer personas. Let's say you forge knives inlaid with gold. You make your own pattern-welded steel. Your handle material is a month's rent for some people. You want to sell your knife so that you can work on your next masterpiece. Perhaps you have not built up a following yet, or your name isn't yet recognized as someone whose work should be collected.

If you're this kind of maker, who is your buyer? He's a collector, but perhaps not necessarily of knives. Maybe he collects antique firearms but is looking for something else to collect. He doesn't flinch at a $10,000 price tag. Maybe he's a lawyer who can tell good whiskey from bad and enjoys a cigar now and again. He's married, has two grown children who are settling into their own married lives. He and his wife like fine restaurants and not-too-adventurous adventure travel—think safaris with white tablecloths at sunset. Money isn't the issue. He's just doesn't know about you—yet. Is your mind thinking up more ways to meet him where he is? Good, because he's not coming to you. Simple "getting the word out" is wasted, untargeted effort, especially if you're only posting to your fellow knifemakers on Instagram.

Go through this targeting exercise for every customer you have. There will be a handful of customer types for every knifemaker. Get detailed. It may be nebulous to try to explain the difference between someone who needs your bushcrafting chopper versus someone who should have your camp knife, but those two audiences are different. The key is to explore what they might be interested in when they're not holding a knife.

Social Media Is Mandatory Fun

Social media has changed the world by changing the ways in which people interact with one another. If you want to meet potential customers, but ignore social media, the growth of your business will be a difficult uphill climb. Social media is first of all social, which means interactive. People interact on social media, independent of their business interests. People who only post sales content and rarely engage with anyone else's posts will feel it in their lack of influence. You can come to the party and sit in the corner if you want to, but don't expect people to pay attention to you when all of a sudden you start hawking your wares, which is rude to do at a social event anyway. Each platform is very different, so know the intent and limitations of each.

Facebook

On the surface, Facebook is about fun, family, friends, and photos, and that's truly where its value lies. Facebook is antiweapon, and even if you consider yourself a "tool" maker, Facebook's algorithms are designed to suppress knife content. Your Facebook page can be a place where you post behind-the-scenes stills, works in progress, spur-of-the-moment videos, and links to news releases and articles. Make no mistake, however. If you sell your knives for money, that's business. You won't even be allowed to advertise knives on Facebook, so don't even try. You'll get caught, and your content will be pulled. If you do try, do make sure to make it a presentable advertisement. There was once a maker who got an ad through the filters and posted a picture of a knife for sale with handle gaps and glue seepage. Don't be that guy.

Whether you keep your business account separate from your personal account is up to you. Either way, you should realize that Facebook can suspend or terminate your account for the knives alone. Be sure to keep records of all your Messenger conversations. Facebook owns Messenger, and if you lose your account, all associated Messages will be unavailable as well. That guy you can't remember who ordered a knife you can't remember, but it's all on Messenger—gone. Don't be that guy either. Copy and paste each conversation into a word-processing document for that client, or use email instead. You could even go old school and take notes by hand.

LinkedIn

LinkedIn is an overlooked platform if you have an affiliation with a professional organization or if you approach knifemaking as a professional as opposed to as a craftsman. If you want to reach businessmen with your gentleman's folder, if you want to get your tactical knife before police departments, or if you're putting on a series of forging classes, then LinkedIn can be a great platform for you. People don't go there regularly, but be there so that when they do, they find you. People come to LinkedIn to network, to learn, or to conduct business, so the tone is always professional.

Twitter

Twitter is the social media platform of choice for journalists. So why be there? Because you want to build relationships with mainstream journalists and citizen journalists (bloggers) so that when you have something newsworthy, you've already assembled a pool of writers. For instance, say you make bushcrafting knives. Start following bushcrafting aficionados on Twitter, and actually read what they write about knives. Comment. Share. Engage. Stick with the ones you can develop a genuine relationship with, and Tweet them when your chopper goes midtech. Unlike whoever covers knives for *Outside* magazine, bloggers are always open to story suggestions. They write more frequently and so need lots of topics. Bloggers are typically not working years in advance, and they aren't locked into an editorial calendar catering to advertisers.

Instagram

Instagram is most recently the social media platform of choice for the knifemaker. Instagram is all about sharing pictures. You can share pictures of your work, of works in progress, of knives available, of your shop, or even of your family. Finding a style and posting regularly are both critical. Your customer needs to see your pictures and immediately recognize the work as yours. Remember that Facebook is antiknife and owns Instagram. Keep doing what you're doing, but recognize that you're not going to expand your audience unless you focus on how your knives are used or made, and forget about the posting-to-sell approach. Code words and work-arounds won't win in the long run. Focus on using Instagram to share high-quality images.

YouTube

YouTube is a great parking lot for your videos, but market forces are working against you. Google owns You Tube, and Facebook and Google are arch enemies. Facebook's algorithms bury anything posted from YouTube. There are a few makers who have built their business through YouTube, but it's not the first place you should focus unless you're already capable of high-quality video content.

Where to Start?

So let's say your mom just got a smartphone, and you want to start using social media, starting with absolutely nothing. Where do you start? I (Jason) suggest that you start by building a personal Facebook profile. Use Facebook, first of all, as it's intended, to connect with people you already know. Post stories and pictures about your life and include a bit of knife content occasionally. Don't try to sell. Once you've built a network of all your high school buddies, former coworkers, and so on, then you can start pointing them toward your work in other areas.

Second, and perhaps simultaneously, start an Instagram account. Remember, Instagram is all about photos, so make your photos good ones. Instagram uses hashtags (that's the symbol formerly known as the pound sign, #) to sort and search the pictures posted there. Explore some hashtags that appeal to you, like #knife or #blacksmith for starters. Observe what other hashtags are commonly associated, and use several appropriate hashtags for each of your pictures. Instagram rewards people who post frequently. Post every day if you can maintain quality content. On the other hand, posting pics of your breakfast just so you can post every day is a waste of time for your knife marketing.

Erin rightly suggests that you should also focus on a website. Social media is owned by companies, and several of those companies are biased against knives. Your website belongs to you and no one else. Build your social media presence on multiple platforms, and use them to drive customers to your website. Your website doesn't have to be a giant For Sale page. It should include information about you and show pictures of your work. You should link to your social media accounts, and should pictures, videos, and instructional material on your website as well. It's from your website that you will collect email addresses for current and potential customers.

All of your media funnel to your website, which captures email addresses for your mailing list. This is the point at which you're allowed to sell. By now, you're not shooting random spam emails; you're emailing directly to customers who have signed up for information about your product.

Don't Burn Bridges

Maintaining professionalism is a very important aspect of any business. Treating your customers and other business connections with respect will go a long way. At times, you may encounter coarse individuals as well as those who try to drive a hard bargain. First off, keep your emotions in check. Most often, an angry response from you (even if well deserved) will take that person off of your potential list of customers. You may find that some people can't be reasoned with, and others have unique ways of dealing that just rub you wrong. Don't lose your cool and become the lesser person in the situation. On the other hand, some customers are more trouble than the potential sale is worth. The guy who calls you thirty-seven times on a two-hundred-dollar order may be a good guy to refer to somebody else for their next project.

One-Hit Wonder or Long-Term Success?

The one-hit wonder may sell some albums (or at least a bunch of song downloads), but those who can consistently produce hits are the ones who do well in the long-term. Congratulations to you for generating a buzz on social media, or for making it into print. These accomplishments are legitimate, but don't immediately lead to long-term success. By diversifying your market and means of income, you will be more likely to maintain a more consistent cash flow. Creativity and keen observation of market trends are also critical to long-term success. Repeat customers, wholesale outlets, online markets, trade shows, and other venues can all be part of a diverse set of channels for moving your knives. If all you have is one stream, what do you do when the stream dries up? Multiple sources of income will help to compensate when cash flow from one area begins trickle rather than flow. Similarly, you should be running multiple marketing streams. You can't just focus on trade shows, and you can't just post on Instagram. Long-term next-level success requires marketing that is both broad, taking advantage of many venues, and deep, consistently putting forward quality content.

You didn't learn knifemaking overnight, and you won't learn marketing overnight either. Follow the same path, of mentors, of formal education, or of trial and error, but whatever you do, *do* something. Passive marketing is about like "imported knife" or "anvil-shaped object." It may look like it's going to work, but in the end, it won't work well at all and will leave you dissatisfied. Attack marketing with the same fervor you attacked learning to make knives, and your sales will continue to grow along with your knifemaking skills.

CHAPTER 20

Getting Published

Joshua Swanagon

THEY SAY, "IF you build it, they will come." When it comes to knifemaking and publication, however, publishers don't simply show up when you start building knives. For someone who has spent their time and effort perfecting a craft of any kind, recognition in print on the national or international stage can make all the difference in the world when it comes to increasing your status in the industry. Increased exposure can translate into an increased customer base, increased sales, and potentially increased prices.

Although we are moving into the digital age there's still a general sense that if something is in print it must be credible—most likely due to the cost of putting something in print, signifying the fact that a reviewer or editor must have faith in it. Although social media can take something viral and get it in front of thousands, or even millions almost overnight, it isn't guaranteed. However, getting your work in print media—or even a reputable online media source—is guaranteed to put your work in the hands of tens to hundreds of thousands of people, which can have a dramatic and almost immediate impact on your customer base and in overall sales

It's a difficult and at times downright frustrating task to get your work out to the masses. There are many different roads to the top, but having your work published in a trade magazine is a great way to fast-track the road to notoriety. Here are some things to consider that you can do to help get your work in front of editors.

Send Your Best and Be Thorough

When you send your work to an editor, make sure to choose your absolute best work and send high-quality beauty shots. You have to think of editors like future customers, except that they are well-educated future customers who see a lot of knives on a daily basis. You must do everything in your power to stand out and impress them. You may have the best knife in the world, but if the photo you send is plain, poorly composed, out of focus, or uninspiring they won't be as likely to bite. Make sure that all photos are professional quality and that all of the knife's specifications are provided with the query. You won't catch the eye of a professional editor with a subprofessional representation of your work.

Another strategy is to pick your best knives from several different categories and submit them all at once. If you send photos and specs of one hunting knife, but the editor you send it to doesn't have immediate magazine space for a hunting knife, he may not give it much consideration. However, if you send photos and specs for a hunting knife, tactical knife, bowie knife, and a bushcrafting knife at the same time, you have a better shot of the editor having an open slot in one of these categories in an upcoming issue that you might fit into.

Make a Knife with a Purpose

A good friend of mine in the publishing industry once told me that every knife should have a story of some kind—that's the selling point. That is advice I have taken to heart, and it has helped me immensely in my own designs and in knife selection. Stories sell knives to customers, and part of treating an editor like a customer is to sell the story.

Whatever design features you place on your knife, you should be able to explain in detail why you included them. Oftentimes, a simple but purposeful knife will do much better than a knife with a ton of bells and whistles that serve no other function than the ability to market the piece as a "multifunction knife." Personally, I've never opened a bottle in the field. In fact, I've never even taken a bottle into the field. Therefore, if a knife marketed as a bushcrafting knife has a bottle opener, I'm going to want to know why. If there's no legitimate, demonstrable reason for it, I'm going to chalk it up as marketing gimmickry and take the knife less seriously.

Along those same lines, if the profile of the blade has odd angles and is completely outside the norm for its marketed intent, each deviation from the norm should have a solid purpose, and you should be able to explain your reasoning succinctly. On the other hand, if it takes too much explaining to understand your knife, you risk losing a large part of your market. Anything you do outside the norm should have an immediately evident, unmistakable purpose that can be seen just by looking at the knife.

Don't include pointless bells and whistles and oddly placed features. Make sure that you make a blade with purpose and avoid doing things just to make it look cool. Oftentimes, less is more, and simple is best.

Remember: every knife you send in for consideration is a sales pitch. You're trying to get the attention of whoever you want to review your knife. Make them want it.

Self-Promotion: The Art of Show and Tell

It may seem obvious, but I believe that it bears mentioning that self-promotion will go a long way toward getting noticed. The more time you spend promoting your work, the more likely someone who can get your knives into the public eye will see them. Especially in the beginning of your journey, unless you toot your own horn, nobody is going to toot it for you.

Consider doing things like creating a YouTube channel and making short videos about your knifemaking process. Also make short videos, testing your knives. Make sure that they aren't too long; about five minutes is an appropriate length. If your videos are too long, people will be less likely to watch them. Most people will watch a five-minute video if you make it interesting.

It's worth your time and effort to attend shows. If you're serious about your work, there's no reason you should be missing any of the local gun-and-knife shows. Put some money into a booth design that will attract people from across the show floor—build a high backdrop out of PVC and invest in an eye-catching banner. If you get more people to your table, you have a better chance of converting a few.

Have business cards out and easily accessible. People may not buy from you on the spot because of budget or personal reasons, but if you have a card and they like your work, they may visit your website later and purchase something at that time. The more knives you get into people's hands, the more chance that other people will see them. Also, you never know what kind of writers frequent your local gun-and-knife shows; I go to them fairly often myself. If you've not been published anywhere before, even a local newspaper is a step in the right direction.

Blade Show is the biggest knife show in the United States and is attended by a great number of media professionals. If you can put some money aside every year and get a booth at Blade Show, your odds of being noticed by a writer will increase greatly. Perhaps even better are the sheer number of attendees that are there with one thing on their mind: buying knives.

While at Blade Show, you must do something to draw attention to yourself. You'll be in a room with hundreds of other knifemakers, and you must work to stand out. Bring a knife or two and do a couple free raffles during the show. This will get a crowd around your booth. When you have attracted the crowd, get them to make a bunch of noise. As a writer, I've given attention to a few different booths at Blade Show just to find out what all the commotion was about. Never be afraid to give away a knife or two for promotional reasons—just make sure that when you do, you make the absolute most of it and do it in a way that will garner the most attention. If you give away one knife but get thirty people to your booth doing it, chances are that you'll sell a few knives to those who didn't win but like what they see.

Whatever you do, do something that gets people talking. If you can get enough people talking, you might get a writer to wander by your table to see what the hype is all about.

There was one year I was at the show and I saw a line of people trying to get to a small booth. I had no idea what was going on and couldn't even get to it to find out. I later came to learn that the owner of the booth had managed to cause such a commotion on social media before the show that he literally had people lining up to buy tickets for the chance to win the opportunity to purchase one of his knives. It was so creative that I met up with him later that night just to find out his secret. He said it was just that he did a lot on social media and endeared himself to attendees that morning by bringing coffee and doughnuts to the people waiting in line to get in.

I'm not saying that this approach will work for everyone, but the more creative you are, the more likely you are to be noticed. Remember: when you're at these shows, you're not a knifemaker; you're a salesman. Be inventive and make yourself stand out in the crowd. Blade Show is packed with booths, and every one of them is selling knives—be bold, stand out.

Utilizing Social Media

Social media is the latest and greatest in mankind's search for the ultimate self-promotion tool. There are many ways to utilize social media to attract the attention of the right people.

Facebook has several viable avenues for showing your work. Check out the different knife groups that fit your style best. If you forge your knives, take the time to join groups specifically tailored to that. If you do kitchen knives, join kitchen-knife and chef groups, and so on. Posting your work regularly is a great way to get noticed. Sometimes writers quietly frequent many of the knife groups and troll for cool work. I have found a few really great makers that I had never heard of that way. Although Facebook is somewhat antiknife and isn't a good venue for knife sales, Facebook contacts can easily become future customers.

Along the same lines as Facebook, Instagram and Twitter are other great ways to get your work out. I personally find Instagram to be better because it's a bit more focused on this type of self-promotion and gives you more words to work with in your posts. There are many hashtags that get a ton of traction on Instagram—start looking around at some of the different trending topics involving knives and post some photos of your work using those hashtags.

Even though social media has become a dominant presence in the digital age, be sure to visit some message boards that are specific to your topic, like BladeForums.com. Many writers and editors continue to troll message boards, sometimes in search of new talent and sometimes just because they love knives too.

You should respect that forums are different than other forms of social media. Social media sites like Facebook and Instagram are built for shameless self-promotion, whereas message boards are built to be a community of people helping each other. If you join a forum, don't just go in and start pimping your work, or you'll find that it will have the opposite effect on potential contacts. People will be turned off to your work, not turned on. When you join a message board, seek first to become part of the community. Give good advice, ask intelligent questions, and get involved in off-topic conversations. Avoid the inevitable arguments and controversies that come with message boards. Eventually, people will get to know you on a more personal level and in turn will be interested in your professional endeavors.

Much like at Blade Show, occasionally be willing to do a promotional giveaway of some kind. Giveaways are a great way to gain followers. The more of a following you can build on your own, the more likely writers and editors are to take your work seriously. If your work has enough merit that you can garner a sizeable following of people who love your work and follow you on social media just to see more, this speaks volumes about the quality of your design and craftsmanship. Not many serious knife lovers will follow the account of someone who does shoddy work. The ability to gain a following simply by the value of your work can tell an editor much of what they need to know about you as a craftsman, your character and attention to your customers

Put Your Knives in the Right Hands

Another way to gain market attention is to seek out an online reviewer that has a solid following, take the monetary loss and put your best work in their hands. At the onset, you may incur a loss, but in the long run, it will gain the attention of more people than you could have attracted on your own. There are many writers and editors who follow these online reviewers and could be seeing your work for the first time.

When trying to select the right online reviewer(s) for your product, a simple online search of knife reviews will give you a good list of reviewers to consider. While researching the right person to send your work to, take a look at some of their videos or online articles. See if their style will work for you. Take a look at the comments they get; if they are generally positive toward the reviewer, they may be a good fit. Also, take a look at how many followers they have. For online personas, the number of followers speaks to the quality of work. Make sure to do your research so you're not sending a high-price product to someone who won't be able to give you any real returns on your investment.

Also, out-of-the-box reviewers can have their place, especially if you need the knife back to sell. But if you really want to get the attention of knife people, send your knife to someone who will really test it hard and report on every aspect of its performance—you'll be able to tell what type of reviewer they are by watching some of their other videos or reading their past blog posts. Many editors like to know that the knife they invest time in will be something that they can recommend to their readers in good confidence.

As with any promotion strategy, patience is required. You may not see an overnight result, and you may have to put your product into the hands of more than one reviewer. It may be that the right people didn't notice the first review, or it may be that they're waiting and watching to see if you're a one-hit wonder. Not that finding that one design that ends up being a unicorn is necessarily bad, but when an editor or writer invests their time or print space, they're investing in you as a maker. They're telling their readers to keep an eye on you for great things. If you can demonstrate high quality, with consistency, it will help to promote confidence in an editor or writer that when they recommend you to their readers, you won't disappoint with your next design(s). If you turn out to be a one-hit wonder, that can make the editor look like they didn't do their homework on researching you. If you damage your own credibility, you damage the credibility of those who have published your work.

Not all writers and editors watch the same reviewers. For the most part, writers all have friends throughout the industry and, most likely, pay more attention to them. The more industry professionals who get your knife in their hands, the more chance you'll have of your knife being seen by a writer. Writers also talk to each other at the major shows, and if there was something that really caught the eye of one writer or reviewer, they're likely to share with their friends in the industry.

Be Prepared to Have Your Knife Tested Hard

You can count on it for sure that when you send your knife to a reviewer of any kind, whether online or print, your knife will be tested hard. Make sure that the knife you send is prepared to go through rigorous tests without failure.

Good reviewers and the good magazines for which they write have built a following based on solid information. Anyone who takes what they do seriously won't just look at a knife and tell their followers that it's a good knife. They'll take it out and use it for its intended purpose and, for the most part, will use it hard. When we tell our readers/viewers that a knife is well built, comfortable, and held up to the testing, our name is on that recommendation, and we take that seriously.

If you send a knife for testing, make it your best work. Also, if you require the knife back, make sure you're prepared to put some work into it to bring it back to any kind of sellable form again. Expect to either write that knife off and let the reviewer keep it or use it to send out to up-and-coming reviewers with smaller but growing followings.

Buy Advertisements

I know you're thinking, *Here it is. I knew it! The game is rigged! Only paid advertisers get attention!* I want to make sure you understand exactly how this relationship works, because it isn't how you may think.

First, advertising dollars pay for publishing print media—subscriptions and newsstand sales aren't enough to cover the full costs of publishing a print magazine. If there were no advertisers, there would be no magazines.

Now put yourself in the position of a person who has paid for an ad. If you continually advertised in a magazine but never saw your products in print, would you continue to advertise with them? Probably not. Therefore, it's indeed true that magazines do have to pay extra attention to advertisers. It isn't backroom cronyism; it's survival. Let's also not forget that when you advertise with a large trade magazine, your knife will be placed in front of their entire reader base, which could prove to be far more valuable than the cost of the ad. The old adage rings true here: it takes money to make money.

Something else to consider regarding advertising is the message that buying an ad sends about you. If you don't believe enough in your product to put money toward it, why should an editor? Space is money in print media. Each magazine only has so many pages per issue, and considering the staggering number of knives that come out every year, editors are faced with the very difficult task of selecting the right knives to cover. There are many variables that go into choosing which knife to put in print—such as how photogenic the knife is, what category it fits in, what features may set it apart from others in its category, the story behind it, and so on—and sometimes it can come down to the small details, such as your own confidence in your work. It doesn't hurt to support a magazine when you're asking them for their support.

Purchasing an advertisement is a fast-track way of making sure that the editor sees your work. You may have great work, but if an editor doesn't happen to stumble on it at just the right moment, online or elsewhere, they may never see it. On the other hand, if they're flipping through the pages of their package to proof for publication and they see an advertisement with a great-looking knife, it may get their attention and make them want to know more.

Even with the symbiotic relationship between advertisers and magazines, advertisers aren't the only people that make it into print. There really is a very fair selection process that goes into what gets published.

Stay the Course

One of the most important things you can do when trying to get your knife published is be patient. You have to keep in mind that trade magazine editors get frequent requests for coverage but are limited in the page count of their magazine. They simply cannot cover every knife or knifemaker that comes their way. Patience is the only thing that will help you maintain your sanity during the sometimes-long road to publication. Often, it takes time and effort to get the attention of the right people.

The knife industry is very large and is growing more and more each year. With every new knifemaker and every new knife to hit the market, the selection process for editors becomes more difficult. I wish I could tell you that there was a simple or quick way to get published, but unfortunately, I cannot. This truly is a case of time and persistent effort ruling the day. The more time and effort you put into getting your work out there, the more likely you will be to have the right people notice it. It can be a long road, but it's definitely worth it. You must be willing to stay the course: don't quit a block from the finish line. What a shame it would be if you gave up early, only to find out later that you were on the brink of being noticed!

If you truly believe that your work is good enough to be published and placed into the hands of tens or hundreds of thousands of people, then it's worth your hard work and effort to make sure that happens. Good luck and I hope to see your work in print someday.

CHAPTER 21

Using Professional Photography

Jim Cooper/SharpByCoop Photography

OF ALL OUR senses, the strongest emotions are elicited through visual images. Look at any advertisement in any media, and the product will be shown *enhanced*: as it should be. Discretionary products that nobody "needs" have to become objects of desire in order for the sale to go through. "**No one needs a custom knife, they have to want it.**" This is where the professional photographer comes in, to highlight your hard work with the perfect high-quality visual images that are necessary to be competitive in today's knife market.

First impressions are a powerful signal, and lasting impressions are even stronger. We live in an age where we're surrounded by quality cameras. We carry one with us all day, and phone cameras now sustain the current hottest promotional format: social media. The process of using phone-camera images on social media is very immediate and easy to access, and the phone manufacturers and media companies work hard to make it so. This ease of use presents a *limitation* for most knifemakers, but an *opportunity* for a few astute makers.

The challenge for the individual maker is how to make your work stand out in a visual ocean of similar interests. The phone camera, however convenient, is only a mediocre source of images. Almost every knifemaker is posting pictures of their work from raw materials, to work in progress, to finished work, all from the convenience of their phone. Even so, everyone gets it: posting phone images to social media is a compromise. Makers get it, and so do the viewers. But—did you *dazzle* them? If you're reading this book, you're taking steps to become better at your work. "Better" implies not only progress relative to your previous efforts, but also better than your peers. The knife work is up to you. My challenge is to make images of your work that dazzle your potential clients.

Whether you realize it or not, your viewers are gauging your knifemaking effort and long-term sustainability through your visual presentations. Those makers who go the extra mile in visual presentation are duly noted. What's new in your product lineup? Have you improved your styles, execution, equipment or models? You need a continuous display of past projects, current models, and compelling new work to you in the forefront. By way of metaphor, consider that the display of your knives with professional-quality images is like wearing a suit instead of blue jeans. The presentation itself increases your status. You want that.

You have three choices when it comes to improving your visual presentation:

1. You can work with a professional photographer like me or one of my competitors.
2. You can try and improve your visual presentation yourself.
3. You can do nothing, and keep on getting what you've always got.

A professional-level knife image will use clarity and creativity to generate a commanding visual presentation. There are many things in a professional photograph that take some education in order to notice, and even more skill and experience to reproduce.

A professional image will have blade lighting, which has no reflections and is even along the entire length. Dark handle materials and edges will be visible without losing distinctiveness in shadowed areas. The knife will be centered in the image, with even spacing around the frame. Textures and rounded profiles benefit from intentional lighting highlights to make them more visible. The image shouldn't be too enhanced, nor too drab, as either is an untrue representation of the knife.

The technique of using multiple images inset into the same rectangle is a *very* powerful visual tool and allows multiple angles or knife elements to be viewed at once. When it's done well, a multi-image makes a statement that compounds visually beyond the attributes of separate images alone.

A Few Preliminary Words about How It's Done

Anyone who has tried to replicate a pro photo invariably determines that it isn't as easy as it appears. I have witnessed my own progressions since 2002 and continue to learn, refine, and improve. To this day, I maintain that professional knife photography is one part tools, one part technical skill, and one part artistic vision.

First and foremost, *directional* lighting is the critical tool of the professional knife photographer. Shooting knives is difficult for a few reasons. There are textures and curves that are left unpronounced with simple overhead lighting. Most knives have bright, shiny, beveled blades and darker absorbing handles. I use three light sources to illuminate a subject. Good knife images need clear, overhead lighting, strong side lighting, and added fill lighting for directing some light back into the darker areas.

Background selection is another significant aspect of professional picture composition. One always wants a backdrop to either enhance or be neutral to the subject. A background should never be a distraction. I cringe when I see a knife alongside a gun for "effect." The gun draws the eye. They say, "Don't bring a knife to a gunfight," and I suggest that you don't bring a gun to a knife photo either. Another amateur mistake is to use a background that is too "busy." If the texture or colors of the background are competing for attention with the knife, your photo won't show off the knife to maximum effect.

Everyone wants to know about cameras for taking quality photographs. I'd describe the camera hierarchy from high to low: medium format, DSLR, mirrorless, point and shoot, and cell phone cameras. Even though there are high-quality and high-cost cameras all the way down to phone cameras, camera selection isn't as crucial as you think. I use a 26mp Canon DSLR, and *only* use fixed (non-zoom) lenses. Telephoto just lenses aren't as crisp as a fixed lens, and I have a $250 50mm macro, which is *much* sharper than my $1,200 telephoto lens. However, use what you have to begin. Onboard cell phone cameras have gotten incredibly advanced, and I submit that I cannot educate you in an area I don't utilize. However, I have seen impressive shots from every format above. It's *more* about lighting than camera quality. Spend your time learning light control, and when you need *even* better pictures, *then* upgrade your camera.

My primary area of visual arts expertise is *photography*. While I don't consider myself qualified to offer technical advice with regard to the use of video for knife promotion, I have made one observation that I've found to be nearly universal for evaluation of knife videos. Neophyte videographers are notoriously long-winded. To captivate viewers and hold attention the video needs to be *short*. There's a famous line by Blaise Pascal who said, "I'm sorry for writing such a long letter. I didn't have time to write a shorter one." Creation of a short video demands efficiency of words and message, and it's hard work to do this. For further examples, one needs only look to how Instagram and Twitter have capitalized and thrived on shorter communication formats.

How to Create Basic Professional-Quality Photos

In order to illuminate and enhance the image, the photographer requires a minimum of two light sources and added fill reflectors. All of these light sources should be directed through a diffuser of some form.

You need one large overhead light source, which is positioned above and slightly behind the knife. This will be the source for the lighting of the blade itself. Drawing the source back ensures that the subtleties of the grinds, hollows, flats, and clips are all distinguished clearly and with the desired dramatic effect.

Another more powerful light, which can be focused smaller by size or position, illuminates the handle and any other area of the knife that has darker color or texture. I have contracted a supplier of Plexiglas mirrors to build an array of fill-in mirrors. They add subtle reflective light that really helps illuminate deep shadows and reveals important details.

A few inches of movement of my lights or reflectors can mask or reveal important shapes. Just like any other skill, practice and experimentation are critical. With the right equipment and a measure of practice, you will develop the skill to elevate your pictures from "good enough" to "exceptional."

Changing the angle of the piece by rolling the knife on its long axis is another area for experimentation. A slight lift of the knife using a bed of 3M sticky putty holds the knife at an angle, which improves the appearance from how it lies alone on a flat surface. This also gives the knife more depth and shadows for prominence within the overall frame.

These three sources are the basis of my photography. In truth, the proper positioning of all three of them, and the camera, is never something I can describe on paper. I beat a path around to adjust them all incrementally until my trials turn into a trophy shot. Consider this work as a puzzle worth solving.

With regard to camera setup, I typically shoot at F18 to F22. You want a large depth of field, and my images are sharp and in focus from tip to butt. High-intensity strobe lights also allow a shutter speed of 1/125th of a second, which allows for handholding the camera and does not require a cumbersome tripod between me and my work.

If you must capture your own work without proper equipment or setup time, outdoors under an overcast sky produces clearer images than harsh light bulbs. Using a homemade diffuser, even with sunlight as a source, is even better. *Professional* knife photography is never done "outside on an overcast day." While those images may be clear and lack the garish reflections of shooting in full sun, they are dreadfully flat, with no contrast where it's needed.

Further Considerations for Advanced Photography

As you move farther down the photography journey, you'll want to set up a dedicated area and maintain dedicated tools. The acquisition of a dedicated area and the tools to take good photos indoors have three main benefits. First of all, they're always ready, day and night, regardless of weather. There's no waiting for the perfect light outdoors, as you're comfortably inside. Second, dedicated equipment can be applied consistently, without the day-to-day variability of outdoor photography. The consistent ability to produce quality images becomes possible with dedicated equipment, with much more consistency than shooting outdoors. Finally, the quality of images you will be able to produce will be well above average relative to the phone shots that most makers post online. I know you don't want to be average, or you wouldn't be reading this book. Don't settle for average.

Equipment Considerations

For my primary lighting, I use strobes. It's hard for me to suggest them, as there's a learning curve; however, the benefits for me are incredibly powerful. Strobes can provide an abundance of light and allow camera settings to be so elevated that it actually becomes easier. My *greatest* need for strobes is so I may work quickly and efficiently *without* a tripod in my way. If you aren't shooting knife after knife, this is irrelevant. The costs of a pair of strobes range from import eBay monolight kits at $300 dollars a set, up to many thousands of dollars for a commercial grade setup. Truth is, for the *occasional* user, less expensive will work fine.

An important aspect about indoor lighting is to have proper daylight-balanced illumination, whether your source is strobe, florescent, or LED. Bulbs that produce light at 5,000K–5,500K are what you need. Incandescent bulbs in any form are a poor choice. They simply cannot produce *white* light. The best modern light solution will be LED lamps. They aren't hot, and can provide a great amount of light, performing just short of strobes. In using fixed LED lamps, you can also see exactly what the camera sees. Strobes use an always-on "modeling lamp," which offers some clue of the final lighting direction, and helps you see the work.

If you don't use strobes that allow you to increase your camera shutter speed, you will *have to use* a tripod. A tripod allows you to utilize the required higher f-stop for focus in standard lighting, which necessitates a longer shutter speed. You cannot steadily hand-hold below one-sixtieth second when you use a high f-stop (above f-16). You don't want any portion of your image out of crisp focus, and lower f–stops are notorious for having portions of the image blurry.

Regarding light boxes, if I saw good images consistently produced by those small cube light boxes, which work for knives, I would recommend them. Unfortunately, the inherent design is wrong for a flat, horizontal, shiny piece of metal. The part of the light box that the blade reflects needs to be lit from behind, *not* from front, top, or the sides. These light boxes are adequate for the hobbyist, at best. This isn't to say you have to lay out tons of cash. My own "professional-grade" diffuser is a composition of parts acquired at Lowe's/ Home Depot and an art supply store. I've built an angular tent with one-inch PVC tubing and fittings, and secured draftsman's vellum acetate tracing paper as the actual diffuser. This can be purchased in large sheets and even in a roll. The PVC frame is created according to the dimensions of the diffuser sheet.

When it comes to fill reflectors, I suggest you experiment with folded white paper, tinfoil, or my favorite: Plexiglas mirrors. I've found a couple of five-by-ten-inch reflectors will make a big improvement. I can't make your work look great without them.

Regarding backgrounds, less is always more. The most successful retailer in the world is Amazon, and they require resellers to offer common products on a plain white background. This setup is a measure of genius: just the product with no extraneous distractions. Our challenge is different from Amazon, however. We aren't just trying to show a product, we are trying to create *desire*. Plain white backgrounds are simply neutral at best and bland at worst.

The colors and light textures of your backgrounds should have enough interest to elevate the viewer's visual senses. I use specialty papers and wallpaper book sample backgrounds. Until you're very proficient, any objects other than your subjects will be a distraction. It's much more important to focus on the development great lighting and technique to enhance your hard work than it is to find the "perfect" background.

When it comes to the shape format of the photo, you'll have to consider whether to shoot landscape or portrait format. Portrait is great for viewing on cell phones and for full-page print displays. Landscape is best for PC browsers and other widescreen formats. Neither format is perfect for all usages. I always ask if the knifemaker has a primary purpose in mind for the image. The final crops to the image ought to be very tight. Fill the image with your knife!

Using Photos to Enhance Your Business

Others even more qualified than me have written a chapter on promotion and marketing, but it's much of my business as well. Here's an adjunct to their dialogue:

1. Show your best work everywhere, whether it's a pro photo or your own. If it's good, let the world see it. *Never*, in your zeal to show off a new exciting piece, take a "crappy cell phone shot" before you take a better shot. You just diluted the all-powerful first-impression hit.

2. The internet now has more impact than print. Your presence is mandatory. Instagram, Facebook, various knife forums, YouTube, and even Twitter offer two-way conversations. If you take a good photo, put it online. If you pay for a photo, part of getting your money's worth is to post it as many places as possible.
3. A clear website is a must. For many of your customers, your website is the final destination before they place an order. You need to link your social media presence to your website. Make your site relevant, brief and *compelling*. From there, point your customer to social media, which is where you may offer an in-depth view into your world. Contrary to social media, your website is a one-way dialogue, and you are at the podium. Speak well, show your work, and show yourself. Sell yourself, not only your knives. On your website, I strongly recommend a quality photo of you looking at your viewers. There's something primal and gratifying looking in someone's eyes. It becomes a connection rather than a display. You will instill trust and disarm a wary viewer through the simple act of looking at them with a smile.
4. Be kind and professional in your online interactions. The internet is the world's most rowdy playground, and it's up to you to be your own best ambassador. Behind every keyboard is a real human being, and it's up to us to move beyond angry fingers to find the heart of your viewers. Your present and future customers are judging you by your responses.
5. Don't overlook the connection between professionals. Editors of both print and online media know immediately what to expect from a Sharp by Coop photo. Editors know that if you've made the effort to purchase a professional picture, they're not only guaranteed a quality image for their publication, they also have an indication that you're serious about your work.

If you choose to invest in a professional image, then the rewards will be noted and returned. At a very real level, good pictures pay more than they cost. While you may eventually learn to take a quality photo, your time in learning these skills may reduce the time you can spend doing something you were better at, like making knives. Either way, don't do nothing. Ship your knife to a professional, or visit one of us at a knife show. At the end of the day, no one may read a thousand words, but they'll see your picture.

SECTION SIX

Advanced Forging

CHAPTER 22

How to Build a Power Hammer in Your Backyard

Jason Fry

I THINK ALMOST EVERY smith wishes at some point that he had a power hammer. They're loud, powerful, and they move metal quickly. They're also the key to improving the production speed of forging and Damascus steel, and speed without sacrificing quality quickly translates into increased revenue and more fun. It's under these conditions that the smith turns to the internet and begins to look for a hammer. Quickly the smith discovers several things.

First, the smith finds stories of people who got incredible deals on a hammer stored in a barn somewhere. These are like hunting stories of giant whitetail bucks, or fishing stories of twelve-pound largemouth bass: the story is true, but it's not likely to happen to you that way. If you're one of the lucky ones who find a running Little Giant fifty pound for $200 bucks at a garage sale, I don't like you, and I don't want to hear your story, LOL.

The next thing the smith discovers is that there are running hammers to be had in the world, and they're expensive. The odds of finding a working hammer in your area are slim, even if you're willing to pay retail. Whether they look at the new production hammers or rebuilt old ones, the price tag is steep, sometimes even five or ten thousand dollars. That's a lot of knives, and for many folks, there's no way to justify the purchase.

Desperate for a tool that seems just out of reach, the smith turns again to the internet and searches "how to build a power hammer."

How I Came to Build a Hammer

I competed on the History Channel's *Forged in Fire* in May 2018. My episode aired September 4, 2018. When you do a deal like that, they don't catch you by surprise. Rather, there's a lengthy application and approval process, and you're in for quite a while before you get your shooting date for your episode. In my case, there were several months between when I found out I would be on the show and when the episode was actually filmed. I thought about several ways to prepare. One way was to practice various smithing techniques. I forged quite a few blades and practiced my forge welding during this time. Another way to prepare is to work on equipment. I built a new forge out of castable refractory suitable for forge welding. I also decided to build a power hammer.

Here was my reasoning, by way of an analogy. If I work hard and lose fifty pounds to go on a vacation to the beach, and then it rains while I'm at the beach, my vacation sucked, but I still lost fifty pounds. Along the same line, I figured that if I made the final two on the show, I'd sure like to have a power hammer to use in the final build. If I was eliminated in the first two rounds, I'd be disappointed, but in the end, I'd still have a tool that few smiths get to have. So I spent five weekends in April and May building a spring-helve power hammer, a style often called an "Appalachian" or "rusty" hammer. Because I had a friend with an epic scrap yard, I was able to build the hammer for under $250 cash. I did end up trading a few knives to my friend for the metal as well. Lest I sound like one of those guys who found a cheap running hammer in a barn, I'd like to point out that I spent about fifty hours of actual work building my hammer over the course of a month. I could have built roughly $2,000 worth of knives during that time, maybe more. Between the time I spent and the knives I traded, I estimate I have roughly $3,500 in my hammer. For that price, I could have purchased a running and functional hammer. The reason for me to take the DIY path was cash outlay: I had more time than money. The following chapter is based off of my experience building this hammer, plus the research I did in the planning-and-building process.

Warnings

If you decide to build a power hammer, don't ever lose sight of the fact that you're building a mechanized tool for smashing stuff with great force, and that your appendages smash easier than steel. There's no risk in me sharing these plans with you unless you get a paper cut turning a page. There's great risk in building and using a hammer, and when you build one, you assume those risks. It won't be my welds that come apart if you build poorly or my hand that gets smashed if you don't design your hammer right: it will be yours.

I believe strongly that in order to successfully build a power hammer, you need several things. First and foremost, you need to be mechanically inclined. Building a hammer from scrap is exactly like building a race car from a tub of Legos, and nothing at all like building the same from a boxed Lego set. In a set, there are step-by-step instructions with pictures, and perfectly shaped pieces that fit together. If you build a hammer from scrap, there are no plans, instructions, or pictures. You'll have to sort through materials looking for a piece that fits or that will serve the purpose you need, just like when you dig through the Lego tub looking for four matching wheels. In addition to size and shape, you'll have to judge if the piece you just found is structurally strong enough for the task. If you don't have the necessary experience in mechanical design and fabrication, if you can't visualize and then build, if you can't anticipate future problems before you weld everything together, my opinion is that you should buy a hammer if you want one.

Second, you need to be able to weld, and you need a welding machine with high enough amperage to weld thick steel. An import 110v wire feed doesn't have the power to weld the sizes of steel that you'll need to build a hammer. I used a 220v 180 amp class wire feed, and it was underpowered for some of the heaviest welds on my hammer, requiring multiple passes to get adequate penetration. It's not what I'd recommend, but it's what I had. I can tell you that I became a much better welder over the course of building my hammer, as I gained experience using my machine to weld heavy steel. Will my welds hold? I think so, but if they don't, it's me who will get hurt, not you. Regarding welding method, stick or MIG or flux core wire feed is up to you, as all can do the job if the machine is powerful enough and you have the skills. If you don't have confidence you can weld steel well enough to hold up under extreme stresses, then you should buy a hammer.

Next, you're thinking of building a machine that is loud and heavy. If you work out of a one-car garage, or live in an apartment, it just won't work. If you have a HOA or live in a city with zealous code enforcement officers, good luck. If you have employees and need OSHA approval or insurance for your shop, you should buy a hammer. If you have touchy neighbors who already don't like the fact that you forge in the backyard because they're irritated by your two-hour hand-hammer-and-anvil sessions on Saturday afternoons, good luck. I'm fortunate to live in a neighborhood with neighbors who think my hobby is cool, in a city with weak code enforcement, and I have a shop in my backyard. All of this is less than ideal, but so far, I've had no trouble running the hammer during lawn-mowing hours. If you're fortunate enough to have a place in the country with no neighbors, hammer away. For the rest of us, we'd better plan ahead and be courteous about the times we make noise. As far as weight, I estimate my hammer weighs seven hundred pounds or so, and it's a light one. With a proper base plate and a heavy anvil, you're building a tool that could easily weigh fifteen hundred pounds. If you work in sales, oilfield, church work, or some other vocation where you end up moving every few years, you need to think about how you're going to move your hammer should the need arise. I personally built mine where there were several bolt-together joints so I can break my hammer down into parts of a few hundred pounds each that can be lifted with an engine hoist.

Finally, a good source of scrap metal is a must if you want to build your hammer economically. If you have to go buy steel at retail, you'll end up spending as much as a new hammer costs. If you can score your steel for cheap to free, you're good to build.

If by this point in the chapter you still want to build a hammer, read on, and I'll talk you through some of the things I learned in my build.

Which Style?

The first thing you'll have to decide is which style of power hammer you will build. There are as many designs as there are folks who build hammers, but they fall into two basic categories: helve hammers and linkage hammers. At the basic level, a helve hammer has an arm that moves up and down on a fulcrum to move the hammer head up and down. A linkage hammer uses a wheel, tire, or disk that rotates and uses the rotation to move the hammer head up and down. The Little Giant uses a linkage, as does the commonly home-built tire hammer. I personally chose to build a spring-helve hammer, because I had access to a variety of leaf springs, and because the design is more intuitive and less mechanically precise. I figured (correctly) that I could make up a helve-hammer design from scratch, but that a tire hammer had some engineering points that would be difficult for me to figure out. If you have access to uniform steel sizes or have to purchase your steel, I suggest a tire hammer. I had good scrap and didn't want to purchase much. My "tub of Legos" was better suited to the helve hammer.

First, Go Find a Unicorn

There are many different things that can make a suitable anvil for a power hammer, and many more things that do not. While it may sound simple to just go to a scrap yard and get something heavy, reality isn't that simple. What you're looking for in an anvil is a solid piece of steel that weighs anywhere from 150 to 600–800 pounds. They don't grow on trees, and they're hard to find. Sometimes you can find solid square or round bar. Some folks recommend railroad axles. Others suggest forklift tines welded together. I've seen sections of two-inch-square bar welded together into a solid six-by-six. I've seen pieces of one-inch plate welded where the hammer strikes the ends. Whatever you can find needs to be solid or able to be welded into a solid, single massive piece, and your welder has to have the power to stick it all together. My personal hammer is built on a thirty-two-inch piece of five-inch round bar welded inside a mud pump sleeve that has a five-inch bore. The total weight of my anvil is around four hundred pounds.

Anvil Assembly

Don't be tempted to think that you can get a piece of something hollow like pipe or square tubing and fill it up and make a suitable anvil. Each stroke of your hammer pounds the steel in between the hammer head and your anvil, pushing your anvil toward the ground. If you have any movement, vibration, or give in your anvil, the force is absorbed by the movement and not efficiently transferred to your workpiece.

When you finally find this difficult-to-find thing, it won't likely be the size or shape that you want. My anvil was round, which doesn't as easily weld to square tubing, for example. I had to deal with it. My anvil was around four hundred pounds total weight. Yours may be more or less. You should design your hammer with a minimum of 1:10 head to anvil ratio. Since I had a four-hundred-pound anvil, I built a forty-pound head. If all you can find is a two-hundred-pound hunk of steel for your anvil, you should stick to a twenty-pound head or so. Design your hammer around your anvil, as the anvil is the hardest part to find.

Another consideration is the base that your hammer will sit on. My personal hammer currently sits on a wood deck in front of my shop, far from ideal. To compensate for the flexibility of the deck, I built my hammer on top of a set of bolted-together railroad timbers topped with a piece of steel plate. I was only able to find quarter-inch plate, far less than ideal, but enough to weld the various components of my hammer to, and then lag screwed into the railroad ties. I'd recommend the thickest steel plate you can find, mounted on the firmest foundation you can muster. If I could have built on one-inch plate, and bolted that to a twenty-four-inch-deep concrete pad set into a concrete shop floor, I'd have done it. I had to make do with what I could find in my "free" scrap yard, and deal with the limitations of my shop setting.

Center Post

For a spring-helve hammer, you need a center post. This post should be heavy enough to withstand the extreme forces involved in rocking a spring arm with a heavy hammer on one end. I used a piece of four-inch tubing with half-inch walls. Others have used thinner walled but larger cross section square or rectangular tubing, heavy-walled pipe, or sections of I beam. Fortunately, straight sections of heavy material aren't all that hard to come up with.

Springs

I used a set of leaf springs for my rocker arm. The arm is also called a "helve." When it comes to selecting your springs, if you have several to choose from, choose a set that is sufficiently stiff. If you have the choice between sets that are more curved versus more straight, choose the straighter ones. If you have a choice between a spring set with more springs that are thin versus fewer springs that are thick, choose the set with the thinner springs. If you have the choice between sets that are longer or shorter overall length, either one will work, but you'll have to consider this dimension as you lay out the distance between the center post, the anvil, and the drive wheel. The length of your spring pack coupled with your stroke length will impact the speed at which your hammer will safely run. I personally began with a single set of rear springs off of a Chrysler minivan. They were wide at two and a half inches, but each individual spring was only a bit over quarter-inch thick. These springs were too soft and flexible. I then added springs from the other side, to make essentially a doubled set of minivan springs, which was still too soft. Finally I added another spring from an unknown set that had similar curvature but was closer to three-eighths inches thick and much stiffer. The combination of all the van springs plus the thick one was stiff enough. The spring action and whip action of the spring set during cycling increases head speed at contact, which improves performance. You'll have the same trial-and-error process I did as you try to tune your hammer and make it run right.

Springs and center swivel

Your spring set needs to swivel or rock on top of your center post. I built my hammer with the springs riding on top of the shaft and the shaft riding in pillow block bearings. Some have built with flange bearings, and others with the shaft above the springs. Any configuration is fine, provided you have the clearance you need for the springs to rock back and forth as the hammer operates.

Your spring set will need a swivel on the end where it connects to the pitman arm (the rod that connects the spring arm to the drive wheel). Like the top pivot, there are as many different designs as there are guys building hammers.

The end of the spring set near the hammer head needs to be connected in a way where the arc of the spring travel is converted into direct, linear up-and-down energy. Again, there are multiple ways to accomplish this. I went with a set of rollers on the hammer head, and the spring rides in and out on the rollers as it arcs up and down. I have seen designs with toggle linkage as well.

Hammer head rollers

Hammer Head/Tup

The entire twenty-five-pound power hammer, they're referring to the tup weight. Again, you're looking for a tup weight that is roughly one-tenth of your anvil weight. I built my hammer with a piece of two-inch solid square stock long enough to make a forty-pound tup. For lighter weight heads, you can use a piece of solid for the contact area and tubing or pipe to make up the extra length you need. While the anvil being solid is critical to the function of the hammer, the hammer head itself only needs to be solid on the end in order to properly transfer the force.

The tup rides up and down in a set of guides. You're converting an arcing spring movement into a linear, up-and-down hammer movement. Again, there are as many different designs as there are hammer builders. One consideration is that your guides need to account for lateral movement in all four directions. The simplest way is for the guide to completely enclose the hammer shaft. Contact surfaces between the hammer head and guide should be lubricated, and steel on steel isn't advised. Bearing surfaces should be made of UMHW plastic, or of bronze. These surfaces benefit from a degree of adjustability to make sure that the hammer head is aligned properly with the anvil. I used set screws and a UMHW plastic cutting board on my hammer, with lithium grease as well. My hammer runs well with fresh grease, and less well without. I grease the hammer shaft at the beginning of every forging session. The vertical position and length of your guides should accommodate the various stroke lengths of your hammer. You don't want the hammer head hitting the bottom of the guide on the upstroke, nor the spring connector hitting the top of the guide on the down stroke.

Pitman Arm

A stiff arm connects the spring pack to the rotating wheel, converting the rotary action of the flywheel to a straight up-and-down rocking motion. This type of arm is called a "pitman arm." It's not important what your pitman is made of, whether solid, pipe, or threaded rod. What is important is that your arm is adjustable for length, as this dimension will ultimately be changed as you tune your hammer by trial and error, or as you adjust your hammer to accommodate varying thicknesses of stock or the use of swages or top and bottom tools. Many designs use a turnbuckle. Again, you're going to have to dig around in your proverbial box of Legos and find parts that will work. The arm will be connected on one end to your spring pack, and on the other end to your rotating flywheel. You'll have to plan for those connections. I used a toggle linkage on the top, and for the bottom of the arm, large bolts welded to a piece of plate which was then bolted to the hub of the tire I used for a clutch. This is another area where your available parts and mechanical experience will dictate your design.

The Clutch

Like a variable-speed hand drill, you want your hammer to be able to run slowly, at full speed, or in between, depending on the task. The simplest way to do this is to use a slipping clutch, and there are two main clutch designs. One design uses a slack belt, a flywheel, and pulleys. The drive pulley rotates within a slack belt. The foot pedal linkage pushes an idler wheel into the slack belt, increasing the belt tension to the point that the belt begins to turn the pulley on the flywheel. Another design uses a tire clutch, where the foot pedal linkage pushes a drive wheel into an automobile tire, with the hub of the tire serving as the flywheel. The most common tire-hammer design uses a similar clutch, but turned the other way and connected to a linkage. For my personal hammer, I had the minivan axle, so I used an integral tire clutch/flywheel assembly. Your available parts will dictate your design.

Tire Clutch

A function of the clutch is to reduce the RPM of the motor speed in order to get the hammer rate of beats per minute (BMP) into a safe and useful range. You want the BPM of the hammer to generally end up between 150 and 250 BPM, although there are many variables that change with each individual hammer. In general, a heavier tup requires a slower BPM, where a lighter hammer can have a higher BPM. You don't want your hammer running faster than you can control it, nor so fast that the inherent forces tear your hammer apart. My particular hammer uses a twenty-four-inch tire and a three-inch drive wheel for an 8:1 reduction of a 1750 RPM motor, yielding a calculated 218 BPM at full speed. Your hammer will run differently depending on your motor RPM, your drive and driven wheel diameters, and the overall design of your hammer. I can also say that my hammer running full speed will overhit uncontrollably on small stock such as three-eighths-inch round bar, although full speed works acceptably well for drawing out Damascus billets. I rarely run my hammer full speed, and the tire clutch gives good speed control.

My tire clutch has an integral flywheel bolted to the hub. On the flywheel I welded several different nuts for attaching the pitman arm. Each nut is a different distance from the center of the hub. This allows me to vary the length of the stroke, in my case between six and a half inches, seven inches, and seven and a half inches, based on where I connect the arm to the flywheel. Coupled with an adjustable length pitman arm, this setup allows a degree of tuning to get the hammer hitting in a way that transfers the power directly to the workpiece with efficiency, and yet in a way that doesn't place undue stress on the hammer itself.

Motors

As far as motors, the size of the motor may vary a bit depending on the overall tup weight of your hammer. For most home-built hammer sizes, a 1 HP or 1.5 HP motor is plenty. My forty-pound hammer uses a 1.5 HP motor running on 110v and does not trip a standard fifteen-amp breaker, suggesting that 1.5 HP is more than plenty for a forty-pound head. Whether the motor runs on 110 or 220 will depend on your shop setup and what you have available, but you'd be best served either way with a motor that runs in the 1700 RPM range, not one that runs in the 3400 RPM range. You will need an on/off switch for your motor. To run the hammer, you turn the motor on and then use the foot pedal linkage to engage the clutch.

Dies

Most power hammers have a set of dies in between the anvil and the hammer shaft. Dies may be built in a variety of shapes and sizes, depending on how you want your hammer to move the metal. Two basic die designs are flat and crowned. Flat dies move the metal somewhat equally in all four directions, while crowned dies will draw out the length of your workpiece perpendicular to the crown on the dies. Some smiths design their hammers to accommodate various top or bottom tools or spring swages as well. On my personal hammer, the dies are built out of 1.5-inch-square 4140 steel bar stock, heat-treated. I have them ground essentially flat, with slightly radiused corners. I'd like to experiment with other die shapes as I progress, but I haven't got there yet. Some hammers are set up with dies that are interchangeable. My particular hammer isn't.

Hammer head and dies

I can't emphasize enough the creativity necessary to build a functioning power hammer from scrap. One thing that was exceptionally helpful for me was looking at pictures and videos online. Each time I hit a design snag, I was able to look at pictures and focus on that particular part of the design. Even though there's huge variability in designs, I was able to see enough different versions of each part that I was able to make it work. It's one thing to watch a YouTube video and think, *It must be nice to have a power hammer.* It's another thing entirely to watch the same video to try to discern how the rocker arm connects to the center post, or how the tire clutch axle is set up. At the time of my hammer build, there was an online gallery hosted somewhere in Eastern Europe that had hundreds of pictures of various home build and factory build hammers. I couldn't have built my hammer without those examples.

My power hammer has become an essential tool in my shop, to the point that I sometimes wonder how I ever lived without it. Even yet I have only begun to explore its full potential. I built my hammer for *Forged in Fire*, and was fortunate to make the final. I was able to come home and use my hammer to build my final weapon. I lost the contest, much like the rain on the beach vacation, but in the end, I still have a power hammer, and I can still take pride in the fact that I built it myself from little more than a pile of junk.

CHAPTER 23

Passing the Journeyman Smith Performance Test

Ed Caffrey, ABS Master Smith

FOR MANY PEOPLE, knifemaking at some point becomes less difficult as we learn how to consistently make tools that cut. Most of us don't routinely make knives designed to bend, and so the American Bladesmith Society (ABS) journeyman smith (JS) test is somewhat intimidating. Let's look closely at the process of making a blade that will pass the JS performance test.

The basic criteria for the test blade include a maximum of fifteen inch overall length, and a maximum ten-inch blade with the blade no more than two inches from spine to edge. The basic elements of the performance test include cutting a one-inch free-hanging sisal rope in one stroke, and then chopping through a two-by-four twice. After the chop, the blade must shave hair along its length as a measure of edge retention. The blade must then sustain a ninety-degree bend without failure. I highly recommend that you read the requirements for the blade and the performance testing multiple times directly from the ABS standards. Don't just take my word for it.

Choosing the proper steel is a must in order to pass the ABS JS test, and I highly recommend 5160. Don't be fooled by it only having 60 percent carbon.

With proper heat-treating, it will easily pass all phases of the test. I will take you through step-by-step explaining the manner in which I would produce a blade to pass the ABS JS test with 5160 steel. Either on an a quarter inches or one and a half inches by a quarter-inch is the best size to start with for a test blade.

Forging Your Blade

Begin forging with the highest heats you intend to use and then progressively reduce the heats throughout the forging process. Pay close attention and don't let yourself be distracted from the forge! This is where most people let their minds wander and, without realizing it, let the blade overheat. Overheating causes the grain to grow dramatically, which can introduce brittleness to your final blade. The reducing heats are intended to refine grain structure as you go through the forging process. Ensure you leave extra "meat" at the edge as "sacrificial" material that will be ground away after the heat-treat process. Remember that you may use either a full or hidden-tang blade for the JS test, but for safety sake, I recommend forging a full tang unless you feel supremely confident that you can make a hidden tang that will pass the bend test.

Normalizing

Normalizing is a critical step in a high-performance blade. Once forging to shape is complete, heat the blade to just critical temp, and allow it to *completely* cool in still air. This has the effect of relaxing all the internal stresses that have been built up during the forging process, and will eliminate 90 percent of warpage problems. Multiple cycles are of great benefit, and you should experiment to achieve optimum results in your shop.

Thermal Cycling

Thermal cycling is basically an "insurance" step that can be used in conjunction with or in place of the normalizing step. This step involves heating the forged blade to *not more* than 1350F, and then allowing it to cool to *below* 900F. If you have a heat-treat oven, these steps can be completed with precise temperature control. If necessary, turn your forge down (provides better control), and then *do not be distracted by anything*. Bring the entire blade and tang to an even heat that is *not more than* 1350F. Visually this will be a *very* dull red, where the red color is just visually perceptible. If you're judging by eye, place the blade in a shadowed area near your forge to better see the actual color. Once the blade and tang are evenly heated to the temperature and color indicated, place it on a rack of some type to cool. *Do not* lay it on its side on the anvil or any other heat sink! Allow the blade to cool to at least 900F. There will be no color in the blade, but it will still be too hot to handle with welding gloves. Allowing it to cool more isn't an issue, but not allowing it to cool enough is. Repeat for a total of three times and then proceed to the annealing step. Proper thermal cycling will "repair" any grain enlargement that occurred during the forging step, and will ensure a fine, tight grain structure for the remaining operations.

Annealing

Once the blade has completely cooled, it's time to anneal. Bring the blade to a little past nonmagnetic, and place in a slow cooling media. I recommend vermiculite. Sand isn't a good insulator, and ashes draw moisture, which can result in hard spots (something you certainly *do not* want at this point). I usually do my annealing in the evening, and allow the blade to cool overnight. Routinely it takes a test blade sized piece of steel six-to-ten hours to fully cool in vermiculite. This step reduces grain size within the steel, and may be accomplished multiple times for added benefit. Like normalizing, multiple annealing cycles are of added benefit to both 5160 and 52100.

Rough Grinding

After annealing, the blade is profiled and the shape refined prior to the final heat treatment. Distal tapers can be refined or added at this point. Ensure you leave enough extra material in the edge so as not to overheat it during hardening. I recommend about the thickness of a nickel. I choose to call this extra material "sacrificial," as it acts like a protective shroud to what will be the working edge of the blade. After rough grinding is complete, ensure you go over the entire blade with at least 120 grit to eliminate the possibility of stress risers that may be caused by large scratches that are left from the course grit belts. Also, ensure that there are no sharp angular transitions in the knife profile, as the point of an angle is another potential stress riser. A stress riser is a point at which a crack may form, causing the blade to break.

Hardening

When it comes to hardening, keep in mind that we are talking about 5160 steel. You will read conflicting recommendations about edge quench versus a soft back draw. While I typically don't edge quench production knives, I recommend edge quenching *only* on a blade that will be used for something as important as the ABS JS test. I *do not* endorse fully hardening a blade, and "soft back" drawing. Most people don't draw the spine back correctly, and so very often a soft backed knife will end with the blade breaking during the bending portion of the performance test.

If you don't already have one, make a "limiter plate" for your quench tank. This is nothing more than a quarter-inch-to-three-eighth-inch thick piece of aluminum that is full of three-eighth-inch holes. At each corner drill and tap a quarter-inch-by-twenty hole and use carriage bolts with the heads facing the bottom of the quench tank, and screwed into the holes at each corner of the plate. This will allow you to raise and lower the quench depth to fit any blade. The limiter plate should be set so that about a third of the blade enters the oil. Preheat the quenching oil. If you're using vet grade mineral oil, preheat the oil to approximately 130F. Be careful here: *do not* quench in mineral oil if the oil is 180F or higher. At this temp the oil won't cool the steel fast enough to achieve full hardness and your blade won't pass the chopping portion of the ABS JS test. If you're using a fast quench oil such as Parks 50, I recommend using it at room temp (50–70F). You will likely have to experiment based on what kind of quench oils you have available.

Using approximately a #3 welding tip on an oxy-acetylene torch, and with a *soft* flame (a flame that does not roar, but has a very mild hiss), start heating the ricasso area near the edge. As soon as the ricasso starts to turn color, then start to work the blade back and forth along the edge until the entire edge area is just past nonmagnetic. I recommend going slightly past nonmagnetic because the actual critical temp for most steels is approximately 150F beyond nonmagnetic. You also must consider that there will be a certain amount of heat lost between removing the torch and getting the blade into the quench oil.

This heating step may also be performed with a salt tank, heat-treat oven, or even the forge, but be forewarned: the chances for mistakes are much greater than if you have practiced edge hardening with the torch. Remember: your only goal here is to create a blade that will pass a given set of circumstances, the ABS performance tests. You're not building an everyday user knife, or even a knife like you would build for your paying customers. Although I'm an advocate of differential heat-treating, and believe with experience and correct application that it creates an outstanding "user," it's certainly not the only way to harden a blade. However, in my experience differential hardening is the best way to harden if your goal is to pass the ABS performance tests.

Once the entire edge is an even temperature just above nonmagnetic, quench by placing the tip into the oil first, for a count of seven, and then rock the rest of edge into the oil for another count of seven. Continue rocking the blade back and forth in this manner until all the "fumes" have ceased. At this point, slide the blade off the limiter plate, and allow it to cool *completely* in the oil, to room temp. Repeat the process twice more for a triple quench. Once the final quench/cool cycle is complete, grind off the scale with a 120 or 220 grit, and get ready to temper.

Tempering

Preheat your oven to 350F. If you're using a kitchen oven, don't trust the dial. I strongly suggest an oven thermometer (I use two just to make sure). Let the oven cycle for twenty-to-thirty minutes to achieve a level, even heat, and place the blade on the middle rack for *at least two hours*. Allow the blade to cool to room temp between tempering cycles, and repeat for a total of three tempering cycles.

Final Grinding

Final grinding is where the rubber meets the road. To this point you have set everything else up for a fine convex grind, and a nice flowing, distal taper. Finish grinding can be a slow process, because you're dealing with a blade that has been heat-treated. You should be grinding bare handed. If the blade gets too hot to hold, then it's too hot period! I start with a fresh fifty-grit belt, cleaning up the tapers and then remove excess material from the flats of the blade. I usually will flat grind with the fifty and then a 120, which will reduce weight and thin down the area just above the edge. Once I hit 220, I go to a convex grind. I do this through a modification I made to the grinder platen, where there's approximately a two-inch area that is slack just below the platen and above the lower contact wheel. Your goal at this point should be for the edge to be very close to "sharp" by the time you finish with a four-hundred-grit belt, as well as having the spine rounded and all sharp corners removed. Sharp corners can, and often do cause blades to fail in the ninety-degree bend test.

Just to make things easier when hand sanding, I often go over the blade with a six-hundred-grit belt to get as many four-hundred-grit scratches out as possible. Once you have completed with the belt grinder, go to the bench and hand sand out all the scratches with four-hundred-grit paper. I prefer the final finish to be lengthwise, with the scratch pattern following the blade's length. Even though the ABS rules state that the blade need not be highly finished, *finish your blade*! I can usually tell when a potential JS walks into my shop to test based on the outward appearance of their test blade as to whether or not they will pass. The level of finish on the blade is an outward and immediate indication of how careful an individual has been with the overall process. To date, my initial predictions have not been proven wrong, particularly in those cases where I have not met the person before prior to the testing.

Handles, Guards, and Bolsters

The test blade isn't required to be a highly finished piece, and therefore guard and bolster aren't necessary. I recommend some type of Micarta or phenolic for the handle slabs. Both materials are very tough, and will lend support to the tang area during the bending phase of the test. Don't use large handle bolts that force you to drill large holes in the tang! This will only serve to weaken the tang, and could cost you dearly during the test. I suggest holding the handle material in place with epoxy, and at the maximum, a couple of one-eighth-inch pins, peened to hold the handles.

The number one thing that will get you through the test easily is paying close attention to details! Superior heat treatment, proper distal tapers to distribute the bending stresses, a fine convex grind, and rounding all sharp corners are all details to be attended to. I personally like to see a test blade that has been etched lightly in ferric chloride to reveal the temper line and the grain structure. This is also key, in that if the blade isn't finished to the point where a light etch will show the temper line and grain structure, I believe it isn't finished enough for the test.

Many qualified smiths may insist on using another type of steel, and that is fine. As long as you have enough experimentation and experience to ensure all the desired characteristics are there, other steels can pass the test. In the past, individuals have passed the JS test with a variety of steels such as O-1 1095, 1084, 52100, and 80CrV2. However, these passing individuals had taken the time and effort to work out the "kinks" of their chosen steel. More aspiring JS applicants have passed the test with 5160 than with any other steel: that should speak volumes!

This article is intended as a general guide to creating a blade that will pass the ABS JS tests, and is in no way a guarantee of success. In the end, your success depends on your understanding of proper blade design in relation to function, and to applying the necessary concentration and attention to detail throughout the *entire* process of creating a test blade. These are proven methods from twenty-five-plus years of bladesmithing experience, and should be of much value to anyone interested in achieving their ABS JS rating.

Good luck!

SECTION SEVEN

Expanding Your Knife Business

CHAPTER 24

Lean Manufacturing for the Knifemaker

John Gulso

IF YOU HAVE ever worked in manufacturing, you're likely groaning inwardly as you read the title of this chapter. You're either mentally preparing to refute what you're anticipating it will propose, or actively turning the page to get to the next section. The rest of you, having never worked in a manufacturing environment, may be wondering why I'd say such a thing. In short, the concept of lean manufacturing has been often perverted and misused by those who don't understand the ultimate goal of going lean before diving headfirst into system-wide implementation. Like many a half-baked plan, that experience often leads people to having a bad taste in their mouth for something that can be extremely beneficial. Lean concepts can be helpful to address many manufacturing concerns, whether you're a sole proprietor or an international corporation.

What Is Lean Manufacturing?

Lean manufacturing is a systematic approach to minimizing waste without sacrificing productivity. Where people go wrong is to apply only portions of the idea, rather than the entire conceptual framework. Some administrators latch onto "systematic approach" and throw out "without sacrificing productivity." Others focus on the "minimizing waste" without a systematic approach. In order to utilize lean, especially for the individual knifemaker, you must embrace the entire concept as a whole, for the whole is greater than the sum of its parts.

Lean is about reducing waste, but what is waste? Waste comes in many forms. When asked this question, I wager most knifemakers would immediately say "scrap material." It's physical, it's easy to see, and you paid hard earned dollars for material you end up throwing away, which is tough to swallow. That idea of waste is right, to an extent. We definitely have waste material, and none of our processes allow for 100 percent material utilization. It's not physically possible. Just because scrap is the easiest to see however, doesn't mean it's the most important waste area to improve.

The Most Important Resource

As an individual craftsman, what is your most important resource? Your most valuable resource is time. If you're anything like me, you waste a lot of time. If you've ever been to the point where you said, "Enough is enough," and you stopped everything to clean your entire shop, put everything away, throw away broken tools, sharpen dull drills, reorganize your belts, chase down all of the scraps of sandpaper, and when you were done you gave a big sigh of relief—and then proceeded to tear it apart looking for that broach that you *knew* was just sitting on your bench before you "hid" everything, you could benefit from a little "5S."

5S is a concept many makers practice at least to some extent. Usually those of us who are already organized people are doing at least a little bit. 5S means sort, set in order, shine, standardize, and sustain. In short, 5S starts with "a place for everything and everything in its place." Many of us fall short at one or more of these individual actions. Personally for me, it's sustain. For others who seem to have, on the surface, very neat, tidy and organized shops, it may be standardize that suffers.

How do the first few projects go for you after your whirlwind shop-cleaning exercise? In my experience, they are almost seamless. That drill I needed was right where it was supposed to be. My workbench had so much space I couldn't mess up my blade finish no matter where I set it down. The vises were empty when I needed them, and I didn't have to dig through ten "some-life-in-these" belts to get to the fresh, sharp belt I really needed at the moment. 5S is about making every day in your shop like that first day after a cleanup marathon. So where do you start?

Sort

Sort out your stuff. Put like items with other like items. Get rid of those things that you don't use, can't use, or really have no value. That well-worn ceramic belt may have cost nine dollars, and it may possibly be useful for that one task, but it isn't worth having to dig past it every time you need a newer belt. At the very least, if you can't bear to part with old, worn, or broken tools, segregate them away from the things you need on a daily basis. You might find that you've never dug into that pile of stuff months down the road, and throwing it out doesn't seem as such a bad idea.

Set in Order

Certain areas of your shop will have specific items needed in those areas. Organize those items and put them in those areas. No one would think it makes sense to store belts on the other side of their shop from their grinder, so apply that to everything. Ask yourself, "Where do I use this too the most?" and then put that tool within reaching distance. Mark out or label the spot, so that if the tool is something you would put away after using it, you put it in the same location. For tools that you use in multiple areas, make their location central so, no matter where you need them, they're within a few steps.

Shine

Shine always gets questioned. Does how does whether things are clean things really impact my productivity? I can answer that question with another question. How many times have you dropped a 2-56 screw, or a Corby bolt, or a pin on the floor? You can imagine how much easier it is to find when the floor is swept clean versus littered with chips from your mill or swarf from your grinder. Clean bench tops don't stain handles or leatherwork or scratch hand-finished 62 RC blades. Clean grinders don't throw plumes of dust in the air each time you turn them on.

Standardize

Standardization is very difficult when you're beginning your journey into knifemaking. You want to try every belt on the market, every technique you read on a forum or in a book, make every kind of blade you can imagine and you want to do it all right now. This is a trap, and because we're drawn to this craft by our personal desires, we inevitably jump down various rabbit holes to satisfy our own curiosity. Playing the field to find the best sixty-grit roughing belt for you is fine. But ordering a different brand or type every time without rhyme or reason other than to try something new isn't productive. Find something that works for you, learn how to use it, buy the same thing next time so you don't have to relearn the intricacies of pressure, speed, tracking, and performance with every new belt order. Apply that to all of your consumables. Apply it to your style of knifemaking. Standardization may be a challenge, but is especially important for a beginner or intermediate level maker looking to become more efficient. Making the same three or five knife styles, from the same materials, over and over may become mundane, but you're forming habits while you do it, and learning seemingly minor things that all add up to being able to "make one of those with my eyes shut." When you get to that point, throw another into the mix. At a certain point, you won't have to "try and see if this works" any longer. You'll be able to put a knife you've never made down on paper with complete confidence that you can complete it, efficiently, just how you've drawn it.

I could write an entire essay on standardization, the elimination of variables and how we're our own worst enemy at times, but for the purpose of 5S, that's probably sufficient.

Sustain

Once you've eliminated the clutter, you've put things in order, you've shined up the shop and you've standardized your work and tools, then comes the hard part: Sustain what you've done. You marked or labeled where things go so you'll put them away when you're done using them. Do it! The next time you order sandpaper, don't toss it on the bench to put away when you get around to it. Put it away! Take the time *every day* to clean up your work area. This is hard to do, especially if you're part time and only have scant hours here and there to work. You don't want to spend it cleaning. But having the discipline to stop working on your project fifteen or twenty minutes before you absolutely have to crawl into bed is worth it. Even if it's more time spent cleaning up measured cumulatively over time compared to a big whirlwind shop cleaning once a month, every second saved by not wondering where you set your caliper this time, or where the last place you used that C-clamp was adds up to a huge savings in both time, stress, and even money. I can't be the only one to purchase something twice because I either forgot I bought it the first time, or put it somewhere it doesn't belong only to be unable to find it when I needed it.

Do this every day for twenty-one days, and it will become a habit. It will become second nature to leave your shop in the same or better condition than when you started, every day. When it becomes habitual, the improvement to your efficiency will become measurable, and the reduction in stress that accompanies it, immeasurable.

How else can the individual knifemaker leverage lean manufacturing to eliminate waste of your most important resource? If you've gone through all the steps of 5S, then you've standardized at least a portion of your work. That opens a number of possibilities to you. Begin evaluating what you should personally have control over in order for your product to meet your standards. How much time do you spend profiling a blade? How much material do you lose doing it yourself? Are the rough cuts the final surface finish on a completed knife? When considered from this angle, the expense of outsourcing your blade profiling to either a water-jet or laser-cutting supplier becomes much more reasonable. When you buy a two-inch-wide stick, at best you're throwing away 40 percent of it after band sawing your profile out. Buying a twelve-inch-wide plate and having a water-jet or laser provider nest your design will get you much better material utilization. Not only that, but also they can place your holes in relative location with likely greater precision than you could by whatever method you use currently. Even if those holes aren't *finished* size, they can be sized in a way that all it takes is a single pass with a reamer for them to be precisely located and sized for your fasteners.

You've gone from sawing, grinding close to your lines with a rough belt, grinding to your lines with a finer belt, laying out and drilling every hole, deburring everything, to taking a nearly finished blank, reaming holes to size and zipping around the profile with a 120 belt to set a foundation for your finish. This is likely a three-to-one improvement in time, depending on the complexity of the blade. Add in some odd shaped cut outs and it's probably four- or five-to-one. You still retained control of the design. You retained control of the finished product. But for twenty-five knives, you reduced your time and material expense significantly. Heat-treating is another example that can be outsourced for that batch of knives. The amount of time and energy saved for what someone like Bos or Peter's charges is incredible, and you've eliminated a lot of variables in your process. It's hard for some of us to do because it takes some of the fun out of what we're doing. But to become more productive, with less variability in the quality of your product, professional heat-treating service is something worth investigating.

To conclude, this is a rather brief overview of how lean manufacturing concepts can help the individual knifemaker reduce variability in his or her process, and become more productive and profitable. I'm by no means insinuating that any of it is necessary, or that even any kind of standardization of work is possible if your entire model revolves around one-off bespoke forgings. My intent is only to shed some insight from my manufacturing experience, and how I try to apply some of that to my work in knifemaking. If your goal is to become more productive and profitable, lean offers some valuable organizational tools to do this. Only you can determine how to apply these concepts in order to strike a balance that you personally can live with. Standardization does not have to be an end state—think of it as a training device. Master this knife before moving on to the next, master this alloy before adding another to your catalog. Doing that will help you progress in your development without unnecessary waste, and allow you to be profitable even without "making it big."

CHAPTER 25

Making a Business out of Knife Business

Shanna Jantz Kemp

SOME KNIFEMAKERS LOOK around at the various businesses they support and begin to think, I can do that, and so want to start a business that supplies or supports knifemakers. Others in the course of their knifemaking develop a new or unique product that provides them an opportunity to enter the supply side of the knife business. Before you take the leap, consider carefully what your end goals are and explore the full implications of entering the world of product manufacturing and sales. Growing up in and around Jantz Supply and working for others, as well as having my own business in another field, has given me unique insights into product sales from several different perspectives. Let me share my parents' story and my thoughts with you.

Ken and Venice Jantz—A Success Story

When my dad, Ken Jantz, started what would become Jantz Supply in 1966, he just loved guns. He was a gunsmith who enjoyed shooting sports and had a passion for working with, repairing, and making custom rifles. Ken's passion for guns and his ability to take a concept, visualize a better way, and then skillfully execute and machine the concept into life led him to develop a safety known widely as the "three-position side-swing safety." Jim Carmichael, then shooting editor of *Outdoor Life*, loved Ken's safety so much he wrote an article extoling the craftsmanship and innovative design. Jantz Supply still gets calls from customers wanting to buy one, although that safety has been out of production for over twenty years. Little did anyone know, but this success with the safety would be one of the first steps on the road to building the world's largest and most comprehensive knifemaking supply company.

In 1968, Ken and his wife, Venice, expanded their business, as Venice laughingly and lovingly says, to "support Ken's gunsmithing habit." Venice noticed how much it cost for tools and supplies to maintain Jantz Gun Service and discovered that many materials and tools could be purchased at a significant discount if they were purchased in quantity. The couple began attending gun shows where Ken showed his custom gun work and Venice sold the excess tools for a small profit, allowing for the purchase of new equipment. In this way, Jantz Supply was born.

They had bigger dreams than small-time profits, and an optimistic vision for the future. Over the next twenty years, Ken and Venice slowly built Jantz Supply one customer at a time, by attending numerous gun shows each year. Sometimes, they even worked two shows in a weekend by traveling separately, each of them with children in tow. As they attended gun shows, they also met knifemakers and began to understand and appreciate the craftsmanship and work involved in making knives by hand. Their vision for Jantz Supply grew to include knifemaking tools and supplies, and eventually knifemaking became the core focus and mission of Jantz Supply.

Building a business is no easy task, as entrepreneurs from many industries can tell you. Regardless of the industry, it takes hard work and dedication to be successful. It was no different for the Jantz family. Jantz Supply was definitely a family endeavor from the beginning. Kenda and Brett Jantz, Ken and Venice's children, and I (Shanna) grew up working in the business. Quite literally, we grew up *in* the business: the main office was in our living room, and the shop was attached to the house. The only phone line we had for many years was the business line. Like many people who begin their own business, Ken and Venice held jobs outside of Jantz Supply to support their family financially while they built the business outside of their everyday work hours. Ken worked as a high school shop teacher until 1979 when he and Venice decided to take a leap of faith and put everything into Jantz Supply. Ken quit teaching while Venice kept her job with Mental Health Services of Oklahoma to retain some measure of security and ensure that the family was fed and clothed, the lights stayed on, and the phone bill paid. The kids were now twelve, nine, and seven, and with everyone in school during the day and the business at home they made the schedule work. We continued to work the gun shows to meet customers and make friendships within the knifemaking community, building a good working relationship and reputation for quality and honesty while selling supplies.

In those days, gun shows were the primary venue for knife and gun makers to showcase and sell their products to the public. Ken talked to knifemakers and studied their products to learn what they needed, wanted and used, with the goal that Jantz would be at the leading edge of providing supplies. He also had the idea that there are people who would want to make knives for their own use or for gifts, and that many of these people were not at the level of the professional knifemaker. To fill that market niche, he created the Knife Kit—a package containing all necessary components to craft a knife, designed to make it easy for the hobby field. These kits were a hit and became a staple of Jantz Supply, offering the everyday man (or woman) the opportunity to put together a knife from a preshaped blade, handle material and simple to install components. By making knife construction accessible, Ken and Venice helped expand knifemaking beyond the well-trained craftsman into a project for people who wanted a hobby and loved to work with their hands.

Gun shows were not the only way Ken and Venice built Jantz Supply. Starting in the 1970s, Ken and Venice advertised Ken's safety, bolt handles, and other gun improvements in *Outdoor Life*, *Shooting Sports* and *Shotgun News*. As their knifemaking supplies increased, they began advertising their tools in *Blade Magazine* reaching more people interested in making and owning knives. Ken and Venice also began publishing a catalog of supplies for customers to order from by phone or mail. Every penny made was scrupulously put back into the business to keep it growing.

In the 1980s Jantz Supply moved out of the family home and into Davis, Oklahoma, first leasing a building on Main Street and then purchasing a building at the intersection of highways 7 and 77. Jantz later went online at knifemaking.com and built an e-commerce store to keep up with the changing times. They continue to publish their print catalog as customers frequently tell them they cannot do without one in their shop and love the printed reference.

People often ask how we did it. If you're reading this chapter with an eye to making a "knifemaking business" out of your hobby, you may be wondering the same thing. How did Jantz Supply become successful and stay in business for over fifty years?

Looking back on the risky years at the beginning after Ken was no longer teaching, Venice says, "I really don't know how we did it. We had three children, worked, started the business, and went to gun shows more weekends than we were at home. We filled orders and purchased supplies during the week and somehow managed to keep dinner cooked, the house reasonably clean, and the business running. It really is incredible to me now how we managed everything. We just did it. We just got up every day and did it, and we loved doing everything and having our family with us and part of it. We put an effort into making it fun by visiting parks, museums, and fun attractions when possible while traveling. When we went to the lake, Ken and I would work at the picnic table while the kids swam or fished."

As everyone knows, there's no single or easy answer to being successful and building a business. One common factor, however, is a willingness to risk everything: there's no reward without risk. When Ken stepped out of his secure position as a teacher and committed himself to building Jantz Supply, they knew they could lose everything. Beyond a willingness to accept the risk and work hard, Ken and Venice were perfect partners in that each of them brought a different set of skills to the partnership, and each recognized and honored the contribution of the other.

Ken often says, "Jantz Supply would not exist without Venice. She managed the daily business, worked with customers, and organized everything. Without her, Jantz Supply would not be the company it is today."

Likewise, Venice credits Ken as the visionary whose ideas, concepts, and ability to look to the future and see the trends that are coming five and ten years out made Jantz Supply successful.

Without the partnership, either might have succeeded or failed but Ken and Venice's combination of skills and abilities worked together to contribute to building Jantz Supply.

Knifemakers Are Innovators

Knifemakers are craftsmen who continually study and hone their skills, always seeking the next level of achievement. Because of this drive to improve, they often come up with pioneering ideas for new products and materials that aren't available or discover new ways to use materials that no one has thought of before. Innovative knifemakers often ask us about what is the best way to share their product with other knifemakers and profit from their idea through sales.

To understand the best way for anyone to profit from the sale of their product, it's important to determine which path to product sales you want to take: building your own business or selling your product through an established supplier.

Before any steps are taken to sell your product to the masses, it's important to understand the level of commitment you're willing and able to make. It isn't uncommon for people to come up with an idea and enjoy making the first ten or even hundred and then realize that manufacturing the same thing over and over isn't really how they planned to spend their days. They want to innovate, to continue making new cool gadgets and knives, not keep making the same thing over and over. It isn't uncommon for creative people to feel trapped by their own invention when they commit to making them routinely for large scale sales.

Understanding what you want to do and developing a long-term plan for the future is important before jumping into any business outlet. Some dreams grow step-by-step and look easy in hindsight. Ken and Venice started out selling excess gunsmithing tools and then expanded into knifemaking tools and supplies based on demand. The story seems simple in concept and from an outside perspective but many, many hours of planning and looking to the next few years went into where Jantz Supply is now. Anyone who wants to start a business should understand businesses change and be always looking forward for the next innovation and opportunity. Much like knifemaking—you have to have a plan before you start fashioning your future.

Choosing Your Path

Once you're fully committed to making the product, then you need to decide your overall business goal.

Do you want to stay small and produce products outside of your financially secure job? You can limit product availability to what is available and sell only what you can make. Taking this route, you remain fully in charge of your product. You must be diligent when limiting supply however as too many people fall into the trap of overpromising and find themselves resenting the workload they never meant to have.

Do you want to sell as many products as the market will buy, expanding your business to meet the demand? If this is your goal then you must decide if you want to be an independent business handling all aspects of manufacture, sales, and distribution or if you want to sell your products through established suppliers.

No matter which of those paths you choose there are a few key elements you must work out before going to market including pricing and branding. Too often, people are so excited about their product or gizmo that they start selling them without really doing their homework or having a plan for the future. An immediate jump start to sales isn't often in the best interest long-term.

Key Decisions

It's important to have your pricing worked out in advance. Know your costs and how much you want to profit. Be realistic about what another knifemaker would pay. Are there similar products in the market already? Suppliers need a good margin to cover advertising, service, packaging, and labor expenses, so don't set a price point so high it cannot be reasonably sold. Jantz will offer advice on retail pricing but we cannot tell you how much your product is worth to you to manufacture and sell.

Make your product as unique as possible. For example, lots of people build fixtures to make grinding easier. What makes your fixture better than anyone else's? Why would we buy and sell yours rather than another manufacturer? Do you have a known name in the industry? The maker's reputation can be a great selling point. If you're a highly respected and known knifemaker people will recognize the name branding. People recognized that Ken Jantz was a master metalsmith known not only for his high-quality metalwork but for his stock work as well. Having a custom gun made by Ken was like having a William Moran custom knife.

Understand your manufacturing ability. How much product can you produce in a certain time period? What is the lead time? If demand increases do you have a plan in place to meet the demand? Some manufacturers can only commit to making a certain number of products per month. By sharing that up front, you establish an order basis and also a demand limit which gives Jantz (and other suppliers) the ability to market accordingly.

Once you understand your cost, manufacturing capacity, and branding strategy, then you must choose how you want to sell your product.

The Highway to Success—Established Suppliers

Selling through an established supplier is the easiest direction for the majority of inventors. Jantz Supply, for example, already has established customers, advertising venues, and a customer service team, and is able to purchase product from vendors in advance of sales to keep products in stock for regular delivery. When you go through a vendor, they will handle all of the advertising, sales, technical questions, and financial aspects of your product. If you work with a reputable vendor like Jantz, you don't have to be worried about getting paid for your product, and products are purchased in quantities at a time, making delivery easier.

The most difficult part of working with suppliers like Jantz Supply is getting your product to us in a way that captures our attention and makes sense for us to bring to market. This is where your work on pricing and branding gives you an advantage.

We recommend making preliminary contact via email with photos, pricing, and information about your product. Email is a great way to make initial contact because you can take your time presenting your product in writing. It's very difficult quite honestly to get a manager on the phone to discuss a potential product unless we have already received some initial information.

Jantz has a dedicated email address for new product submission: newideas@knifemaking.com. If you don't hear back right away, don't worry. Give it a couple of weeks and then follow up if you don't hear back. If we have a project going on, it may take precedence over new products. Be prepared to send a sample or several of your product. No one likes to give away product, but remember this is an investment in your sales strategy. We don't sell samples ever, and likewise, we don't return samples. We test them, check the quality, and determine if it's a marketable product. We won't ask for samples unless we think there's potential based on the photos and initial information.

Be prepared for rejection. Sometimes, we receive a good product but cannot bring it to market for a variety of reasons, such as if we have already committed to buying a similar product from another vendor or are already are making a similar product ourselves and don't believe there's enough difference to warrant carrying both lines. The price point might also be unattainable. When that happens, we're direct about it to give makers an opportunity to review their costs and see if anything can be adjusted, but if customers won't pay for it, we cannot buy it.

Understand there are no guarantees. The only guaranteed sale you get is the first order. Jantz doesn't go to all the effort of adding new products to our line without the intent that they will be strong sellers but occasionally, for reasons not always clear, a product just doesn't move. If it doesn't sell, we won't reorder.

Be Your Own Boss

What if you really want to sell your product independently? We understand. After all, Jantz Supply was born out of a desire by Ken and Venice to pursue a passion, make a great living for themselves and their children, and be independent. Taking your product to market independently can be immensely rewarding or completely draining depending on what you really want to do on a day-to-day basis.

Consider what you want to get out of the process. What is it that drives you to move forward? What skills do you have to accomplish the various tasks of getting a product to market? Do you want to work with customers, contracts, payments, and the daily agenda of sales along with the manufacturing of the product?

Working independently means you take all of the risk in manufacturing, advertising, sales and service. You will be responsible not only for making your product but also for selling it, shipping it, and handling the complete customer transaction from start to finish. Some people love this (we do) while others shudder at the thought of being responsible for every step of the process.

Having support resources can make all the difference in a successful independent venture and failure. Financial support is essential. It's possible to be your own financial support by having savings you can rely on or a job outside of your independent venture. Ken and Venice balanced the financial aspect when Ken stopped teaching, but they had also worked for years establishing the base of the business by this point.

Having business strategy support is also essential. Ken and Venice had each other and balanced their skills set, but your partner doesn't have to be a spouse. Knowledgeable friends or a business partner whose skills are different from yours can be a great resource. There are also many entrepreneur groups you can join to learn marketing and business strategies to help you build sales and market presence.

Before you take any steps be sure to protect yourself. Check out the laws in your state/country for starting a business. Register your business with the secretary of state and study all the paperwork and requirements for running a business. Find out the rules about sales taxes and how to collect and submit them to the state. In my opinion, it's also important to set up a limited liability company to do business under to protect your personal assets. An LLC is fairly easy to set up yourself through your state, but you can also hire a lawyer to do it for you if you don't want to mess with the paperwork and have the extra funds.

Hard Work Pays Off

If you decide to move forward into the supply side of the business, be prepared to work and work hard. In my experience knifemakers as a rule are hard-working folks so this concept is nothing new, but there's something different when you're working for yourself. The journey is both rewarding and frightening, as your success is all your own but so is any failure. No one else will ever care as much about your business as you do. At Jantz, we have team members who have been with us for years and are like family. That is about as close as it comes, but no one who works for you can be as emotionally invested as you will be.

CHAPTER 26

Transitioning into High-Volume Production

Nathan "The Machinist" Carothers

FOR MANY KNIFEMAKERS, a dream come true might look something like this:

- You have a large and growing following of users and collectors who want your work.
- You can make whatever you like, and there will be someone who wants it.
- You can make as many knives as you can, and it seems like you can never meet demand.
- You can apparently earn a living doing this. Wow. What a fantastic dream come true.
- You just need to scale up.

Everything is going so well there's no way it could possibly end badly.

There are more makers who find themselves in this position than you might realize. You may have never heard of many of them because they figured out a way to fail before you heard of them. This may be you right now, on the verge of becoming "big" and the time is perfect to position yourself where you want to be in the custom or high-end knife market. But you're also venturing outside of your core competency. Let's face it; you're probably a better knifemaker than you are a businessman. You're transitioning into a proper "knife manufacturer" rather than simply "a guy making stuff" in your garage, so you're also in the perfect position to be blindsided by things you don't anticipate.

The Entry-Level Thought Process

If you can sell everything you make, you simply need to ramp up to make more and become a knife manufacturer. All you need to do is take a bunch of orders, get a loan, buy some CNC equipment, and start cranking out the knives. Within a few months, you'll buy another machine and then another, and within a few years, you'll somehow have a respectable business with employees, bank accounts, P&L statements, and a building with a loading dock and a break room with one of those water coolers in it. How is all that stuff going to happen? Who knows? But you're smart (your mom said so), so you'll figure it out.

Before I go into my thoughts on this, please let me fill you in on my background so you'll see where I'm coming from. My degree is in industrial design (product design), and I worked as a design engineer and a product design/engineering manager and production manager for a midsized contract manufacturer and a design-and-manufacturing consultancy. I spent about fifteen years in the field, and during that time, I worked in the chemical, agricultural, and medical industries among others working with functional businesses getting things into production. I was involved in the product development process from early pie-in-the-sky concept development through the R&D phase of product and process testing and optimization and all the aspects of production from design/process/engineering documentation, quoting, purchasing, production lines, hiring and training personnel, implementing a quality system, packaging, and shipping. And even with that significant background in manufacturing, I still feel unqualified advising other knifemakers on how to navigate the transition into real manufacturing. I've been doing this for a while, and it still scares me. So if you're running headlong into this transition filled with confidence and pure optimism but no real experience, you need to pause, get a reality check, and proceed cautiously. In the real world, even when working with seasoned professionals, nothing ever works the way you think it will. If you get overextended financially or move off into a manufacturing realm that you can't navigate, you can very easily fail, and frequently while holding other people's money. Don't do that.

Everyone comes into this from different directions and has different goals so what has worked for me may not work for you and vice versa, but I hope you can take something from my experiences or at least gain some insight into the direction you want to take.

My migration into knives and knife production was unplanned. I had opened shop as an independent consultant and was operating a small prototyping machine shop with low-volume production. I was simply making knives on the side as a hobby. We had a few CNC machines already. My transition to knife manufacturer began by putting knife production on open machines for "fun and profit," and eventually knifemaking evolved into our primary business. You should respect that I'm unusual as a knifemaker because I already had a shop with CNC and heat treat before I started making knives. I wouldn't actually say this was an advantage, but it certainly had me coming into this from a different direction than most.

It took a few years but we eventually found our way into that "dream come true" predicament many makers reach. I needed to decide whether to keep knifemaking fun and small and a side business or to pursue knifemaking as a serious focus. The fact we were already engaged in small scale production (of other things) made the transition less treacherous to navigate. Even so, it still took a significant restructuring of our business to do it right, including selling CNC machines suited to prototyping and replacing them with production machines. We also had to reorganize the shop for the efficient flow of our knife-manufacturing process. It was almost like starting from scratch.

We've been successful and have grown steadily and safely and have so far avoided any fatal pitfalls. I'll describe some of the things I've done that have helped get us here.

Time to Ramp It Up!

If you've made it to this point in this chapter, you're either just curious, you're planning to go toward manufacturing at some point, or perhaps you're here now and are contemplating your next move. If you're already "here," you already have a market for your knives, and you've made a lot of good choices and have done a lot of good work. You're making a lot of knives, and it's still not enough. If that's you, great. If that's not you yet, but it's where you want to be, here are a few things to consider.

There's no point to scaling up to produce lots of knives until lots of folks want to buy them. How do you build demand? Hype, social media marketing, and traditional advertising are commonly seen in this industry. Offering a good balance of value and performance in a desirable product that you can demonstrate will perform what the end user wants is another way to build demand. If you make a better product at a better price and can demonstrate your performance, you'll probably do well. That's capitalism 101, and it's the "good-product-for-a-good-price," "honest-pay-for-an-honest-day's-work" approach to business that I strive for. In my opinion, it's the best way to do business because there will always be people who want a good product at a good price, and this approach has never failed to put food on my table.

I'm not a better knifemaker than most, but I consider our knives to be among the best of their kind in the industry. They're also reasonably priced for a high-end knife which is why we have the demand that we do. Our success isn't due to some super-secret "special sauce" but a simple and systematic approach to design and refinement as applied in many, many other industries. You can apply a similar approach to your own work and over time develop a highly desirable product that can be sold in higher volumes.

The primary approach involves identifying variables, designing constrained experiments, and rigorously applying simple and repeatable testing with the goal of developing a better and more desirable product that will work and sell better. It's really very simple, but for some reason, there's still quite a bit of low hanging fruit in the knife industry. Really, the industry standard is frequently so poor that some random schlub working from their garage can often figure out something better than what has been done before if they apply some systematic logic to their project. It's amazing the extent to which knife production isn't really difficult, but people aren't picking this low-hanging fruit. Let's look at some examples of this approach to product optimization (which is done in every industry) as applied to knives:

Regarding Heat Treatment

By this point you have selected an alloy to use to make your knives. Maybe it's an alloy you're already known for using. You're using the industry-standard heat-treat protocol for that alloy and it's working reasonably well. But could it be better? That protocol was probably developed by a pretty smart metallurgist with an understanding of heat treat that you will never have. It's common to assume that their recommended heat treat will be the best heat treat for this alloy, with the recommended variables to control the hardness the only adjustments you can make. But the fact is, there's some low-hanging fruit here. Chances are that general purpose heat treat was never optimized for knives but instead may have simply been a cheap, reliable, and safe way to hit a particular hardness range in a stamping tool where minimizing part growth and reducing risk of cracking was a much higher priority than maximizing edge stability in an acute knife edge.

Martensite, the body-centered cubic structure that makes steel hard, is actually less dense than austenite (a face-centered cubic structure of steel that is soft) and is increasingly less dense the more tetragonal (stressed and hard) it is. This means that a tool can grow as it's quenched and hardened. This growth includes warping, cracking and dimension changes that are unacceptable in a thick complex stamping tool. Consequently, industry quench rates are often only fast enough to get "under the nose." Fortunately for us, these problems are almost totally irrelevant in a simple shape like a knife blade.

Who was that industry-standard heat-treat protocol designed for? It probably wasn't knifemakers. A knife-specific heat-treat regimen is one thing you can use to differentiate yourself from other run-of-the-mill makers to drive sales into volumes that justify scaling up. It turns out that for many steels the retained austenite that is built into the steel design and the secondary hardening and overtempered martensite used in things like stamping tools and extruder screws in order to reduce the dimensional changes of the hardened workpiece also reduce the edge stability in a narrow knife edge. This is probably one reason that some modern super steels have a reputation for mushy, crumbly edges compared to the old simple carbon steels. This edge stability is probably more important than wear resistance to the edge retention in a knife for many people, and it's not something that industry has done a very good job of developing.

So this is one of the ways we developed interest in our work, by optimizing a heat treat for the steel we were using for a knife-edge application in order to achieve better edge retention than the other guys. We did this by making a matrix of the interrelated variables related to heat treat and evaluating the effects that combinations of those variables had on edge stability. This matrix included steel condition going into heat treat, variations of a grain refinement process used on complex steels called prequenching, austenitizing times and temperatures, quench rates and depth, the timing of and application of cryo cycles and tempering temperatures. You don't have to be a metallurgist and know that certain steels will put certain amounts of carbon into solution under certain conditions and form lath or plate martensite to notice that the steel behaves differently depending on your austentizing temperatures regardless of the hardness you finally tempered to.

In the end, you don't need to know why something works to recognize a property that you want. You don't need to be a metallurgist to optimize a heat treat for your application, but you do need to tightly control your variables (heat treat and geometry of test specimens) and make meaningful and reproducible measurements in order to learn something. If you're testing edge stability by cutting certain materials in a certain way and comparing the results to certain standards, you have to do things like make those cuts in a very reproducible way and control the edge angle of the cut specimens very closely. Otherwise, the signal-to-noise ratio will obscure your results, and you'll waste a lot of time. It was during this process that I learned how easy it was to burn the very apex of a knife edge while sharpening dry. It turns out it doesn't take much. That heat during sharpening was a variable in my testing that I didn't recognize at first. So a side effect of such close scrutiny of your process is you will often learn something you didn't expect. For me, optimizing a heat treat led to an optimized sharpening process as well.

Get a Handle on It

The same iterative approach to heat treat can be applied to any other part of the knifemaking process. Use a similar systematic approach to analyzing the effect of different blade shapes, bevel geometries, edge geometries, and handle shapes on the cutting ability, cutting characteristics, and durability of your knife that you hope to reproduce and mass produce. Everyone knows that a narrower edge angle, a thinner bevel behind the edge, and a narrower grind angle will cut better but be more fragile. You can generate more interest in your work if you take the time to find the sweet spot for these variables for your different patterns. The more you do this, the more you'll come to accurately predict values for certain applications.

Something I've never been able to get right the first time is knife handles. This area can be particularly tricky for those going into mass production because you're either still grinding them out one at a time and need develop a fast and repeatable process, or you're using CNC-machined handle scales. CNC will repeat nearly perfectly from handle to handle but is fiendishly difficult to model and program in an ideal way and dial in for a particular knife. It takes multiples. You have to try an assortment, and you have to use them under real conditions in order to determine what's best. It's not enough to just feel them and shake them around because you'll find a handle that felt the most comfortable in the shop might not work the best in the field once you're putting certain loads on it and using it for certain tasks.

In my opinion, the handle is the area where otherwise excellent knifemakers moving into higher volumes miss the mark the most. If you go around a knife show and handle the midtechs and go by the custom makers with both handmade and midtech knives on their tables, you'll see what I'm talking about. They're almost universally bad. It's appalling how little refinement some otherwise highly competent makers put into their midtech handles. There's lots of low-hanging fruit there where you can grow your business if you do it right. If your handle is simply straight or is basically flat with a round-over, consider revisiting it.

You've Started, Now Don't Fail

Moving on from looking at ways to grow your business into a larger enterprise, let's look at ways to preserve it. In my opinion, the biggest pitfall (not a hurdle to overcome but a trap to avoid) for the knifemaker moving from low-volume handmade production to higher-volume production is being unable to navigate modern manufacturing in the United States by exposing themselves to unknown risks working with outside vendors. It's almost universal that someone making knives in his garage gets into trouble when he branches out and gets blades water jet somewhere, heat-treated somewhere else, ground some other somewhere else and gets them in-house (literally in his house) and attempts to assemble them with hardware from some other somewhere else that nothing fits and there are a number of other practically irrecoverable problems.

Whether inappropriate heat treat, poor grind finish, scales geometry problems, the maker invariably ends up scrapping much of the first batch or fixing it by hand with more time invested than it would take to start over. Even worse, some end up selling the resulting second-rate product to trusting customers. Modern manufacturing production in the United States is hard and tuition is expensive. I feel bad for the people who take out a loan and go bankrupt or worse take payment for preorders they'll never be able to fill, cheating their friends and customers and ending their future in this industry. One could write a book about the Dunning Kruger effect (look it up) among knifemakers choosing to "go into production." Sometimes it works, but it often fails because they fall into a trap along the way. When a process is out of control, success or failure is largely due to random luck. Nearly as bad as the man who fails is the man who is successful the first time around without understanding why and loses it on the next (larger) round.

What Manufacturing Could Look Like

Let's look at some hypothetical examples of things that commonly go wrong, that hopefully hit you early in the process when you're still dealing with manageable numbers and not later on when it can bankrupt you.

You have a successful knife pattern that you have made hundreds of by hand. It's a knife that you're known for, and you want to be able to continue to produce this pattern for your customers, but you're sick of making them one at a time. You want to work on other things, so you decide to bite the bullet and go midtech on this one pattern. What could go wrong?

You happen to be very good at CAD and can create a CAD file in your computer that is a good representation of your knife. You send a DXF file to your water-jet cutter to cut the blanks. They cut them to their normal standards, which are poor. They substitute some NURBS splines with different geometry to reduce their program size without telling you, so some areas will never match the scales the other shop is making. At the same time, you don't realize there's an angled kerf to the water jet, so the tang is going to stand proud of the scale on one side and the scale is going to stand proud of the tang on the other. Also, there's a little bump left in all of the tang holes where the cut doesn't quite go all the way around, which you'll find later when you go to put the pins in. These blanks go directly to the heat treater, who uses the industry-standard heat treat that hits the right Rockwell hardness number but doesn't have the edge stability your customers expect from your work. You get good results from your plate quench that you don't realize is much faster than their standard atmospheric quench. You never notice this problem until customers bring it up to you later. Those heat-treated blanks go to the blade grinder, who leaves weird undulations out on the bevels and a coarse grind on the flats. They scrap 10 percent.

You get the blades in and realize the pins won't fit the holes, so you buy a better drill press and a reamer so you can chase them out while waiting for the scales to arrive from the machine shop. You hurt yourself when a blade binds on a reamer and helicopters, slicing your palm because you don't really know how to do this safely. You burn up a lot of reamers before you realize you need carbide for this because the blades are hardened, putting the tooling on a credit card that is now nearly maxed out. The scales arrive (late) and even though the holes are accurate relative to each other so they do bolt onto the tang, the holes in the scales aren't accurate relative to the rest of the scale so they sit funny on the knife. You bring this up to the shop, who fixtures the profiling operation inaccurately from the hole drilling operation, and they ask you where was that dimension and tolerance on the drawing? It wasn't there.

It doesn't matter because you were going to need to grind the profiles flush to the scales anyways because of the aforementioned angled kerf. But this messes up the tumbled finish you paid for. So you borrow money and buy your own tumbler, grind flush, temporarily remove the scales, and tumble the blades, keeping track of which scales go on which knife. Your tumbler is under powered and your finish sucks, it gets shiny and you can see all the grind marks and waves from the blade grinder. So, you regrind the blades by hand and basically finish the knives out with the exact same amount of effort as if you'd made them from scratch.

These were preorders, and they're late, so your customers are getting angry. You finally ship and some of them are breaking in use. It turns out the water-jet cutter arranged them randomly in the sheet and you were using an alloy with a pronounced grain direction that has very different transverse strength, but you never noticed this before because you always bought it in strip. Then a few months later, the knives start coming back as returns because the "Micarta" the shop used was a cheap Chinese import with poor stability and it's shrinking from the tang. Even that hardly matters because the scale design was just flat with a simple round-over that you never really tested in the field, so they're so uncomfortable to actually really use that nobody was using the knife anyways. Between the so-so heat treat and the shrinking scales these knives that took just as much time and effort to make as your regular handmade work and cost you more to make despite being sold for less will likely be the last time you try to do a midtech. Hopefully, your customers are understanding. It's about this point that you start to question some of your life choices when it comes to knifemaking.

This version of events is actually a pretty good outcome because you can still recover. Your business can survive that. You're paying your tuition. A worse outcome is when everything goes right at the beginning and your preorders get bigger and bigger without you learning about these and other pitfalls until it's a large order and you've mortgaged your house on it. Holes can come in oversized so your scales shift around in use. The blade grinder can burn your heat treat, and unless you're testing for that, you may not notice it, though your customers will. Someone can use the wrong steel. Unless you're prepared for these kinds of mishaps (that do happen) and checking for them and creating enforceable agreements with your vendors, it's only a matter of time before something happens to you. I guarantee something will happen. These kinds of things happen all the time. It's a matter of when you catch the problem, your degree of preparedness, and the ultimate severity of those problems that can determine if you're going to fail.

How We Manufacture a Knife

I'll describe some details of my knifemaking process. It's not the ultimate "right way," and I wouldn't recommend it as an approach for most folks, but it's how we do it here, and it does address some of these pitfalls. Most of our knives are made with some variation of this process.

I buy sheets of steel with certifications directly from the steel mill where it's rolled out. I have these sheets rolled to my specifications. They come in, and we saw the plates into bars. These bars get loaded into a large mill where they're set in vises and decked down to width in two operations. These blanks then go onto an automatic surface grinder where they're ground to thickness in two operations. These accurate blanks go into a machining center where holes are spotted, drilled, circular interpolated for position, and reamed to diameter. These holes are extremely accurate, which helps with other fixturing and the final assembly. We also engrave our makers mark, skeletonize the tang, and cut chamfers. The blank goes to another machine that fixtures it from those accurate holes where we cut the belly of the knife in preparation for milling the bevels. It then goes to another machine were we mill the bevels and another fixture where we trim out the final profile. We typically have some milled jimping on a thumb ramp that's added during trim out. When it emerges, it's fully machined with chamfers, maker's mark, and bevels. We put them in a tumbler for a short time to lightly deburr and then heat treat.

Following heat treat, the knives either receive a grind on a shaped platen or go straight into a longer tumble for finish. When the finish is right, they're fixtured and sharpened at a specific angle under flood coolant, at which point we have a very accurately machined, very sharp, and well-finished hardened blade that will have the very predictable and repeatable cutting and performance characteristics that we're known for. At this point, the sharpened blank is ready for scales.

Our scales process involves a sheet of high-quality laminate material that we order from a domestic manufacturer, pulled down to a vacuum fixture in a CNC machining center where we use a stubby carbide drill to cut holes in accurate locations. This is followed by a pass with a short, stiff carbide reamer that opens those holes to size accurately. The holes are countersunk with circular interpolation and a V mill. The entire sheet then goes to another machining center that has sump filters and is built to tolerate the abrasive mud generated by cutting synthetic handle materials. From this machine, the scales are slowly carved into shape with 3-D tool paths that create the complex geometric shapes our handles are known for. After they're washed, these scales are attached to the accurately machined tangs and sheathed, finishing a Carothers Performance Knife ready to ship.

Production Tips and Tricks

The lightweight linear-way CNC machines that knifemakers tend to gravitate toward aren't stable enough to take heavy cuts in knife steels. The high load tears up both the machine and the carbide cutters. The use of heavier, old-box way mills allows us to take a rough profile cut around a knife blade in one pass without steps or multiple peels. This allows the use of older, used end mills where the tip was consumed in another step and axis shift tweaks allow the entire length of the cutter to be consumed. We'll often rough with one area of the end mill and shift for the finish. This makes profiling steps fast and simple and keeps CNC machining, which is often a relatively expensive process, fast and cost effective compared to other approaches. I can CNC a blank cheaper than you can get one water jet, and CNC milled is ten times better.

Cheap carbide isn't cost effective in the long run. As you're developing processes, you may make compromises on tooling costs. Once you have your process dialed in and predictable and you start experimenting with better cutters, you'll find better economy with better tools.

When evaluating a potential hire, I think it's often better to train a knifemaker to run a machine tool than to train a machinist to make a knife. The knifemaker better understands the final product, while the machinist just understands the use of the machinery.

Many of your hires won't be long-term, but any damage they accumulate to their body while working for you may be. Knifemaking and machining can be hard on ears, eyes, fingers, and lungs. Their long-term health and safety is your responsibility as their employer. Take safety seriously.

Writing a full book about launching a real business about larger-scale high-end knife production would include chapters about business (licensing/

permits, financing, insurance, employees, payroll, corporate status, advertising/marketing, and sales/distribution) as well as developing and marketing a desirable product to enable the higher volumes needed to recoup the development costs as much as setting up a manufacturing system from which to produce the knives. From that point of view, very little of the knife-production business is actually knifemaking, and quickly goes outside of the scope of this chapter.

Get Down to Business

Starting a business making knives is like starting any other business—house painting, pressure washing, laying carpet, and so on. Because knifemaking has a low cost of entry, virtually anybody can get started in it. But unlike other easy-to-get-into businesses, it's also something a lot of people do for fun, and many of your smaller competitors are happy to do it at a loss. From this point of view, you'd have to be crazy to venture into this industry for a living. You'd be better off opening a hot dog cart. Many full-time knifemakers are poor for a few years, fail, and then go get a real job. Even really good ones.

That said, I can think of a few examples of makers that are doing pretty well for themselves. Most of them happen to be pretty good at something related to running a business or running production. The skills are different, so that success doesn't come from just being a good knifemaker. Earning a living manufacturing knives can be done, but you have to have a well-developed and desirable product, and you have to run your business as a business. At the end of the day, you could be manufacturing anything; it just happens to be knives. If you can't approach your knifemaking this way, you should stay small and do it as a hobby. But if you have a following and the ability to run a business and can handle the perils of manufacturing in this day and age, I can think of no other manufacturing endeavor that brings you as close to your customers and is as rewarding as being a medium-high-volume, high-end knifemaker. I can't imagine any other way that I would prefer to earn a living.

More Random Thoughts on CNC from Nathan

Crashes That We All Have to Make

Knifemaking is becoming increasingly CNC-oriented, particularly when it comes to folding knives. This shift toward CNC has a lot of folks feeling their way around in a new skill, and there's a learning curve.

I've been through all of this, and I've trained people who have been down this road. One common theme I've found is that errors are common and costly, and it seems like the only way people really learn is to make a mistake and learn some fear from it before their subconscious subsystems kick in and they recognize that something might cause a problem before it actually does.

I've come to realize that when training a new machinist, they need to be in control in order to learn. Mistakes are inevitable, and it's best to supervise them in a way where the mistakes can happen, but the broken tools are small in order to preserve the machine tool.

The knifemakers learning machining and CNC alone in their shops don't have someone looking over their shoulders to prevent the catastrophic crash that wrecks a mill or causes an injury. I've compiled a list of the mandatory muck ups that everyone seems to do so you can at least have the chance to mull it over. Perhaps, having thought about it in advance, you might reduce your learning curve and the related tuition.

This is my list of mistakes that every rookie makes and learns from:

- tall workpiece slips in vise, breaks end mill
- executing a tool change over a tall workpiece with long tooling, such as a drill, and having the tool (or a neighboring tool in the carousel) crash into your work during the tool change
- retract plane in drill cycle too low, breaks drill in counterbore or similar
- send wrong program
- zero the workpiece or tool incorrectly
- load wrong tool
- inadequate tool stick out and tool holder collides
- a parallel moves during machining and a drill exits the back side of the workpiece and hits the parallel

- face mill stalls the spindle
- tool pulls down out of tool holder in a heavy cut
- plastic or wood part pulls up out of the vise
- hitting the work stop that you think is set safely to the side with a big face mill
- tapping deeper than the hole is drilled
- and if you're using a CAD/CAM system, cutting on the wrong side of a surface or trajectory (sending the cutter through the part, not the air beside the part)

There really could be a whole book about this, but I'm going to try and talk about some of these. If you're new to CNC or you're thinking of getting into this, stop and really think about how it might apply to your work flow.

1. Tall workpiece slips in vise. What happens here is a tall workpiece set up sticking up out of the vise and you're cutting on the end of it. Being CNC, you're climb milling. The nature of climb milling is it wants to pull the workpiece into the cut. The longer your workpiece, the more torque it can put on your work holding. If it's long enough, and the workpiece is perhaps not perfectly square or otherwise not well retained, the cut can lean the work into the cutting tool. When it does, your chip load might go up from .004 to .040 and break your cutter.
2. The Haas minimill is one of the most popular CNC mills that a maker might buy. They're cheap (around $35K), they fit under a seven-foot garage door, they're easy to use, and have first-rate motion control. But they only have ten inches of Z travel. And it uses some of that travel to execute a tool change. The tool change height (and the carousel full of tooling) is down in the working envelope. So when using long tools like drills and reamers, you have to learn to double-check and if necessary move your work away from the ATC before executing a tool change.
3. Retract plane in drill cycle too low, breaks drill in counterbore or similar. This one still gets me sometimes. When countersinking holes in the bottom of counterbores, I remember to change my retract plane

in the CAM system, but I forgot to change the output so that tweak occurs in the mill itself. So when it retracts to rapid over to the next hole, it's still buried in the work.

4. Send wrong program. This is easy to do. Double-check the time stamp on the file before sending it so you're certain you're sending the right file. And engage the gear between your ears when you press the green button: Is that the cutter and RPM you're expecting? We get complacent over time, and this last double check has saved my butt many times.
5. Zero the workpiece or tool incorrectly. Just go ahead and assume you have. When it's a new program and a freshly loaded cutter, pause the program just before the cutter reaches the work and look at the "distance-to-go" screen and make sure you don't have another five inches of rapid z move while you're hovering an inch above the workpiece. This saves my butt with some regularity.
6. Inadequate tool stick out and tool holder collides. Every rookie does this. It surprising how frequently they hear a problem but don't know what it is. Or they can see the work is messed up but don't know why. People get so wrapped up in looking at the cut they fail to look at the tool holder. Once bit, they start using too much stick out.
7. A parallel moves during machining, and a drill exits the back side of the workpiece and hits the parallel. You need to tap your workpiece down into the vise so your parallels can't move. If in doubt, I'll put a spring in there to hold the parallels against the jaws. Some holes are close to the edge, and you need to allow for that.
8. Face mill stalls the spindle. You're a knifemaker facing the scale off some Elmax (nastiest stuff most machinists ever deal with) on the tiniest little mill. Yeah, it may be a seven-and-a-half HP "industrial" machine tool, but it doesn't make that much power down at 400 RPM. As the inserts dull and the steel work hardens, the cutting forces go up, the RPM drops out of the power range and you stall the spindle. When the spindle bogs down on a big face mill and the table keeps feeding, you can Brinell your spindle bearings in a single muck up. If you're near 100 percent on the load meter, pull some inserts out

of the face mill and slow your feed rate accordingly or get a smaller face mill. Recognize that your little Haas minimill isn't really made for this and adjust your expectations accordingly.

9. Tool pulls down out of tool holder in a heavy cut. Rookies never see this coming. Heavy cuts and inadequate tool clamping pulls the cutter down out of the tool holder, making the cut that much deeper and leading to trouble.
10. Plastic or wood part pulls up out of the vise. You can't clamp across soft materials like you can steel. And it's tempting to use the high helix cutters designed for aluminum because they cut so well. But the helix of the cutter can pull the work up out of the vise and then throw it at you. Sometimes in this situation, you need to use router bits because they have a low helix. You can also super glue sandpaper to your vise jaws to give them more grip.
11. Hitting the work stop that you think is set safely to the side with a big face mill. Again, you get so involved with your cutter and workpiece that sometimes you forget to look at what else is on the table.
12. Tapping deeper than the hole is drilled. Obviously, you can screw this up the old fashioned way, but you can also run into trouble tapping on a machine without rigid tapping and having the tap overshoot while the spindle reverses. Or using saved parameters for tapping and forgetting to update the thread pitch. If you tap a 10-24 hole with parameters for a 10-32 hole, it's going to overshoot the bottom.

Some Other Words of Wisdom

Never interrupt a tool change. If you do, go ahead and assume the machine has lost track of the spindle status and remove the tool manually. It only has to think the spindle is empty once and try to pick up a tool while there's a tool already in the spindle to ruin your day.

When you clamp the workpiece, both it and the fixed jaw are going to distort a little. This is important when flipping to side two of a part. Go ahead and assume things will move a little and add .001-positive Y tweak. You might need more that than, but you'll seldom need less.

I like to add tweaks to the global offset (G52). (Fanuc, Haas will do this with a parameter change.) I like adding this to global so the values in G54 are what I measured, and the tweak is easy to see.

Learn to start a program in the middle of the program. You can use the search function to find the tool you're on in the program and start the program from the top of that tool.

Standardize your tool length offset plane and compensate either in your programming or in your work offset. Touching off tools in the carousel again when changing to another part is a foolish (but common) waste of time. Don't use feeler strips. Use a lighting touch probe. They're faster, more accurate, and more forgiving.

Use a torque wrench to set your vise. It takes the guess work out of the equation and leads to consistency. You'll know with experience, "This part needs twenty foot-pounds," and your work is more accurate and less dented.

If you're driving a nice car and have a crappy band saw, your priorities are out of whack.

I hope some of my experience is helpful to one of you guys starting out down this road.

ABOUT THE AUTHORS

In order of appearance.

Jason Fry- Editor- Chapters 1, 2, 3, 14, 15, 19, 22

Jason makes knives part time for the last 13 years, working as a behavior analyst for developmentally disabled persons as his day job. He is married with four boys, ages 16, 15, and 3-year-old twins (As of May 2020). His knife hobby supports a full schedule of fishing, hunting, church work, and playing with his kids. He is a voting member of the Knifemakers' Guild, an Apprentice in the American Bladesmith Society, and the president of the Texas Knifemakers' Guild. He was runner up on Forged in Fire season 5, episode 26. He forges his own Damascus and builds knives by both forging and stock removal. His work can be seen at www.frycustomknives.com or @frycustomknives on Instagram. He is the author of "Knifemaking Hacks: Tips to Make a Knife Like the Pros" available through Gun Digest.

Salem Straub- Chapter 4

Salem is a Washington State based bladesmith and teacher, specializing in culinary knives, daggers, and various integral forged blades. His main areas of interest are in the historical work of Europe and Asia, in vivid and interesting materials, and in exploring new boundaries in all styles of pattern welding. He was fortunate enough to have been a protege of Ken Onion- besides that, is been mostly self taught and holds no affiliations with professional organizations in the trade. A 2016 Forged in Fire Champion, Salem is a full time maker whose books are currently closed for custom orders. He has been making knives since 2004 and plans to continue until he can›t pick up a hammer.

Tracy Mickley, Chapter 5

Tracy is the founder, owner and operator of Midwest Knifemakers Supply llc, dba www.USAknifemaker.com established in 2006. He transitioned to the knife making supply business after 30+ years in retail management for his second career. He has been making knives for 25 years using both stock removal and forging. Tracy is involved in R&D of new materials and tools related to knife making. He has published several tutorial videos on knife making and is owner of www.Knifedogs.com forums.

Geoff Keyes- Chapter 6, 7

Geoff is the sole maker at 5 Elements Forge in a small town in the Cascade foothills of Washington state. He received his rank of ABS Journeyman in 2007 and intends to stand for Mastersmith. As the child of teachers, he has an interest in history and archaeology and many of his blades are based on examples out of history, especially early American styles. His work has been featured in Blade and Knives Illustrated and in many issues of the Knives Annual. He was a contestant on Forged in Fire season 5, episode 25.

Larrin Thomas- Chapter 8, 9

Larrin is a steel metallurgist who develops automotive sheet steels. In his free time he tests and writes about knife steels. He developed his interest in knife steel through his father, Devin Thomas, who makes pattern-welded Damascus steel. Larrin loves steel so much he got a PhD in Metallurgical Engineering and won't stop telling strangers about iron-carbon phase diagrams. You can read more from Larrin at www.KnifeSteelNerds.com. He is the author of "Knife Engineering" available on Amazon.

Brad Stallsmith- Chapter 10

Brad is the chief heat treater at Peters Heat Treating in Pennsylvania. Peters heat treats hundreds of blades per day, as well as various other machine parts for manufacturing and aerospace industries. www.petersheattreat.com

Dave Ferry- Chapter 11

Dave is an experienced knife maker, leather craftsman and cattle rancher. These three things combine in Horsewright Clothing and Tack, a business that he owns and runs with his wife Nichole, a fellow leather worker. Everything that Horsewright makes and sells is designed "for the saddle, from the saddle" and is hand made by Dave and Nichole. Dave has lost track of how many knife sheaths he's made but knows its north of 17,000! What really got him developing his designs and working on knife retention for a using sheath was watching Nichole, years ago, ride a bucking horse and seeing her knife go flying and hitting the dirt a few jumps before she did.

Tom Lewis- Chapter 12

Tom is a retired school teacher who makes knives full time. Tom grew up in Phoenix AZ where his Father had a well equipped shop. Tom learned to use tools at an early age and has always had a interest in knives. He sold his first knife in 1980 and makes knives with both the forging and stock removal method. He forges pattern welded Damascus, chain damascus, wire rope damascus and canister Damascus. He uses CPM154, 26C3, W-2, AEB-L steels for stock removal. After forty years of making and selling knives he has a well equipped shop. Four drill presses, eight 2"X72" grinders, five band saws, a hundred pound little giant power hammer and a twenty-five lb power hammer, a hydraulic press, metal lathe, milling machine, etc. He has a wife of 52 years and four married children with 9 grandchildren. Pictures of Tom's knives have appeared in Blade Magazine and a number of Knife annuals.

Bob Ohlemann- Chapter 13

Bob is a knife maker from Sanger, Texas specializing in handmade custom folders. His unique style has garnered numerous awards including "Best Tactical Folder" at the International Custom Cutlery Exposition and a double award at the Texas Custom Knife Show for "Best Art Knife" and "Best of Show". He is a member of the American Bladesmith Society and serves on the Board of Directors for the Texas Knifemaker's Guild. Bob's knives are created using modern computer aided design and high-tech materials blended with old world craftsmanship and more traditional materials. Bob credits his "interesting" life experiences as the catalyst for his creative, highly functional designs. He is a retired twenty-year veteran of the U.S. Army with many deployments around the globe. When Bob isn't in the shop, he enjoys shooting, photography, and spending time with his wife and their two Doberman Pinschers.

Bob makes his knives under the trade name Rangermade Knives and can be found at the following:

www.RangermadeKnives.com
www.Facebook.com/rangermadeknives
Instagram- RangermadeKnives
YouTube channel- Rangermade Knives

Mark Bartlett- Chapter 14

Mark grew up in a small town in Maine. After leaving the Army in 2002 he moved to Tennessee. His knives have been published in several magazines internationally. He is currently in preparation for ABS Journeyman testing and eventually Mastersmith testing. He has always had an interest in building things. His work background is in maintenance on agricultural equipment, heavy equipment, and trucks and also building drag cars, motorcycles, and pulling tractors.

Ed Braun- Chapter 16

Ed is a former literature professor turned full time knifemaker. He works closely with New Jersey Steel Baron developing and testing heat treat regimens for NJSB steels.

Lin Rhea- Chapter 17

Lin is a Master Bladesmith in the American Bladesmith Society and lives with his wife Kay in Prattsville, AR. He is retired from the state of Arkansas and is working from his home shop. He is also a bladesmithing instructor for the University of Arkansas at both Hope, AR and Texarkana, TX. His website is www.rheaknives.com and his email is lwrhea2@windstream.net

Erin Healy- Chapter 19

Erin is the associate editor of the NRA Hunters' Leadership Forum. She edited a lifestyle magazine on Cape Cod for 14 years prior to working for BLADE magazine, the world's No. 1 knife publication. She also provided marketing services for a guntry club as well as to a start-up distribution firm. She served in the U.S. Army, breeds Jack Russell Terriers and lives in the mountains of northwest Georgia.

Dustin Rhodes- Chapter 19

Dustin currently operates a shop and teaches forging in Central Illinois. He began forging in 1993, and now is a full time bladesmith specializing in early American style blades. He appeared on Forged in Fire S4E2 and Master of Arms S1E1. He operates Dustin Rhodes Forge Works, Church of the Forge.

Joshua Swanagon- Chapter 20

Joshua has studied survival in both urban and wilderness environments in Colorado and Michigan for most of his life, while also adding experience in harsher terrains abroad. He combines this experience with years of diverse martial arts and combatives training and real-world application as a published freelance writer and Field Editor for various magazines in the fields of knives, survival, self-defense and tactical subject matters. After his resignation as Editor and Subject Matter Expert for Knives Illustrated Magazine, Joshua applied his years of experience in this role to focus on his webzine Knife & Gear Society, LLC www.Knife-Gear.com

Jim Cooper- Chapter 21

Jim is the owner of Sharp by Coop photography, and is one of the premier photographers in the knife industry. His work has been featured in every knife publication since 2007. A typical monthly issue of Blade Magazine will feature several of his photographs. His primary business site is www.sharpbycoop.com and his picture gallery is www.knifegallery.com/index

Ed Caffrey- Chapter 23

Ed is an ABS Mastersmith, a retired USAF MSgt and is a full time bladesmith in Great Falls, Montana. He produces forged blades from user through collector grade. He has taught bladesmithing throughout the world and offers one on one instruction at his shop. He is married to Cindy (Saltsman) Caffrey for 37 years as of May 2020. www.caffreyknives.net

John Gulso- Chapter 24

John currently manages operations at a heavy plate metal fabrication facility. His love for making has driven his professional career through widely varying industries, from casting iron waterworks to building progressive dies for stamping hard drive read/write head suspensions. John sees the ability to make and manufacture, to build and create, from the same philosophical point of view he sees the right to keep and bear arms - not simply a right, but a necessity for one to be truly considered a free person.

Shanna Jantz Kemp- Chapter 25

Shanna has worked on and off in the knife supply business since she was a child when her parents, Ken and Venice, founded Jantz Supply. Since Venice's retirement, Shanna works with her dad (Ken), sister (Kenda), brother (Brett), and husband (Jerry) to continue the legacy her parents built. Before returning to knife making, Shanna built a career as an Autism Specialist in Austin, TX teaching supporting social and behavioral change. Shanna has 1 child who will turn 23 this year (2020) and 1 exuberant puppy who will turn 2. Shanna enjoys playing in the shop to learn new skills, fishing, camping and cooking with her family. www.knifemaking.com

Nathan Carothers- Chapter 26

Known on the internet as "Nathan the Machinist," Nathan has developed CNC machining techniques for knifemaking. He took a simple hobby and turned it with technical precision into a viable business. His work has been published multiple times in Blade Magazine and the Knives annuals.

www.ingramcontent.com/pod-product-compliance
Lightning Source LLC
LaVergne TN
LVHW041113080826
845145LV00007B/1793
9781732193048